E

MUHAMMAD &
THE IDEOLOGICAL FOUNDATION OF
THE NATION OF ISLAM
by
Adib Rashad (James Miller)

WITH CONTRIBUTIONS FROM:

- Dr. Alauddin Shabazz
- Dr. Dorothy Blake Fardan
- Dr. Na'im Akbar
- Dr. Sulayman Nyang
- H. Khalif Khalifah

U. B. & U. S. COMMUNICATIONS SYSTEMS
912 West Pembroke Ave. ● Hampton, Virginia 23669
(804) 723-2696

FIRST EDITION ● FIRST PRINTING

JUNE, 1994

ISBN#1-56411-065-6   Y. B. B. G. #0070

Printed in the U. S. A.

U. B. & U. S. Communications Systems
P. O. Box 5368 ● Newport News, Va. 23605
(804) 723-2696

CONTENTS

DEDICATION

I dedicate this book to the memory of my deceased son, Ahmed Immanuel Nasser, whom I love with all my heart. I also dedicate this book to my beloved mother, deceased grandfather, and to my other sons and daughters. I make a special dedication to my hearts delight, my youngest son, Jamil Adib Rashad.

To all the Muslim pioneers who sacrificed with the Honorable Elijah Muhammad, may Allah grant all of you a place in paradise.

ACKNOWLEDGEMENTS

I am extremely grateful to a number of special people for their assistance in the completion of this work. I begin by deeply thanking my wife, Amira Rashad (Cheryl Lane-Miller) for her research and word processing skills. I also thank her for her patience, tolerance, support, and being a good mother to our son. I thank my heart felt friend, Aisha Farida (Lenora Johnson) for her library assistance, xeroxing, and constant encouragement. I am extremely grateful to my tall brother and serious archivist, Oduno Tarik, who supplied me with some very important documents. I am grateful to Brother Danial El-Amin, Muslim pioneer and proprietor of Shabazz Barber Shop in Washington, D.C. for putting up with me and the many questions I asked him. He was always very accommodating. I thank Dr. Sulayman Nyang, always for his constant confidence and encouragement. To Dr. Abdel Alim Shabazz, I am grateful for your sharing your experiences as a minister under the Honorable Elijah Muhammad. I thank and appreciate my intellectual father, Dr. William P. McDonald, for his input and confidence in everything I undertake. I am appreciative to Ms. Linda Kirksey for sacrificing her time to put certain chapters into the computer. I am deeply pleased that Dr. Alauddin Shabazz agreed to advise me on this entire project. He made everything much easier. To Brother Seifullah-Ali-Shabazz, I highly appreciate the long and many informative conversations that we had regarding this book and for his scholarly and insightful taped interviews. I am deeply grateful to Dr. Dorothy Blake-Fardan for her confidence, and scholarly input. I thank Dr. Náim Akbar for always expressing an interest in my endeavors and for always being willing to contribute. I am grateful to Dr. Farid Muhammad for his encouragement. I am also grateful to Dr. Lewis Sabree (Wright) for his input and inspiration. And last, but certainly not least, I am deeply grateful to my publisher, H. Khalif Khalifah, of United Brothers and United Sisters, for his confidence and respect for my work. I thank the entire staff at the Schomburg Center for Research in Black Culture for publishing excerpts from this work that was presented at a symposium in May 1992. Most of all I thank Allah for giving me the mental and emotional fortitude to finish this project. It was indeed a grueling task.

ELIJAH AND MALCOLM:
AN INTRODUCTORY DISCUSSION AND ANALYSIS

The Honorable Elijah Muhammad laid the foundation for the longest lasting, and most enduring, and I believe, the most influential black religio-nationalist movement in American history. His genius lay in the fact that he was able, without formal education, to synthesize a Black Nationalist Christian tradition, messianic-nationalism, and quasi fundamental Islamic tenets. He also syncretized selected biblical versus with selected Quranic verses for the purpose of mentally liberating African Americans from white Christian incarceration. He, through painstaking effort, managed to transform the moral and spiritual lives of black people (Malcolm X included) who otherwise would have been continually discarded as human refuse. Furthermore, he unconsciously employed the Weberian philosophy of the Puritan work-ethic, and Booker T. Washingtonian economics to advance his early followers and subsequently his Nation of Islam to a level of economic independence.

History has repeatedly told us about great men and their accomplishments. History shows us, if we look carefully, that great men in fact make history. Elijah Muhammad made history when he dared to unconditionally and uncompromisingly challenge the "white establishment." He made history when he, through the use of psychology, systematically and paternalistically addressed the slave mentality of black people and its deleterious impact on the necessity for black unity. He made history by showing the world that genius does lay in the so-called dregs of society. Equally important, he made history by unknowingly and indirectly contributing (through the assistance of Malcolm X as his chief spokesman) to the social, political, and civil rights climate of black America. Most importantly, his greatest contribution to history was his uncompromising love for black people. I believe that history will indeed absolve Elijah Muhammad, and other men of his stature but I believe even more so that right-minded people must assist in that process.

Elijah Muhammad's mission and message was designed to attract and uplift black people that had fallen into a moral, spiritual and economic quagmire. What is most important to note, but gets overlooked, is the fact that he frequently stated that he came to pull black people out of the fire, and the one after him would teach the religion. Therefore, he was not a preacher or Imam of Islam in the strict sense of the word; he was by contrast a social and moral reformer who initially was called the "Supreme Minister," and later took the title of the "Messenger of Allah."

Orthodox Muslims (indigenous and immigrant) have maintained their angry denunciations and disavowal of his influential leadership, namely, because of his allegiance to Farad Muhammad, his racial rhetoric, and, his unmitigated temerity to proclaim himself the Messenger of Allah. He never referred to himself as a prophet in the sense of one who received divine scripture or divine revelation. However, he strongly believed that he was the Messenger of Allah to black people. And in actuality when his historical record is pulled and objectively assessed -- I hope this book serves that purpose -- it will show that he was, from the English definition, a messenger to dispossessed black people. In a very real sense, the Nation of Islam under Elijah Muhammad's leadership advocated and practiced more Quranic injunctions than many so-called orthodox Muslims, including those in Mecca, Arabia.

As I indicate in the text, Elijah Muhammad exercised his leadership in a dialectical manner. He was an uncompromising "race leader" who utilized aspects of Islam, and white Christian eschatology to divorce black people from their slave mentality. On the other hand, he acknowledged and taught fundamental aspects of orthodox Islam. Study his words on page 72 of his book, **Message to the Black Man**:

> "The God in Islam is not a national or tribal god, but as the Holy Quran describes Him in the opening words, "He is the Lord of the Worlds." This conception of God is best, since man's belief is by nature, that there must exist somewhere in the universe one who has and can exercise a greater power than can he or the object that he is bowing to as his god."

Mr. Muhammad, contrary to accepted belief, taught his followers the five fundamental principles of Islam and constantly stressed the importance for uniting his Nation of Islam with the universal community (Ummah) of Muslims. Moreover, it was Mr. Muhammad who popularized what was once considered "strange" terms like Islam, Muslims, Holy Quran, Mecca, and Prophet Muhammad.

His first name was Elijah Karriem. Master Farad Muhammad changed Karriem to Muhammad.

2

On another level, the Honorable Elijah Muhammad passionately preached the brotherhood of people of African descent; however, his initial emphasis was on African American brotherhood. Black unity -- regardless of one's religion -- was an all encompassing concern for Muhammad. Contrary to popular belief, Malcolm X was not, after he returned from Hajj, the first to announce the significance of a universal brotherhood in Islam. In fact, and I am deviating for a moment, Malcolm always knew that there was universal brotherhood, or different colors and races in Islam. This fact was always made conspicuous in the Nation of Islam, through the many Eastern Muslims who visited and worked for the Honorable Elijah Muhammad, and even more so in 1959, the year Malcolm went to the Middle East to prepare the way for the Honorable Elijah Muhammad to make his minor Hajj (Umra). Elijah Muhammad stated this in his celebrated *Message to the Blackman*, (p. 138 - 139) regarding the subject of universal brotherhood in Islam:

> "Thus, prayer promotes social relations between the different sections of the Muslim community. Far more important than this, however, is the leveling of social differences brought about by means of congregational prayer. Once within the doors of the Mosque, every Muslim, feels himself in an atmosphere of equality and love."

In another passage, Muhammad is even more poignant on the brotherhood question and the lack of color and class distinction in Islam by stating:

> "Nay, the king or rich man standing in a back row will have to lay his head, prostrating himself before God, at the feet of a slave or a beggar standing in the front. There could be no more leveling in the world. Differences of rank, wealth and color vanish within the Mosque and quite a new atmosphere, an atmosphere of brotherhood, equality and love, totally different from the outside world, prevails within the holy precincts.

The Honorable Elijah Muhammad willingly sent his son, Akbar Muhammad, to Al-Ahzar University in Cario, Egypt; that clearly shows that he understood and respected true Islamic theology.

3

As I just pointed out, Elijah Muhammad's ambiguous or dialectical teachings are quite clear for those who steadfastly scrutinize his principles regarding the oneness of God. Yes, he presented Master Farad Muhammad as Allah in person and understandably, the orthodox Muslim world considered this a violation (shirk), but what is usually overlooked or obscured was his strong orthodox Muslim position regarding the infinity of Allah and the final prophethood of Prophet Muhammad. This position cannot be overly emphasized because it demonstrates how skillful he was as a race leader, on the one hand, and a believer in pristine Islam on the other. Examine his words on page 72 and 74 of **Message to the Blackman**:

> "The number one principle of Islam is a belief in Allah (God); the belief in a power higher than man. It is the fundamental principle of the religion of Islam to believe in Allah, the One God. According to the belief, the teaching and preaching of the prophets of Allah is of One God."

The last paragraph of page 74, same book, Mr. Muhammad contradicts his stance regarding the deification of Master Farad Muhammad, and actually accuses the people of the book (Jews and Christians) of practicing shirk:

> "Both Jews and Christians are guilty of setting up rivals to Allah (God), Adam and Eve accepted the guidance of the serpent instead of that of Allah (Genesis, 3:6). They made a golden calf and took it for their god and bowed down to it (Exodus, 32:4). The Christians have made imaginary pictures (There was a standard picture of Farad Muhammad reading the Quran in the homes of Mr. Muhammad and some of his followers) and statues of wood, silver and gold -- calling them pictures and statues of God. They bow down to pictures and statues alleged to be of Jesus, His mother, and his disciples as though they could see and hear them."

He enhances his belief in the uniqueness of Islamic monotheism and Prophet Muhammad on page 75, same book, he states, "Muhammad took hold of the best, the belief in one God (Allah) and was successful. Fourteen hundred years after him, we are successful, that is, we who will not set up another god with Allah."

Mr. Muhammad resolves and yet sustains the contradiction in his teachings on page 167, of *Message to the Blackman,* by boldly reciting the Kalimah Shahadatin:

> We say, Allah is God. We say in the Arabic language, Allah Oou Akbar. We say in the Arabic language, La illa ha illah lah, Muhammadin Rasoull Allah.

Imam Warith Deen Muhammad made what I believe is an irrefutable point when he argued that Master Farad Muhammad presented himself to the black masses as a god because he wanted to dismantle the Europeanized form of god. Therefore, Elijah Muhammad perpetuated the Farad idea as a means to a justifiable end. The justificatory scenario went according to this: Farad Muhammad had an original black man for a father and a morally pure caucasian woman for a mother; thus this god was genetically akin to black people and was the Father or Author of their religion, Islam.

It is imperative that the reader be informed that Muhammad's contradictions regarding Farad Muhammad and the unadulterated teaching of Islam will be repeated in the text.

It is most befitting to cite Dr. Alauddin Shabazz, comparative religion scholar, who brings a great degree of intellectual clarity to the issue of Farad as god:

> "The Nation of Islam didn't produce itself. Its founder was not Elijah Muhammad, but a Muslim from the East. If any misleading took place, the Nation of Islam was the misled and an "Eastern Sunni Muslim," the misleader. No sane intelligently, sincere Muslim can be found with a heart void of sympathy for those who are mislead. The state of the Muslim world warrants our sympathy and our remorse. There is all kind of shirk in the Muslim world. Some Arab rulers worship and fear "Uncle Sam." They rely on Uncle Sam's protection and distrust the protection of Allah. They submit to the will of the "white" man in the "white" house and disregard the will of Allah (Holy Quran: 5:54, 58-60/3:100, 149/4:92 - 93).

Dr. Shabazz continues:

"Monarchy, nepotism, and kingdoms are all repugnant and unIslamic. Family run Muslim countries are contradictions. Shirk and anthropomorphic concepts by no means are restricted to the Nation of Islam."

Through the use of skillful psycholinguistic projections, Elijah Muhammad reversed the inferiorization of African Americans by imparting that inferiorization to European Americans. Black people were no longer savages, but gods who came with creation. Caucasians were no longer founders of civilization, but were grafted collective devils and savages.

Moreover, the one word that Europeans were able to use with profound results was "nigger." This word with its psycholinguistic and emotional impact can and does sever the humanity from African Americans. Andrew Hacker in his timely and timeless work, *Two nations* (p. 42) has this to say about the use of the word "nigger,"

"When a white person voices it, it becomes a knife with a whetted edge. No black person can hear it with equanimity or ignore it as 'simply a word.' This word has the force to pierce, to wound, to penetrate, as no other has. There have, of course, been terms like 'kike' and 'spic' and 'chink.' But these are less frequently heard today, and they lack the same emotional impact. Some non-ethnic terms come closer, such as 'slut' and 'fag' and 'cripple.' Yet, 'nigger' stands alone with its power to tear at one's insides. It is revealing that whites have never created so wrenching an epithet for even the most benighted members of their own race. Its persistence reminds you that you are still perceived as a degraded species of humanity, a level to which white can never descend."

Black people could not retaliate against caucasian's use of nigger with any appreciable degree. They tried with the use of honky, whitey, cavey, and cracker, but devil put caucasians on the defensive.

The reader should know that there were other leaders before Farad who proclaimed themselves to be god, they will be discussed in the text, but they were Christians who advocated a continued belief in Christianity.

Interestingly, there were times that Elijah Muhammad refrained from the use of devil and referred to caucasians as the "enemy." His ministers used this invective more than he did.

Elijah Muhammad not only denuded the psycho-emotional content of the word nigger, but he also infused the words black and Africa with metaphysical, historical, and cultural substance. Black was (is) associated with bestiality, heathenism, barbarism, etc... Africa, to this day, does not hold any geopolitical significance. In fact, the term "dark continent" is synonymous with unenlightenment, and primitive existence.

Mr. Muhammad took black and Africa as other terms that caucasians attached primarily negative connotations to and dialectically focused on the contexts in which black and Africa became the source of life and humanity.

As just stated, Elijah Muhammad reversed the psycho-emotionally based content of the words, nigger, black and dark continent by labeling the caucasians who believe(d) in the negative or pejorative aspects of those words as "devils," that is people who were beneath Africans in the hierarchy of humanity. It was this phase of his leadership, more so than his affront to Christianity, that removed him from historical consideration by African Americans. Most African Americans could not and did not contest the Farad as god concept because they believe(d) that a caucasian (Jesus) was the son of god. This they could either ignore or mildly tolerate, it was the scathing attack on caucasians that emotionally provoked black people.

The Honorable Elijah Muhammad and the pioneer Black Christian Nationalists attacked racism and its image of a Europeanized god by replacing it with an all-encompassing Black god. They, without the knowledge of psychology, accomplished decades ago what contemporary psychologists and psychiatrists are just beginning to intellectualize about. Dr. Francis Cress Welsing has discussed the psychodynamic of racism through the control of the image of God. If one examines the following statement carefully, one can and will see in the text the exactness of arguments enunciated by pioneer messianic-nationalist leaders such as Father Hurley, Marcus Garvey, Father Divine, Prophet Cherry and Mr. Muhammad:

In *Lost - Found Moslem Lesson No. 1* the question is asked: Why did Musa have a hard time to civilize the devil in 2,000 B.C.? The answer is because he was a savage who had lost the knowledge of himself and was living a beast life.

"Most fundamental and absolutely critical to the white supremacy system of religious thought was the formation of the image of a white man as the son of God. This white male image was then referred to as Christ; it doesn't matter that the prophet Jesus was a black man. Because of the nature of the human brain that functions on logic circuits, once a white male image is established in the brain computer logic as the son of God, then the brain computer at deep unconscious levels automatically concludes that God the Father is also a white male, since black or other nonwhite males would have produced a nonwhite son. Thus, any person accepting the Christian religion -- whether conscious of it or not -- has the image and concept of God as a white man."

Thus, psychologically speaking, Muhammad posited that the white man could not possibly be God because he was the opposite of God. The black man was the original man on the planet; therefore, the black man was God, conversely since white is the opposite of black and black is synonymous to God; therefore, white is synonymous to the enemy of God, the Devil. This was the psychological paradigm that Elijah Muhammad utilized to reverse the control of image type racism that caucasians have executed for centuries.

Imam Warith Deen Muhammad raises a profound philosophical question that speaks directly to this issue of controlled images and the qualities of self-negation and inadequate social development that it engenders. His question and concern, however, is directed to caucasians

"What would happen to the minds of Caucasian people if Black people would suddenly come into power with their mentality, with their love for their religion? What would happen if nappy-headed, Black Jesuses were put all over their land and throughout their homes, and in all of their churches? What would happen to their minds over a period of three-hundred years if they were kept coming to churches and seeing our image as their redeemer, seeing our image as their prophets, their apostles, their angels? They would be reduced to inferiority because the image before them of the supreme model of superiority would be 'Black' and not 'white.'"

Dr. Francis Cress Wesling, *The Isis Papers* (Third World Press, Chicago, 1991, p. 163 - 178.

Obviously, Imam Muhammad also places this issue within the context of a psychological hypothesis.

Dr. Náim Akbar enhances this subject with a succinct analysis:

"The influence of this Caucasian image on the psyches of non-Caucasian people is no worse than would be the influence of a Black image on the psyches of non-Black people. The reduction of people to a state of inferiority represents a reprehensible form of mind control of the worst kind. It also becomes the basis for insuring the continued psychological enslavement of any people under such an influence."

There is no doubt that black people -- especially in America -- have an uncanny and despicable love for European Americans. Therefore, I believe that most black people who reject(ed) Muhammad did and do so because they perceive(d) him to be an anti-white racist. On the other hand, they lionize Malcolm X because he supposedly divorced himself from Muhammad and his racial rhetoric, and accepted a universal brotherhood.

Malcolm's words on the question of Muhammad being a racist should be savored for clarity:

"All that Muhammad is trying to do is clean up the mess the white man has made, and the white man should give him credit. He shouldn't run around here calling Muhammad a racist and a hate-teacher. White man, call yourself a hate-teacher because you invented hate. Call yourself a racist because you invented the race problem."

Unlike, Frantz Fanon, the trained psychiatrist, who postulated that the European oppressor, having become the oppressor through the practice of violence, only understands and yields to counter violence, Muhammad, the uneducated psychologist, postulated a psychothe-

W.D. Muhammad "A Message of Concern To The American People," Chicago: *American Muslim Journal*, Regular Feature, 1980 - 1983.

Náim Akbar, *Chains and Images of Psychological Slavery*, New Minds Productions, Jersey City, N.J., p. 67.

rapeutic program that nonviolently emancipated black people from economic, cultural, historical, and psychological oppression.

Many Eastern, and some African Muslims do not and choose not to understand the Honorable Elijah Muhammad and his leadership tactics. These Muslims, for the most part, were not imposed upon by slavery and dehumanization, nor were they systematically victimized through a process of gradual Euro-Centric internalization. Needless to say, most of the language and some of the practices expressed in the Nation of Islam was (is) annoying to these Muslims who lacked proper understanding of the psycho-idiomatic projections of the Nation.

On the other hand, had these same Muslims, before and after the ascension of the Nation of Islam, conducted meaningful dáwa in the black community; perhaps, the teachings of Farad Muhammad would not have gained fruition. Most of these Muslims never identified on moral principle with the African American struggle for legitimate rights. To this day, unless they are in the black community as commercial agents for pork, whiskey, and drug paraphernalia, they do not offer themselves as fellow comrades or brothers against nonwhite oppression.

In essence, a number of Eastern Muslims are race and color conscious insofar as African Americans are concerned. However, they have historically been in the European American community playing the academy award winning role of "submissive and ingratiating lackeys."

Muslims are duty bound to stand firmly on rightness and righteousness; however, many Muslims who immigrate to the United States opt to wrestle with a dual heritage: They are Muslims who have a culture, but they are desperately trying to internalize or assimilate European American or Euro-Centric values of the host country. This dialectical paradigm obviously presents confusion. The only way to extricate themselves is by developing an Islamic diagnostic program. Thus it is wrong to prejudge the Nation of Islam whose members displayed an understanding of the nature of their Euro-Centric victimization and moved to react against it.

The Nation of Islam always took a strong anti-imperialist position, and stood steadfast in behalf of oppressed people of color; furthermore, the Nation never waved the flag or kowtowed in front of the White House. Hence, the Nation refused to be Uncle Tom Muslims. Personal-

Granted, there are some Eastern and indigenous Muslims that are fiercely, based on an Islamic program, struggling against Euro-Centric ideas and values.

ly, I think there is a lesson to be learned from such boldness.

I refused to discuss Malcolm X at length in the text simply because he has become a "cult of the personality," a larger than life figure, but in actuality was no more than an intellectual organizer and spokesman for Elijah Muhammad. He did not bring or offer anything new to the black independence movement. I knew and loved Malcolm, but I love truth and honesty more. If Malcolm must be honored, and he should, let us honor him within a proper historical context. The height of Malcolm's greatness, for example, came during his twelve-year sojourn in the Nation of Islam. Moreover, what is most important to note is the fact that Elijah Muhammad's program manifested its full potency after the death of Malcolm. Therefore, the belief that Malcolm was primarily responsible for the growth and success of the Nation of Islam is patently false. It can safely be said that Minister Louis Farrakhan successfully filled the void that Malcolm left in terms of promoting Elijah Muhammad's message of black redemption and economic independence.

It is a known fact, that even after Malcolm disconnected himself from the Nation, he continued to pay homage to the Honorable Elijah Muhammad: "I still credit Mr. Muhammad for what I know and who I am; he's the one who opened my eyes." On another occasion, he stated, "I still believe that Mr. Muhammad has the best solution to the American so-called Negro problem."

Reverend Albert Cleage, contemporary Black Christian Nationalist, sums up this subject with objective candor:

> "I believe that the basic truths that Malcolm X taught came from the basic philosophy and teachings of Elijah Muhammad and the Black Muslims."

Cleage adds to this:

> "At the beginning when he was with the Muslims, there was a power base from which he operated, philosophical foundation upon which he could build. And he built well and he operated well in terms of a power base.

"Malcolm's position on third-world or non-white unity and American politics bears testimony to Reverend Cleage's assertions that Malcolm did indeed operate within Elijah Muhammad's basic philosophy and teachings. Malcolm's ideological stance regarding the non-European international community was nurtured during his tenure in the Nation. The seeds of his international view were actually enunciated.

The above comments are excerpted from a speech that Reverend Cleage gave in Detroit, February 24, 1967.

11

and contained in the doctrine of Marcus Garvey and Elijah Muhammad. Muhammad taught that the world was (is) divided into two groups of people: the caucasians (Yakub's grafted race) and the black nation (original people). The black nation comprises the entire world population of the "black, brown, red, and yellow races." These different races were genetic sub-components of the original black race.

As indicated earlier, years before Malcolm's hajj, Muhammad raised the subject of Islamic brotherhood within the context of the Holy Quran. In Muhammad's lesson on the *Brotherhood of Islam* he stated that Islam abolishes all invidious class distinctions "surely the most honorable of you with Allah is the one among you most careful of his duty" sounds a death knell to all superiority or inferiority based on rigid caste or social distinctions." Mankind is but one family according to the Holy Quran, which says: "O mankind, surely We have created you from a male and a female and made you tribes and families that you may know each other" (49:13).

Compare the following statements of Malcolm after he returned from Mecca with Muhammad's lesson on brotherhood:

"The colorblindness of the Muslim world's religious society and the colorblindness of the Muslim world's society: these two influences had each day been making a greater impact, and an increasing persuasion against my previous way of thinking." *The Autobiography of Malcolm X*, p. 338 - 339.

I think, considering the fact that Malcolm was always exposed to different races of Muslims while he was in the Nation of Islam, he used the issue of colorblindness or universal brotherhood to convince the civil rights leaders -- namely Dr. Martin Luther King -- that he had gotten free of his so-called racism, and therefore deserved consideration as an ally.

On a contrary note, Malcolm's realistic grasp on American black-white brotherhood was revealed with these statements:

"It was in the Holy World that my attitude was changed, by what I experienced there, and by what I witnessed there, in terms of brotherhood -- not just brotherhood toward me, but brotherhood between all men, of all nationalities and complexion, who were there. Now that I am back in America, my attitude here concerning white people has to be governed by what my black brothers and I experience here, and what we witness here -- in

12

terms of brotherhood. The problem here in America is that we meet such a small minority of individual so-called 'good,' or 'brotherly,' white people. Here in the United States, notwithstanding those few 'good' white people, it is the collective 150 million white people whom the collective 22 million black people have to deal with! Why, here in America, the seeds of racism are so deeply rooted in the white people collectively, their belief that they are 'superior' in some way is so deeply rooted, that these things are in the national white subconsciousness." *The Autobiography of Malcolm X*, p. 362 - 363.

The above conjecture pertaining to Malcolm's interest in working with civil rights leaders has merit in light of the fact that he maneuvered to get expelled from the Nation of Islam. This point is made crystal clear in his so-called autobiography (p. 305):

> "Any Muslim would have known that my chickens coming home to roost statement had been only an excuse to put into action the plan for getting me out and step one had been already taken: the Muslims were given the impression that I had rebelled against Mr. Muhammad. I could anticipate step two: I would remain suspended (and later I would be isolated) indefinitely. Step three would be either to provoke some Muslim ignorant of the truth to take it upon himself to kill me as a religious duty -- or to isolate me so that I would gradually disappear from the public scene."

I am completely convinced that the above is self-explanatory.

Elijah Muhammad discouraged involvement in the American political system, but he gave verbal support to progressive politicians such as Adam Clayton Powell Jr. -- Malcolm enhanced that support. Muhammad believed in the process of registering to vote for Muslim politicians. As far as he was concerned, Muslims would make the best politicians. His comments pertaining to this touchy subject were as follows:

"The strongest politicians of our kind -- or the person who comes nearest as far as I know, to giving us political justice in the white courts (if he had our complete backing) -- is Congressman Adam Clayton Powell, Jr., though he is not a Muslim. A Muslim politician is what you need, but Congressman Powell is not afraid and would not be easily bribed, for he is not 'Hungry.' There are two other good politicians, but I will not mention them by name at this time. If they could shed their fear, they would make excellent political leaders to guard our interest. We must give good black politicians the total backing of our population." *Message to the Blackman*, p. 173.

Malcolm echoed the same sentiment except he took it a step further when he argued for an independent political leadership not tied to any of the major political parties, not connected to the philosophy of integration, and, most importantly, having an independent economic base in the black community.

Muhammad appealed to black politicians to work for tax exemption status for black people. His outline of the *Muslim Program* titled "What the Muslims Want" number eight, states:

"We want the government of the United States to exempt our people from ALL taxation as long as we are deprived of equal justice under the laws of the land."

Afterwards, Malcolm suggested that an independent black lobby be built in Washington, D.C., in order to accrue political power.

Ironically, there are some Malcolm devotees who erroneously or deliberately use Malcolm's "Ballots or Bullets" speech to advocate continual black support for the Democratic Party.
The speech is clearly against such an action; however, the following statement clearly removes any possible equivocation on this issue:

"I wouldn't have put myself in the position of voting for either candidate for the Presidency or of recommending to any Blackman to do . . .Don't register. That's intelligent. Don't register and vote for a dummy, you can vote for a dummy, you can vote for a crook, you can vote for another who'd want to exploit you. "Register" means being in a position to take political action anytime, anyplace, and in any manner that would be beneficial to you and me; being in a position to take advantage of our position. But as soon as you get registered and you want to be a Republican or Democrat, you are aligning. And once you are aligned, you have no bargaining power -- none whatsoever."

Muhammad also made the following comment regarding political endorsements:

"He would have to be in sympathy with us and he would have to have some knowledge of the aims and purposes of Islam in America." *Message to the Blackman in America*, p. 316.

Another prevalent fallacy revolving around Malcolm was the false claim he made during his Middle East tour and hajj that he never learned how to pray properly (Salat), "Imagine, being a Muslim minister, a leader in Elijah Muhammad's Nation of Islam, and not knowing the prayer ritual." *Autobiography of Malcolm X*, p. 326. The significance and manner of Salat (prayer) was taught in the Nation of Islam at various times. Additionally, Muhammad devoted several chapters to the meaning of prayer in Islam in his *Message to the Blackman in America* (pp. 135 & 160).

On the subject of prayer ablution (Wudu), he stated:

"Each part of ablution requirement has some significance. For instance, the Muslim washes his hands to "get rid of any evil" they might have committed. This also signifies that the Muslim thus

(*Malcolm X Speaks* on the 1964 Johnson-Goldwater Presidential Campaign, p. 43, Second Edition, 1989.
Malcolm X Speaks, First Edition, 1965.)

Unfortunately, political success led to Congressman Powell's political decline. Later, Elijah Muhammad bitterly attacked him for transforming into an "Uncle Tom" politician. Malcolm X criticized Powell for his political indecisiveness in Powell's later, more fun-filled days: "It is hard to tell which direction Congressman Powell moves in. He moves in one direction one minute and another direction another minute."

asks Allah to wash his hands in the spirit of Forgiveness." *The Supreme Wisdom*, Volume Two, p. 65)

Muhammad gave an elaborate, yet brief explanation on the meaning of the various steps of Salat (prayer):

"The various 'steps' of the Muslims prayer -- turning, bowing, sitting and prostrating -- all have a beautiful meaning." *The Supreme Wisdom*, Volume Two, p. 64)

Muslims regard prayer as an out pouring of the heart's sentiments, a devout supplication to God and a reverential expression of the soul's sincerest desires before the Creator. In Islam the idea of prayer, like all other religious ideas has its highest development. Prayer, according to the Holy Quran is the true means of that purification of heart which is the only way of communion with Allah. To a Muslim, prayer is his or her spiritual diet of which he or she partakes five times a day in as much as he or she feeds the body of bread for its physical growth.

Islam, therefore, enjoins prayer as a means of the moral elevation of man. Prayer degenerating into a mere ritual and into a lifeless and rapid ceremony performed with insincerity of hearts is not the prayer enjoined by Islam.

Elijah Muhammad, according to his detractors, did not have an inkling of an understanding of the all-encompassing value of prayer. However, an objective study of Muhammad's comments on prayer clearly demonstrates, I think, how profoundly knowledgeable and sincere he was regarding this heartfelt subject:

"The five prayers of the day are spiritual refreshments and he who cleanses himself in and out leaves no filthiness. It would be an insult to invite His Lord's holy spirit into a house the outside of which was filthy."

Another noted contradiction to Malcolm's statement appears on pages 193 and 194 of his autobiography in which he elaborates on performing ablution (Wudu) with his brother Wilfred. This occurred, mind you, in 1952.

16

Notice that Muhammad uses the term "holy spirit," which again contradicts his teachings that God was not and cannot be a spirit. He continues:

> "Why should we not pray five times a day to our Maker since we feed our bodies three times a day? What is so important that would keep us away from prayer to the Originator of the heavens and the earth? Let us give praises to our God and submit ourselves to the Lord of the worlds and learn how to pray in the right manner. Let us serve the One True God, whose proper name is Allah, in the right state."

In the above, he is clear regarding the necessity for learning the proper way or manner to pray. Undoubtedly, these comments refute Malcolm's statement regarding his ignorance of how to pray while he was a minister in the Nation of Islam. As stated before, Muhammad had an extremely deep love and appreciation for Islam and prayer.

Muhammad urged the study of the Holy Quran on prayer:

> 20:30, 17:78, 17:116 and 29:45. He further added that the object of a Muslim's prayer is the purification of his or her heart which is necessary for spiritual advancement. *Message to the Blackman in America*, p. 136.

Mr. Muhammad believed that the essence of Al-Fatiha (The Opening) of the Holy Quran was one of the best prayers for the so-called Negroes because of its magnificent exaltation of Allah, The Lord of the Worlds. Muhammad indicated that the spiritual profundity of Al-Fatiha in the Holy Quran was an excellent prayer for black people who were (are) lost from the right direction.

Lastly, Muhammad continued to reveal his belief, love, awareness of the proper prayer ritual (Salat) in Islam and the oneness of Allah. His -- surprisingly to some -- profound comments are these:

> "Since learning of the prayer service of Islam -- the religion of entire submission to the will of Allah -- we see him now not only trying to keep his internal parts clean, but the external parts too. He washes his face, his hands, and all the exposed parts of his body before going to prayer. Never before has he done such under the cross (Christianity). (The 'he' is referring to the black man) prostrating himself with his shoes off and his

17

forehead kissing the rug or the bare earth in praises and humble submission to the will of Allah (God). He thanks Allah for the knowledge of words to say, to know Him to be the true God, to believe in and worship Him alone and not to set up a rival to Him." *Message to the Blackman*, p. 152.

I surmised earlier that Malcolm's calculated ploy to get expelled from the Nation of Islam was probably based on his interest in working with civil rights leaders. His following statement validates my conjecture:

"I am prepared to cooperate in local civil rights actions in the south and elsewhere and shall do so because every campaign for specific objectives can only heighten the political consciousness of Blacks and intensify their identification against white society."

Malcolm, unlike Elijah Muhammad, who basically remained an urban based religio-nationalist, sought to internationalize the civil rights struggle to the level of human rights under the Human Rights Provisions of the United Nations Charter. Malcolm was desirous of getting close to the civil rights movement for the purpose of radicalizing it.

In an effort to actualize his goal, Malcolm tried to gain the support of eighteen African countries at the Summit Conference of African prime ministers. He delivered an eight-page memorandum condemning American racism; however, the memorandum did not get the adequate attention it deserved from the delegates at that session.

Malcolm should have known from historical observation that his memorandum, which comprised a scathing criticism of America's racist policies at home and abroad, would be too politically sensitive for those newly emerging independent African countries to consider.

As a result, the State Department, the Justice Department, and the Central Intelligence Agency placed him under twenty-four hour

Elijah Muhammad compiled a booklet, entitled, *Muslim Daily Prayers*, that addressed all aspects of prayer (Salat) and the spiritual significance of Obligatory (Fard) and traditional (Sunnah) prayers, and he described the prayer step (Rak'ah). This was published in February 26, 1957. Thus, if Malcolm did not know how to pray it was because he did not put forth any effort.

surveillance. There was even an effort to poison him in Cario, Egypt prior to his presentation of the memorandum.

There is a very unique and interesting precedent to this subject that deserves a brief discussion. But there is another point that begs for immediate attention at this time. Excluding the fact that African heads of state did not openly endorse Malcolm's memorandum, those influential Muslim countries with whom he came in contact did not render or offer any support either. He did receive the endorsement of orthodox Islamic leaders for his Muslim Mosque, Inc., but that was limited.

Moreover, these Muslim leaders were more interested in seeing to it that Malcolm gained a correct understanding of Islam than in Joining an anti-American racism campaign.

Understandably, the rationale for these countries lack of active involvement was the cold-war ideology that was so prevalent at that time. What these countries were precariously able and willing to do was to verbally link up with Malcolm's agenda on a superficial level.

Paradoxically, some of these same countries -- particularly Muslim countries -- not only gave guarded verbal support to Elijah Muhammad, but also donated millions of dollars to his Nation of Islam program. As a matter of fact, Abdul Basit Naeem, Editor-Publisher of *The Moslem World and the U.S.A.*, was very instrumental in the years 1957 and 1959 for focusing attention on Elijah Muhammad and his Nation of Islam. Naeem's magazine was anti-colonialism, anti-imperialism, and prorevolutionary Arab/African leadership. Equally important, it was an organ that imparted positive information about the accomplishments of members of the Nation.

Aside from Mr. Muhammad's teachings, and news about his followers, which comprised considerable space, Naeem was primarily responsible for interpreting the Nation of Islam. Here is just one major statement he made regarding his respect for Muhammad, his followers and their gradual knowledge and understanding of the Holy Quran and the proper prayer ritual (Salat):

> "As far as I am concerned, I consider the differences between Islam of the East and teachings of Mr. Elijah Muhammad to be of relatively minor importance at this time, because these are not related to the SPIRIT of Islam, which I am sure, is completely shared by all of us. A Moslem from Pakistan, Indonesia, Iran or Egypt only has to meet some of Mr. Elijah Muhammad's followers to be convinced of their love utmost

devotion and passion for all that is the true Islamic Spirit. Not many of Mr. Elijah Muhammad's followers have had the opportunity to read and understand the Holy Quran or fully comprehend the concept of Moslem prayers, fasting, zakat (alms-giving) and the institution of hajj (pilgrimage to Mecca). However, I am in a position to say, most authoritatively, that Muslims, under the leadership of Mr. Muhammad have now BEGUN to make serious study of Allah's Divine Word and to grasp its true meaning. Very soon, I can further state, they will also start receiving instruction in the daily prayers and other Islamic duties. I know of what I have just said, in the preceding paragraph, because I am the humble individual through whom Mr. Elijah Muhammad's followers are obtaining their copies of the Holy Quran and other Islamic literature, and I know that they have already acquired more copies of the Holy Quran than might be in the possession of all the other Moslems in the U.S.A.!"

Afterwards, Mr. Naeem became the General Secretary of a group known as the American Islamic Education Society.

Mr. Naeem continued his support for Muhammad for many years; he even wrote articles for *Muhammad Speaks* after the discontinuation of his *Moslem World*.

Muhammad had more than fleeting acquaintances with African, Asian and Arab leaders. He was always very selective about whom he gave his organizational support; he was openly respectful of anti-America and anti-Zionist leaders such as President Gamal Abdul Nasser, Muamar Quaddafi, and Kwame Nkrumah.

I must, out of responsibility, say that Naeem was just one major foreign-born Muslim who broke introductory ground for Muhammad and his followers. Needless to say, Muhammad was never totally acknowledged as a Muslim social reformer. But he did get enough recognition to make him a conversational force to be reckoned with until the day he departed.

Elijah did not tamper with ideological international politics as did Malcolm; however, he, through a nationalist tradition, always concerned himself with international affairs. The *Muhammad Speaks* newspaper never faltered in this noble task.

Out of respect for historical continuity, it is imperative to briefly compare and assess other attempts by African American leaders to address the issue of American racism via the Human Rights Provisions of the United nations Charter which undoubtedly inspired and motivated Malcolm.

Ralph Bunche, regardless of what one wants to accept about him, used his United Nations and international experiences to passionately argue against colonialism and imperialism in the so-called third-world, and to raise the question of human rights worldwide, especially within the United States. In a Lincoln Day Address given February 15, 1951 at Springfield, Illinois, Bunche found a tactful way of expressing himself about the conditions of America's African American population. He fused it to the United Nations concern for human rights, freedom, and justice throughout the world. In that speech, portions will follow, he cleverly examined his convictions as a United Nations official and as an African American citizen:

> "Race relations is our number one social problem, perhaps our number one problem. It is no mere sectional problem; it is a national -- indeed an international -- problem. For any problem today which challenges the ability of democracy to function convincingly, which undermines the very foundations of democracy and the faith of people in it, is of concern to the entire peace and freedom-loving world."

In another part of his speech he said this:

> "Throughout the nation, in varying degree, the Negro minority -- almost a tenth of the population -- suffers severe political, economic, and social disabilities, solely because of race."

Concluding parts of the speech were as follows:

> "The United Nations ideal is a world in which people would practice tolerance and live together in peace with one another as good neighbors. If this ideal is far from realization, it is only because of the mind of mankind."

The late, venerable, Charles P. Howard, was very instrumental in addressing international issues in the *Muhammad Speaks*.

21

Paul Robeson, for example, echoed the inescapable fact that the American domestic issue was inextricably connected to the international question of peace. Robeson and other moderate and progressive black leaders turned to the United Nations to protest the injustice meted out to Willie McGee, the case of the Martinsville Seven, and the conviction of the Trenton Six as a conclusive manifestation of United States institutionalized racism. William Patterson initiated the drive to present a formal petition -- "We Charge Genocide" -- to the United Nations as a means for publishing the terrible toll of racism in the United States. Influential black leaders such as Bishop W. J. Walls, Reverend Charles A. Hill, Dr. Du Bois, Charlotta Bass, Ben Davis, Jr. and Mary Church Terrell supported the aim of the petition. Robeson spent tireless hours with Patterson drawing up the petition, and making sure the language coincided with the language of the United Nations Charter. They made sure that their use of the term "genocide" was sanctioned by the United Nations' own definition of the term, as established in its Genocide Convention, which in 1951 remained unratified by the United States.

In its final form, Robeson and Patterson's petition extended beyond the understanding of genocide to mean state-sanctioned mass murder, including bodily and mental impairment to individual members of a national, ethnic, racial, or religious group. Their petition, interestingly, embraced the concept of "economic genocide," the "silent, cruel killer."

Both men presented their petitions simultaneously; Robeson to the United Nations Secretariat in New York and Patterson to the United Nations General Assembly in Paris. Needless to say, the United States via its world influence thwarted their efforts; therefore, the charge of genocide was never discussed.

In 1947, Dr. Du Bois appealed to the United Nations in behalf -- a year before, he urged the United Nations General Assembly to consider human rights abuses against Africans -- of African Americans as editor of the NAACP's statement on the Denial of Human Rights to Minorities in the case of citizens of Negro Descent in the United States of America and an appeal to the United Nations for Redress.Du Bois, after winning reluctant approval from Walter White

Bunche was also part of an editorial assistance team that worked with W.E.B. Du Bois in drafting an anti-racism petition to the United Nations. Ironically, Adam Clayton Powell and Malcolm would call Bunche an "international Uncle Tom." *Ralph Bunche - The Man and His Times*, Edited by Benjamin Rivlin (Holmes & Meir, New York, 1990, p. 241, 242, and 245).

and the NAACP, and taking his incentive from the National Negro Congress pressed forward with this momentous project. He consulted with United Nations Secretary General Trygire Lie on the substantive procedures of filing a petition. He also enlisted the editorial assistance of such prominent blacks as William Hastie, Earl Dickerson, Rayford Logan, and, of course, Ralph Bunche. He hastened to get support from imminent black religious leaders, newspaper publishers, black fraternities, and the endorsement of NNC which actually set the petition idea to the United Nations in motion. Dr. Du Bois did not ignore the black left on this subject and invited some of its most politically conscious leaders. Other members of the non-left that were invited and eagerly accepted were Mrs. D. S. Smith and Mary McLeod Bethune.

What is most impressive as we compare historical notes to Malcolm's so-called political ascendancy is the fact that Du Bois' petition received wide endorsement abroad -- namely from third world countries. The Trade Union Congress of Jamaica, Jomo Kenyetta of Kenya, Caribbean Labor Congress, National Council of Nigeria and Cameroons, Nnamdi Azikiwe, Kwame Nkrumah, C. Matinga of the Nysasland African Congress, the African country of Liberia lent its support and Joseph France of the St. Kitts-Nevis Trades and Labor Union.

Other colonial countries such as India, Egypt, Haiti, Mexico, and China, gave overwhelming support to the petition. The reader must bear in mind these countries were themselves struggling for liberation and human dignity. Therefore, it stands to reason that their sentiments would be the same as oppressed African Americans.

Dr. Du Bois, as early as 1941, had conceived of assembling a group to prepare a presentation on the plight of African Americans, Afro-West Indians, and Africans at the Next Peace Conference. This idea was an inspiration to Afro-West Indian scholar, Richard B. Moore, who took up the cause and prepared "An Appeal on Behalf of the Caribbean Peoples."

George R. Murphy, Jr. drew up the third such petition to the United Nations on behalf of black Americans. The first, which will be discussed next, was presented by Dr. W.E.B. Du Bois, the second was presented by Patterson and Robeson.

Malcolm was scheduled to meet with Robeson, but unfortunately, he was murdered a month before the meeting was to take place.
Martin Duberman, *Paul Robeson* (Alfred A. Knopf, New York, 1988, p. 397, 527 & 705).

Du Bois attended the first meeting of the Commission on Human rights escorted by Ralph Bunche. The petition was given to John Humphrey, Director of the Commission on Human Rights, who was asked to take action on the petition. Unfortunately, Humphrey's political hands were tied. Nonetheless, the commission formulated "an International Bill of Rights" and drew up for the United Nations clearer definitions of "human rights and fundamental freedoms." Du Bois engaged in intense lobbying after the Humphrey encounter, but the subcommission voted down the proposal made by Soviet Russia to investigate discrimination against black Americans; the vote was four to one with the United States delegate Jonathan Danials voting no and seven nations abstaining.

Surprising to some, Eleanor Roosevelt who was a member of the United Nations Economic and Social Council and a board member of the NAACP not only complicated the entire process, but also refused to even consider Du Bois request for consideration. Thus Du Bois' petition became bogged down in the quagmire of Cold War politics.

It is safe to conclude that Du Bois' actions and the other black leaders were paramount in helping President Truman to take some steps toward civil rights.

Another petition was presented to the United Nations by Mrs. Mary Church Terrell on the 21st of September 1949 on behalf of a black woman named Mrs. Rosa Lee Ingram and her two sons. The details were stated and drafted by Du Bois and a number of black women supported it. As a result, the previous death sentence meted out to Ingram and her teenage sons were commuted to life imprisonment. In August 1959, they were paroled; in 1964 the sentences were commuted with full restoration of rights.

The global cross cultural sameness of oppression and exploitation qualified the United States "race problem" as a denial of human rights and not merely a civil rights violation. Thus, Malcolm, as we have just seen, had some unique examples from which to choose. His desire to present the cause of African Americans before the United Nations was undoubtedly predicated primarily on the attempt by Dr. Du Bois and I am almost certain that Du Bois' philosophical position pertaining to colonialism and imperialism acted as a spring board for Malcolm.

NAACP Annual Report for 1947, p. 49 - 50.

NAACP Annual Report for 1948, p. 65.

Elliot Rudwick, *W.E.B. Du Bois Voice of the Black Protest Movement,* University of Illinois Press, Urbana, 1982, p. 291 - 292.

Malcolm's anti-Viet Nam War remarks were very much akin to Paul Robeson who also spoke out against the U.S. imperialist war machine.

Malcolm's major speech regarding the necessity to plead the African Americans' case before the United Nation was as follow:

> "One of the first steps we are going to become involved in as an organization of Afro-American Unity will be to bring the Negro problem before the United Nations. We feel that the problem of the black man in this country is beyond the ability of Uncle Sam to solve. We must internationalize the problem and take advantage of the United Nations Declaration of Human Rights and on that ground bring it before the world body wherein we can indict Uncle Sam for the continued criminal injustices that our people experience in this government."

Despite the contextual similarity to DuBois' earlier United Nations petition, Malcolm obviously went beyond a black nationalist and Pan-Africanist perspective to address the plight of the so-called third world. He often spoke of Latin-American brothers and 800 million Chinese brothers supporting such a legitimate United Nations resolution. Unfortunately, as indicated before, the Cold War program of the United States with its designs on world hegemony destroyed any possibility of such an occurrence.

A great deal of emphasis is placed on the impact of the African and Middle Eastern experiences of 1964 on Malcolm's religio-political thinking. As was pointed out before, Malcolm had been exposed to a number of third world revolutionaries in the Nation of Islam during his ministerial tenure. Equally important, we should remember that Malcolm's father was a Garveyite, and Garveyism has always had, as an objective, the cultural, political and economic connections of the plight of Africans throughout the Diaspora. Malcolm was also a frequent visitor and student of Brother Lewis Michaux, Black na-

Gerald Horne, *Black and Red W.E.B. Du Bois and the Afro-American Response to the Cold War 1944 - 1963*, State University of New York Press, 1988, p. 80 - 81

Against Racism Unpublished Essays, Papers Addresses, 1987 - 1961 W.E.B. Du Bois Edited by Herbert Aptheker, The University of Massachusetts Press, 1985, p. 261

tionalist and Garveyite owner of the National African Memorial bookstore "The House of Common Sense and Home of Proper Propaganda," which was situated at 125th Street and Seventh Avenue in Harlem, New York. Professor Michaux hosted a number of progressive nonwhite revolutionaries and black nationalists at his bookstore.

Repeating for emphatic clarity, in the Nation of Islam, Malcolm was always exposed to the interconnections between the African American problem and those of the "original people" or "Asiatics" as Mr. Muhammad referred to all nonwhite peoples. Before he went to Africa and the Middle East in 1959 as an emissary for Mr. Muhammad, he had a lot of contact with African, Asian, and Arab Muslims, and he met and hosted a number of nonwhite revolutionaries such as Fidel Castro in 1960 at the once famous Theresa Hotel. As a matter of fact, Malcolm's proposal to take the case of racial oppression in the United States before the General Assembly surfaced when Che Guevara warned that "The time will come when this Assembly will acquire greater maturity and demand guarantees from the United States government for the lives of the Negro . . . population . . . in this country."

Guevara sensing the emergence of an Afro-Asian, Cuban revolutionary bloc reminded those in attendance that "those peoples whose skins are darkened by the different sun, colored by different pigment, constitute the majority within the United Nations and the world."

Furthermore, Malcolm was intrigued by Robert Williams, NAACP, president of the North Carolina branch, who was one of the first Black Americans to advocate armed self defense and to live in Cuba and China. Williams initiated and organized the Deacons for Defense against Ku Klux Klan violence in North Carolina; he was subsequently forced into exile. Williams was a shinning example of black manly courage, and the *Muhammad Speaks* always reported on his activities.

George Breitman, Editor, *By Any Means Necessary* Pathfinder Press, N. Y., 1967, p. 57.

Castro, The Blacks and Africa by Carlos Moore, University of California, Los Angeles, 1988, p. 192. The Deacons for Defense were also organized for armed self defense.

26

All of these experiences, and involvement with such notables previously mentioned as well as his Black Muslim orientation were important elements in the nationalist and internationalist development of Malcolm X. Professor Essien-Udom sums it up best when he pointed out that during the last phase of Malcolm's life the ideological strands of Garveyism merged with a modified version of Elijah Muhammad's doctrine of the Black Nation to form the core of his thinking about the Afro-American's struggle and its relationship to Africa and the world.

The influence of Garveyism in Malcolm's thinking was made obvious on March 12, 1964, when he announced his break with the Nation of Islam. He never relented in his belief that Mr Muhammad had the best solution to the race problem in America, and, like Garvey, advocated the return of African-Americans to Africa as a long-range solution. He later spoke in terms of a cultural and spiritual return -- which was similar to Muhammad -- to Africa while remaining in the United States.

In Elijah Muhammad's Nation of Islam, the peoples considered as constituting the Black Nation corresponded in a political reality to the colonized and neo-colonized peoples of the world. Malcolm's predisposition to this ideology compelled him to regard the African American liberation struggle as part and parcel of the black revolution of the so-called third world revolt against the United States economic hegemony and cultural supremacy.

The following statements by Malcolm unequivocally demonstrate that he had been properly prepared to be a recipient of the significance and importance of African cultural consciousness:

> "One of the things that made the Black Muslim Movement grow was its emphasis upon things African. This was the secret to the growth of the Black Muslim movement. African blood, African origin, African culture, African ties. And you'd be surprised -- we discovered that deep within the subconscious of the black man in this country, he is still more African than he is American." February 14, 1965.

Another fallacy that Malcolm presented was this, "Elijah Muhammad had taught us that the white man could not enter into

Black Crusader, A Biography of Robert Franklin Williams, by Robert Carl Cohen, Lyle Stuart, Inc., New Jersey, 1972, p. 16, 154 and 155.

Mecca in Arabia and all of us who followed him, we believed it. . ." First of all, Muhammad always taught that there were "white complexioned Muslims," but they were only Muslims by belief and not Muslims by nature. Nevertheless, Muhammad stated that these so-called "white Muslims" would on judgment day, be blessed by Allah. Secondly, I think all we have to do is review history to concur with the fact that a Christian white man, with a white mind, and a white attitude most certainly cannot enter into Mecca to make hajj. The historical example is Sir. Richard Francis Burton who painstakingly disguised himself so that he could make hajj, and according to his accounts, even though his disguise as an Arab was convincing he still feared exposure and for his life.

Reiterating what was discussed previously, Malcolm met and socialized with white complexioned Muslims from Turkey, Albania, and the Middle East while he was a minister of Muhammad. Minister Malcolm hosted, at the request of Mr. Muhammad, a number of Muslims of all colors, who came to New York and Chicago to meet him and Elijah Muhammad and to assess the curriculum at the then Universities of Islam. Some of these Muslims even gave support to the schools, and politely debated Islamic doctrinal policies with Muhammad and Malcolm. As a matter of fact, Malcolm often justified Muhammad's version of Islam by stating: "We are teaching the Islamic faith that is applicable to the peculiar condition faced by the American black man." Malcolm would remind these Eastern Muslims that Muslims throughout the world differed from each other according to their environment. Malcolm, however, clarifies his position by differentiating between "white Muslims" and "white Americans."

> "When I got over there and went to Mecca and saw those people who were blond and blue-eyed and pale-skinned and all those things, I said, Well, but I watched them closely. And I noticed that though they were white, and they would call themselves white, there was a difference between them and the white ones over here. And that basic difference was this: In Asia or the Arab world or in Africa, where the Muslims are if you find one who says he's white, all he's doing is using an adjective to

28

describe something that's incidental about him, one of his incidental characteristics; there is nothing else to it, he's just white. But when you get the white man over here in America and he says he's white, he means something else. You can listen to the sound of his voice -- when he says he's white, he means he's boss."

Considering the above comments by Malcolm, it can be concluded that he did not change his views towards whites in America because he knew that the white American society had not changed.

There were two factors that Malcolm missed about Muslims in the East: One, because he witnessed and felt brotherly love from white complexioned Muslims during hajj, this was not a basis for concluding that Muslims in the East were free of color consciousness. Prophet Muhammad had been critical of Arab Muslims who thought that they were better than non-Arab Muslims. Prophet Muhammad taught that: "An Arab is not more privileged than non-Arabs, nor white than black. Spiritual excellence and true piety are the only distinctions amongst humans recognized by God."

This spiritual teaching did not prevent a number of Arabs from practicing racism during his prophetic era. In fact, Arab racism motivated Al-Jahiz of Basra to write *The Boast of the Blacks against the Whites* or *The Glory of the Black Race* which was a defense of black people. Not only did color prejudice and forms of racism exist during Prophet Muhammad's time, but in the Holy City of Mecca, Saudi Arabia, Africans were (are), for the most part, on the bottom of the socioeconomic scale.

The second factor that Malcolm missed or willfully refused to comprehend was that a Muslim man is allowed to have up to four wives as decreed in the Holy Quran. By understanding this decree, he would have realized that Elijah Muhammad committed no moral transgression by having another wife or more than one wife, if this was indeed the case. Malcolm, out of anger and confusion, judged Muhammad on the basis of Western and Anglo-Christian standards, or he used this allegation as a vindictive tactic.

The Algerian ambassador who proclaimed to Malcolm that black nationalism alienated him because he was white was manifesting that he had internalized a racist identification with the French colonizer.

Malcolm X Speaks, Grove Press, Inc., New York, 1965, p. 162 and 163.

There was legalized slavery in Saudi Arabia during the time that Malcolm made hajj.

Moreover, Malcolm was too close to Elijah Muhammad not to have known about these alleged unions that coincided with Islamic theological tradition. If any infidelity or immorality took place, why did not Sister Clara Muhammad, Elijah's first wife openly object? The most important question is why did Malcolm wait until he was suspended before he raised this issue? Also, if these secretaries who supposedly filed paternity suits against Muhammad were so enraged about their supposed mistreatment, why have they not come forward and claimed what is rightfully theirs, or even better write a book, and go on television? Again, I think, Malcolm used this as a tactic to rebel against his suspension and to try to sway as many of Muhammad's followers away from him as possible. Bear in mind, that Malcolm was desperately trying to establish himself as a newly transformed leader.

Let us deflect those rumors with some degree of fact: as just indicated, if the marital allegations are true, Muhammad was married in an Islamic tradition. According to Dr. Alauddin Shabazz, Palestinian scholar, Ali Baghdadi, was supposedly a witness at one marriage procedure. From what we are told, the only acknowledged wife of Mr. Muhammad is Sister Tynetta Muhammad who is also a follower of Minister Louis Farrakhan. Once again, according to Islamic precepts, Mr. Muhammad operated within the context of the Holy Quran.

The judgment about Muhammad's moral character usually come from, whom I consider, black and white hypocritical Christians that preach morality and monogamy, but practice immorality and voluptuousness. Furthermore, some of America's presidents, lawmakers, celebrities, and theologians were (are) practitioners of mendaciousness, child abuse, (sexual and physical) homosexuality, and martial infidelity. As far as black people are concerned, all we have to do is look at some of our Christian ministers and some of our noted celebrities and scholars who practice homosexuality, infidelity and self-hatred. No human being is infallible, and a human being's errors do not remove him or her from God's graces or historical greatness. The only so-called illegitimate children that Elijah Muhammad was responsible for were the twenty-two million African Americans that he was so passionately trying to rear and nurture into an independent, progressively conscious people.

We must remember that noted or popular figures are almost always vulnerable to slanderous accusations. Since the writing of this book, Minister Farrakhan has brought to the public the Muslim wives of Mr. Muhammad. They graciously acknowledged their husband and his children.

Malcolm was a bitter, angry and a confused man at the time he was making those allegations about Muhammad's moral character. He supposedly persuaded two women, Lucille Rosary Karriem and Evelyn Williams, who claimed Muhammad fathered their children, to file paternity suits against him. However, according to known reports, nothing resulted from these lawsuits. The women never got the papers served and the litigation languished. From what we are told, there were some officials -- such as the late Captain Joseph of New York and Minister Louis Farrakhan -- who supposedly were aware of Muhammad's alleged polygynous situation. If this is true, the question arises again, why did it take Malcolm so long to find out, considering the fact that he was like a son to Muhammad? Furthermore, some members within the Nation of Islam circle were surprised that Malcolm made so much of the allegations in the first place.

In concluding this aspect of our discussion, it should be pointed out that Malcolm often preached against allowing yourself to be coerced by the so-called Devil (white man). However, he became the victim of his own preachments when he went to Mike Wallace and other members of the caucasian press with those scurrilous rumors about Muhammad's so-called infidelity.

Malcolm was temporarily suspended from public speaking because of his untimely statement regarding the assassination of President John Kennedy. Every minister in the Nation was requested to remain silent about the death. Because Malcolm was so vocal and visible, he was particularly admonished to refrain from public comment. Unfortunately, he made his "chickens coming home to roost" statement and was subsequently suspended from his national ministerial duties. It was not the statement in and of itself; it was the fact that the Nation had never before been confronted with the assassination of a president and with the emotional furor that followed it. The terms of the suspension were that Malcolm could go on governing the daily affairs of his mosque in New York, but was forbidden to speak or grant interviews.

Malcolm, initially alleged that Muhammad had fathered children with nine or six of his secretaries. But he only managed to produce two.

When Malcolm was asked if he had proof of his charges against Muhammad, he only invited his doubters to ask Mr. Muhammad "and see if he denies it. . .See if he can give you a yes or no answer."

Surprisingly, Malcolm accepted the terms of the suspension and admitted that it was best for the safety of the Nation of Islam, and for his own as well. He told one Nation of Islam official that Mr. Muhammad had probably saved his life; his chickens coming home to roost statement was a half-cocked statement and if Muhammad had not disciplined him first, the public might well have killed him for it. This is what Malcolm devotees need to understand, and realize that Malcolm was not suspended entirely, nor was he suspended because Elijah Muhammad was envious of his ascension. It was obviously a wise decision on Muhammad's part because of the climate of the country and the nature of the statement.

During the final days of the suspension, Malcolm made several overtures to Muhammad by letter and by phone for a hearing. In other words, and this is documented, Malcolm wanted to be reinstated, but he continued to violate the ninety-day public speaking ban. Thus, when he did receive a hearing, Mr. Muhammad bluntly told Malcolm "Go back and put out the fire you started."

There were agents in and out of the Nation that were working feverishly to prevent Malcolm, the son, and Elijah, the father from ever getting reunited.

Malcolm realized near the end of his life that the Muslims were not under any directive from Muhammad to murder him.

He also changed his mind about the Muslims being responsible for the bombing of his house. Obviously the man who had a hand in the killing confessed that he was not a Muslim in the Nation of Islam. Again, he acted independent of Elijah Muhammad, or any official in the Nation. Furthermore, one can easily conclude that he and his accomplices were aided and abetted by the New York City Police Department, and the FBI. Malcolm was constantly pursued by agents; some of them dressed as Muslims, and thereby harassed him to the point of making him paranoid of all of Elijah Muhammad's followers.

One can argue persuasively that to a certain extent, Minister Louis

Peter Goldman and some former Nation of Islam officials concur that Malcolm confessed that he had been undercutting the "Messenger" among his followers over a two-year period and asked what he could do to make up for it. It was at that point that Muhammad told him to go put out the fire. *The Death and Life of Malcolm X*, Petter Goldman, p. 135 and 136.

Farrakhan, set the rhetorical tempo for Malcolm's death, but almost every minister in the Nation was enraged with Malcolm's antics. It was Farrakhan's high visibility, and his passionate rhetoric which set the pace for the agents to accelerate. I think Farrakhan's honest explanation for his actions deserve respect and forgiveness because every major minister at that critical time was in a very precarious situation.

Lastly, interested parties should read page 418 of the *Autobiography of Malcolm X*, (1965), and analyze what Alex Haley said about high government officials being interested in Malcolm's statements abroad, and what he might do when he returned to the United States.

Ideologically, Malcolm wavered, religiously, he was always a Muslim. This was his greatest triumph. His unyielding devotion to Islam, freedom and Allah was what made him the man that he was. In addition, Malcolm's devotion to the Honorable Elijah Muhammad should be assessed within the larger context of his devotion to the economic uplift and freedom of black people and the religion of Islam. "The Honorable Elijah Muhammad gave me the ability to respect myself." As a total black man, Malcolm said, "Before hearing of him. . ., I had nothing, knew nothing, and was nothing, I was addicted to and enslaved by the evils and vices of this white civilization -- dope, alcohol, adultery, and even murder." Muhammad had elevated him up from "the very bottom of the American white man's society," where, he said, "I. . .was buried up to my neck in the mud of this filthy world, with very little hope, desire or intention of amounting to anything." "I was walking on my own coffin." Muhammad transformed Malcolm, stood him up in an erect position as a proud, dignified black man and Muslim, and then gave him a platform to speak on behalf of

---

Another widely circulated error is that Malcolm took the name Malik after he made hajj. Malcolm received the name Malik El-Shabazz around 1961 from the Honorable Elijah Muhammad. This is also documented. Professor Essien-Udom even mentions this in his classic work *Black Nationalism*, p. 195.

Talmadge Hayer, the trigger man, maintained that he was not and had never been one of Elijah Muhammad's followers nor were his accomplices. He also confessed that they had been hired to carry out the assassination; he also said that the man who hired him was not a Muslim. George Breitman, Herman Porter, and Baxter Smith, *The Assassination of Malcolm X*, Pathfinder Press, New York, 1976.

freedom, justice and equality for black people.

On this same note, Professor Harold Cruse, more than adequately shows the crucial importance of historical continuity with this statement:

"The Black Power exponents who uphold Malcolm X, yet cannot come to terms with either Booker T. Washington or W.E.B. Du Bois as historical leaders, understand neither the break between Du Bois and Washington, nor the break between Malcolm X and Elijah Muhammad. These two breaches are historically related and stem from the same root in Afro-American history, albeit under different circumstances. Malcolm X broke with the Nation of Islam because of Muhammad's refusal to participate in the broad struggle for human rights, as Malcolm X explained it. But W.E.B. Du Bois, the turn-of-the-century radical broke with Booker T. Washington's leadership school for the same reasons. Du Bois said that Washington shied away from participating in the struggle for the Negro's manhood rights. Malcolm X's break was that of a radical nationalist with the conservative nationalism of Elijah Muhammad, the latter inherited from Booker T. Washington, by way of Garvey who had "radicalized" Washington's economic philosophy."

I think it is somewhat safe to say that the differences among those men were rooted in educational levels, social orientations, and geographical locations -- urban-based conditioning versus rural-based training.
Harold Cruse, *The Crisis of the Negro Intellectual*, p. 563.

34

MALCOLM'S ABIDING BELIEFS

Some of the major beliefs of Malcolm were the same as when he was a minister in the Nation of Islam:

1. Blacks can get their freedom only by struggling for it.

2. America is intrinsically racist and will not grant black people total freedom.

3. Integration is not the answer for the black man's problems; it does not offer true freedom, justice or equality.

4. Uncle Toms must be exposed and opposed.

5. Black people must rely on themselves and control their own destiny.

6. Blacks must select and support their own national and community leaders.

7. Blacks must defend themselves when attacked. This position influenced the Black Panthers and the Revolutionary Action Movement (RAM).

8. Blacks must own and control the economic and political resources in their community.

PREACHERS OF SALVATION

Elijah Muhammad is one of the most misunderstood, maligned and vilified black leaders in history. Rarely is he analyzed within the context of his rural southern background, his limited educational background, or his unswerving allegiance to his "Savior, Master Farad Muhammad."

He was born in Sandersville, Georgia on October 7, 1898 (the date is questionable). His father and grandfather were Baptist preachers and sharecroppers. Mr. Muhammad only received a rudimentary education (third grade) before he was compelled to go to the fields to help his family earn a living. Mr. Muhammad (Elijah Poole) later worked as a laborer for the Southern Railroad, and as a builder for the Cherokee Brick Company. His puritan work ethic, which he imparted to his followers, earned him an appointed position as foreman.

He was highly regarded for his dutifulness and honesty which was a result of his early Christian background and his impressive awareness of biblical scripture (which he employed throughout his leadership). He married Clara Evans (later known as Sister Clara Muhammad) and they had two sons while still residing in Georgia. In 1923, the family of four moved to Detroit and there the family increased to four more sons and two daughters. Mr. Muhammad worked for the Chevrolet Auto Plant in Detroit from 1923 to 1929; however, the Great Depression forced the family on relief for two years, 1929 to 1931. It has been alleged that as a result of these extremely difficult times, Elijah began to consume alcohol, which was not uncommon for migrant blacks at that time. Despite his alleged bout with alcohol, he still managed to keep a strong sense of personhood. He often attended lectures given by the Universal Negro Improvement Association (UNIA) headed by Marcus Garvey. Some scholars say that he was an actual member of the UNIA. I contend that just because a person attends an organization's meetings on a regular basis is no indicator that he or she is an active, bonafide member.

The UNIA, Moorish Science Temple, and Farad Muhammad gave him a sense of pragmatic organization that addressed the needs, wants and aspirations of impoverished black people. This is basically why the Nation of Islam was always of paramount concern to him. The UNIA enhanced his southern work ethic through the philosophy of economic self-sufficiency. However, the Great Depression of 1929 forced him and his family to accept welfare for two years, compelling him to view dependency on the white man as psychologically demeaning. Throughout his leadership, he forcefully taught the "Do something for yourself" And what is equally important is the fact that he forbade his followers to seek any welfare assistance.

Additionally, his acquaintance with the Bible enabled him to accept and appreciate the UNIA's exhortation against a European concept of God and Jesus. Bishop Alexander McGuire, chaplain of the UNIA, sought to replace all vestiges of *Anglo-Saxionized versions of Christianity with an Africanized version.* Mr. Muhammad utilized that concept, but advanced it to another psychological level. More will be said about that and some of the above information later. It is worth mentioning at this point that a careful analysis will show that there were esoteric and nationalist elements in the Moorish Scientists' (Nobel Drew Ali) teachings and in the teachings of Elijah Muhammad. This claim stands up to reason considering the fact that Garvey and Drew Ali were close contemporaries. Thus Muhammad became the recipient of three distinct, and yet varied philosophies: 1. Master Farad Muhammad's religio-symbolism, 2. Noble Drew Ali's esoterocism, and 3. Garvey's economic nationalism. Each one of these concepts will also be discussed and the impact they had on Mr. Muhammad's leadership direction.

As I indicated earlier, Muhammad's rural Southern experiences shaped and molded his ideological and philosophical outlook. He often commented on his witnessing the hanging of a black man when he was a young boy. That heart wrenching scene would plague his mind for many years. I remember his stating: "I saw enough of the white man's brutality to last me 26,000 years." Some black people passively endured white racism, some struggled against it through a Christian belief that a better day was coming. And some responded by migrating north and embracing a race conscious philosophy.

Southern segregation and its attendant white racist oppression as well as northern economic deprivation contributed to Elijah and other blacks search for emotional and psychological solace in black organizations that offered economic and spiritual uplift.

Each one of these organizations gave Black people a God-filled euphoria. Some such as the Peace Movement of Ethiopia supported repatriation to Africa. The National Movement for the Establishment of the 49th State sought to create a black state within the United States. In addition to the UNIA and the Moorish Science Temple, which offered blacks a strong sense of racial pride, there was the Father Divine Peace Missions. Father Divine (George Baker) was shrewd enough to capitalize on the economic crisis and the spiritual

37

void of these illiterate southern migrants. As I briefly state Father Divine's philosophy and program, I think it will serve historical consistency to look at and understand the economic and religio-political commonalities of these major black organizations. This should permit us to see more clearly the influence on Elijah Muhammad and the eclectic Fardian approach he utilized in the advancement of the Nation of Islam.

Father Divine ordained himself one specially guided by God. He preached a fusion of mysticism and Christianity; he was so adept that his congregation believed him to be God in person. He was clever enough to know that when you feed a person when he or she is starving you have indeed won his or her loyalty. Thus during the depression, Father Divine provided his followers with employment through his Sayville Employment Center, and he provided them food, shelter and weekly prayer services. To the rejected and despised blacks, their prayers were answered, and as a consequence his followers worshiped him as God. He subsequently changed his name to Father God Major J. Divine, Dean of the Universe. He called his followers "angels" and they were required to adhere to strict moral discipline. He promised his true followers eternal life, for he considered death the final weakness. His sacred text was called *The New Day*.[1]

Another person who emerged on the scene at this time was one Marcelino Manuel De Graca (Sweet Daddy Grace). He came to America in the 1900's from the Cape Verde Islands. He proclaimed himself a healer of mind and body. There is no doubt that he had some knowledge of herbs and African theological systems. Also, because of his mixed ancestry (African and Portuguese), his physical demeanor appealed to most of those blacks that had internalized a caste concept.

His followers believed he was capable of performing miracles such as bringing the dead back to life as well as healing. He taught from the Bible and accentuated his doctrine on the Biblical word "grace." He told his followers that he was the "grace of the world" and only he had the divine power to wash away their sins.[2] He did not advocate an African or nationalist philosophy of any kind. Nevertheless, his success lay in an emotional need of his followers that required illusionary fulfillment. For Daddy Grace, religion was the quintessentiality of his persona. Thus he is exempt from this comparative study. But he undoubtedly capitalized on the existing conditions of the black masses in the same manner as his contemporaries.

In the beginning, Father Divine referred to himself as the "Messenger" of God. At that stage of his leadership, he taught his followers that God is in every person, but later he changed from this conception of God to the idea that God is in Father Divine. As a leader, Divine created a patriarchal and messianic image of himself that transcended his theological and intellectual limitations by denying the pervasiveness of color or race, as well as the dominance of white society and the marginal nature of black society. He went on to assert that everyone could be a part of the American society provided it was transformed into a colorless society. However, this could only be actualized in a government under God, and Father Divine was god.

Father Divine was conceptually contradictory. On the one hand, he was attracted to white America, and he even married Euro-American women, on the other hand, he accentuated and actualized Garvey's position which stated that black was basically superior and white was basically inferior. Divine declared that he was Negro and God dwelled in him; to his followers and black people, he declared that they were also Negroes and they were like unto him. Therefore, they were superior to white.

Obviously, Father Divine adopted some black nationalist elements and his philosophy and program manifested some ideological contradictions; however, what is interesting to note is the fact that most of the pioneer black nationalists up to Garvey and Muhammad reflected contradictions in their program and philosophy. Black nationalism, for example, advocated the physical separation of the races which usually referred only to a simple institutional separatism, or the desire to see black people making efforts to sustain themselves in a proven antagonistic environment. Thus black nationalism was usually contradicted by the assimilationist attitude of the nationalists themselves.

Marcus Garvey, to a certain extent, resolved one aspect of the black nationalist contradiction by developing a "Back to Africa" movement; however, he still looked favorably at Christianity as a "civilizing cultural instrument" for Africa.

Elijah Muhammad, on the other hand, maintained the contradiction, but it was religio-nationalism linked to a segment of Islam. Muhammad preached separation within the territorial boundaries of the United States; furthermore, he preached that black people must "do something for themselves" using every legal and available means inside the United States. Muhammad did not advocate emigration to Africa, nor did he initially enunciate a programmatic position that urged closer contacts and cooperation between Africans at home and abroad through cultural and economic ties. Muhammad -- the uncompromising religio-nationalist that he was -- placed emphasis on the rise of the "so called American Negro" and rejected the fanciful African Fundamentalist philosophy that dramatized the need for foreign mission work in Africa before domestic mission work in black America. He made this passionate statement:

> "It would be a shame on the part of any independent nation's government to come here begging for help from the so-called Negroes whose status is that of free slaves . . . If you have extra money to send abroad, why not use it on SELF and your people here in America . . . First, help yourself and then if you are able, help others if you want to."

Despite his "charity begins at home before it spreads abroad" philosophy, Muhammad was and remains to this day one of the most fierce Africanist or religio-nationalist in black American history.

Another contradiction that deviated from the black nationalist philosophy was Muhammad's use of the term Asiatic black man as opposed to African man or African black man. More will be said about these terms later. Next there was the contradiction of his stating that the earth was called Asia and not Africa. Additionally, his acknowledgement of certain Arab Muslims, Gamal Abdel Nasser for instance, and not certain African Muslims heightened the contradictions for the so-called orthodox black or African nationalists. it was these aforementioned factors which, I believe, estranged or alienated the contemporary nationalists from the Nation of Islam, and needless to say, Father Divine in spite of his effective program was not a subject worthy of discussion.

Undoubtedly, some of these preachers of salvation exemplified contradictions in their programmatic approach to the socio-economic liberation of black people. What should not be overlooked or dismissed is that all of these men, including Father Divine, to some extent, shared a domestic self-help philosophy and program. They instituted a collectivist economy among their followers; they rejected white dependency, they rejected the white Christian concept of God, and they differentiated their followers from the black American subculture.

Excerpt taken from the *Pittsburgh Courier*, September 13, 1958, "Mr. Muhammad Speaks."

Some scholars such as the late sociologist, Robert E. Park and Manning Marable posit that black religion presented a dialectical consciousness in that it fostered both accommodation and protest. Marable expresses this contradictory facet of black religion when he notes that the "conservative tendencies within black religion reach for a spirit which liberates the soul, but not the body, whereas the radical tendencies or consciousness within black religion was concerned with the immediate conditions of black people. The juxtaposition of these opposing themes of protest, and accommodation is present in all dimensions of African-American religions. The messianic-nationalist sects have emphasized protest, and most of the Spiritual churches paid more attention to accommodation, or other worldliness.

World War I increased the demand for labor, and that demand was fulfilled to a great extent, by the migration of southern blacks. Furthermore, the availability of these black migrants as a labor reserve allowed northern industrialists to undercut the demands of an increasingly militant caucasian working class for higher wages and better working conditions. This was also another aspect of the ongoing debate between Booker T. Washington and W.E.B. Du Bois.

Although it fluctuated throughout the succeeding decades, falling during the Depression era and rising again during World War II, the migration pattern that started among blacks in the 1920's continued well into the 1970's. By 1970, only 52 percent of blacks were located in the South, and the majority of blacks in the North and the South were located in urban areas. In the South, black people had occupied the lowest rungs of the rigid class-caste system. In the North -- even though blacks possessed in theory more rights -- blacks became a type of subproletariat, or what is today called an underclass.

Muhammad was, by definition, a nontraditional ideologue. He was an unorthodox Muslim and to some people an unorthodox black nationalist. Contemporary African Fundamentalists have failed to analyze why those contradictions existed with Muhammad and his predecessors, and whether or not they resolved them.

Manning Marable, *Blackwater: Historical Studies in race, Class Consciousness and Revolution* (Black Praxis Press, Drayton, Ohio)

Stanford M. Lyman, *An Analysis and Interpretation of the Early Writings of Robert E. Park Militarism, Imperialism and Racial Accommodation* (University of Arkansas Press, 1992)

Black northern migration encountered overwhelming problems of adjustment that grassroot organizations were more than willing to handle. The harsh impersonal world of the city coupled with centuries of forced servitude, and the cruel economic reality of everyday existence exacted its toll on these non-suspecting victims. Charles Johnson in his *The Shadow of the Plantation* points out that the southern sharecropper had long been conditioned by a plantation tradition. They were completely dependent on the landowner for guidance and control in most facets of life which were related to the world outside. Therefore, these grassroot organization leaders provided these immigrants with personal authority and personal direction. Therefore, a revitalized religious concept married to a concept of economic autonomy gave birth to hope and dignity to these sons and daughters of former slaves. This is one reason why Father Divine became a personalized deity to these desolate migrants. He offered them benevolence and respect; human qualities they rarely experienced in the south.

One common theme that those grassroot religious organizations expressed was the need for a deliverer. Many black migrants were therefore attracted to the Holiness, Pentecostal, Spiritual, Judaic, Farad Muhammad and the Temple of Islam, Father Divine's Peace Mission, Garveyism, Moorish Science Temple, and African Orthodox Church and other sects which proliferated not only in the industrial North but also in many cities of the South.

The objective of the grassroots religious movement was to establish a religion which could make the new and strange burdens of harsh urban life somehow tolerable. Hans A. Baer in his classic study, *The Black Spiritual Movement: A Religious Response to Racism* (p. 12 - 17) contends that the grassroots religious organizations -- sometimes called cults and sects -- were a spiritual movement based on the black religious experience which exhibited a common theme, namely the element of protest against the racist and socially stratified structure of American society. It then becomes clearer why Marcus Garvey and Father Divine were spiritually exalted. Garvey was hailed as the mighty prophet; his mission and work was compared to that of Jesus.

On another level, his followers looked upon him as a demigod from heaven to dispense political and economic salvation to a rejected, exploited and despised people.[3] Of course, Father Divine was both a "Messenger of God" and later honored as "God." Before engaging in a brief comparative discussion about Garvey and Divine, it is most important at this juncture to discuss their contemporary, George Willie Hurley, popularly known as Father Hurley.

Father Hurley (George Willie Hurley) was also a self-proclaimed god. However, Hurley and Father Divine were by no means the first black men to claim to be God incarnate. As early as 1899, blacks in the country side of Savannah, Georgia, began to worship Dupont Bell, a self-proclaimed son of God. Bell was later committed to an asylum; immediately afterwards, other self-proclaimed gods or messiahs appeared in various parts of Georgia until 1916. It is highly possible that George Baker (Father Divine) as a young man born and raised in Georgia, could not have failed to hear of his messianic precursors. Additionally, while serving as an assistant preacher in a Baptist church in Baltimore, Maryland, Baker met and later became the disciple of Samuel Morris, a black man who also claimed to be God. Around 1907, Morris took on the name of Father Jehovia and designated George Baker "the Messenger."

John Hickerson, also known as Bishop St. John the Vine, was an assistant to Morris who later severed his connection to him, and subsequently established his own church. Interestingly, Baker (Divine) was forced to leave Georgia on the premise that he was a public menace. He traveled to New York where St. John the Vine was teaching his congregation the belief that God resides in everyone and therefore everyone is in essence god or part of god. This, I believe, was the beginning of the god-incarnate concept that permeated the religio-nationalist movements. (Baer, p. 140 - 142).

In all likelihood, Farad Muhammad who appeared in 1930, seven years after Hurley, who was also hailed as Allah in person probably was influenced by the teachings of Hurley. As we will see, there are some striking similarities to be found in Hurley's teachings to those found in the Nation of Islam and other messianic-nationalist movements. However, the emphasis will be on the Nation of Islam.

For the sake of informational clarity, it is imperative that we now scrutinize the similarities between Hurley and other religious or messianic-nationalist groups. The major similarity between Father Hurley and Noble Drew Ali is their use of Levi Dowling's *Aquarian Gospel*. Hurley frequently quoted from the Aquarian Gospel and encouraged his followers to study its passages. Similar to Noble Drew Ali, Hurley claimed to have been a mason and a former member of the Mystical Brotherhood of India. He, too, synthesized disparate concepts into an operative wholeness. He utilized, in addition to the Aquarian

Gospel, astrology, esotericism, theosophy, messianic-nationalism, Christianity in the form of black spirituality, aspects of Masonry and other belief systems. Father Hurley called his places of worship temples and assigned numbers to each one. Drew and Elijah did the exact same thing.

Referring back to masonry, Father Hurley established a mason like association in which students were enrolled in the school of Mediumship and Psychology. They were taught spiritual advising, counseling, communicating with the spirit realm and other so-called secrets. Once the student successfully completed the curriculum, he or she became an uncrowned medium and would be given a wand bearing hieroglyphic inscriptions. Once a student successfully completed the master's curriculum, he or she became or was crowned an adept. There was, on special occasions, a ritual in which accomplished students wore specific colors to symbolize their respective learning prominence and spiritual power (Baer, p. 88).

The school was dedicated to the injunction "Man Know Thyself." Father Hurley taught that the school was a branch or an extension of the Great School of the Prophets which Jesus attended during the early periods of his life (Baer, p. 86).

The Knights of the All-Seeing Eye was a secret masonlike auxiliary of Father Hurley's Universal Hagar's Spiritual Church. Unlike most Masonic organizations, which are gender separated, the Knights was open to both male and female. The most Royal Exalted Master and the Royal Noble Mistress were the national heads of the Knights. Each chapter or branch had an Exalted Knight (male or female) and Exalted Scribe. On special occasions, members of the auxiliary wore a scarf, an apron and a fez with a picture of the All Seeing Eye.

The influence of Garvey, Noble Drew Ali, and Farad Muhammad on Father Hurley is difficult to ascertain; however, one of the early temples of the Moorish Scientists was located in Detroit and perhaps predated Hurley's arrival in 1919 and his establishment of his Universal Hagar's Spiritual Church in 1923. On the other hand, one factor seems quite clear and that is by the time Farad Muhammad had started his Temple in Detroit in the early 1930's, Father Hurley had established temples in several other cities. Thus it seems more convincing that Farad was in all probability influenced by Hurley. And at some points during Hurley's mission Farad's doctrine had an impact on the programatic direction and thinking of Father Hurley. One thing is definite and that is that the linkage or continuum of these messianic-nationalists remains unsevered.

Noble Drew Ali devised his own version of a Koran; similarly, Father Hurley -- who incidentally like Drew Ali also referred to himself as a prophet -- devised his own version of the Ten Commandments. Upon scrutiny of these Mores, Baer considers them to be a dogma, one can see compelling similarities to aspects of Garveyism, Faradism and Drewian teachings:

1. Thou shall believe in Spirit (God) within matter.
2. Thou shall ignore a sky heaven for happiness and a downward hell for human punishment.
3. Thou shall believe in heaven and hell on earth.
4. Thou shall believe in the fatherhood of God and the brotherhood of man.
5. Thou shall believe in what you sow, you shall also reap.
6. Thou shall believe that the Ethiopians and all Nations will rule the world in righteousness.
7. Thou shall believe that the Universal Hagar's Spiritual Church was revealed to Father G. W. Hurley for the blessing of all nations that believe in him.
8. Thou Shall not pray for God to bless your enemies.
9. Thou shall ask God to give you power to overcome them.
10. Thou shall believe that our relatives and friends, whose spirits have departed from the body, is within our own bodies to help us overcome all difficulties in life.

Father Hurley's movement was very much akin to the above groups insofar as dietary habits. Each group was commanded to abstain from pork and pork byproducts, tobacco and alcohol. However, Hurley allowed his followers to consume wine in moderation at special church functions. Each group encouraged fasting for health purposes as well as for spiritual advancement (Baer, 107 - 108). It does seem rather apparent that Drew Ali had an influence on Father Hurley.

According to Baer, Garvey's movement was the most influential source for Hurley. Baer is convinced that by the 1920's, if not earlier, Father Hurley and some of his early followers became members of Garvey's Universal Negro Improvement Association. Furthermore, Baer's research leads him to believe that Hurley was personally acquainted with Mr. Garvey. Baer is academically veracious enough to admit that he does not know that exact period during which Hurley was a member of the UNIA; however, there is ideological exactness as to the fact that Garvey had a definite impact on a number of black groups (some ex-Garveyites). Theodore Vincent in his *Black Power and the Garvey Movement* (1971, San Francisco Ramparts, p. 221 - 222) writes the following:

> "Among the hundreds of thousands, perhaps millions, of black people who had joined the Garvey movement, few were willing to reject the movement's philosophical, political, and cultural outlook. When the UNIA could no longer coordinate this sentiment, its members moved to build new organizations based upon what they considered important in their Garveyite experience. Columnist Samuel Haynes condemned these deserters bitterly in the Negro World. "Former Garveyites are now enrolled in the Moorish American Society, in the various Africa movements, most of them founded by ex-Garveyites themselves," wrote Haynes, who also saw a move of "thousands" to "new religious movements claiming to be associated with Garveyism. Former Garveyites see in Father Divine, evangelist George Wilson, Bishop Grace and others the incarnation of Marcus Garvey."

Like Garvey, Hurley presented himself as a savior for the race. Like Garvey, Hurley referred to blacks as Ethiopians and whites as Gentiles. Like Garvey, Hurley expressed a strong disapproval of interracial marriage and dating and held a certain contempt for mulattos. Moreover, Hurley seems to have, in part, adopted the word universal from Garvey in naming his religious group Universal Hagar's Spiritual Church.

Another obvious similarity between Father Hurley's group and the UNIA were the colors of their flags. Hurley's church carried the red, black and green as did the UNIA. Lastly, Hurley had a secret fraternal auxiliary within his organization, which, as was mentioned, masonic in content. However, Vincent (p. 103) seems to believe that Garvey's Noble Order of the Knights of the Nile (1922) may have been the source of inspiration for the Knights of the All-Seeing Eye, (Baer, p. 146 - 148).

Garvey's Universal Negro Improvement Association was curiously similar to the Universal Association for the Moral Improvement of Mankind established in 1905 by the Haitian Pan-Africanist, Benito Sylvain.

Notice that Hurley used the name Hagar for his church; she was the mother of Ishmael, who was according to religious history the father of the Arabs and was most definitely a Cushite (African).

Apostle Elias Dempsey Smith might have been another source of Ethiopianism for Hurley's ideological growth. Smith founded a church called Triumph the Church and the Kingdom of God in Christ of which Father Hurley was also a member. Smith's international church body included a church in Ethiopia, where he resided for a time. There is a prevailing assumption that Smith opted not to return to the United States. His doctrine also emphasized a theology for understanding the reality of God in man and a clarifying perspective on how God's presence is expressed through man. He established his church in January 20, 1904.

With the exception of the probable influence of Drewian esotericism and messianic-nationalism and the striking impact of Garveyism on Father Hurley, Hurley to a certain degree, influenced Farad Muhammad. What is important and relevant to note are the dates of Hurley's ascension as a church organizer versus his gradual self-elevation as God incarnate. In 1924, he established his Mediumship and Psychology school which became a part of each congregation in the Universal Hagar's Spiritual Church. He established his church in Detroit in 1923 and expanded to about 95 churches, and a considerable number of sub-churches called temples spread to several other cities. In the early period of his church leadership, he was called Prophet Hurley, and as a Holiness minister, Elder Hurley.

Around 1933, perhaps earlier, Hurley began to teach his followers that his "carnal flesh" had been "transformed into the flesh of Christ."

At other times, he referred to himself as the "black God of this age," and the "Christ, the God, the Savior, the Protector of the seven thousand-year reign of the Aquarian Age."

Around 1938, he taught that Christ came into the world as a "thief and robber by night into a black body." He taught that although minor prophets would be raised up to carry on his mission after his death, his prophethood would be the last gospel to be preached on the earth. Father Hurley would reign as the God of the Aquarian Age for 7,000 years, and "his name was destined to be universal in the year 6953 A.D.

Theodore G. Vincent, Editor, *Voices of a Black Nation: Political Journalism in the Harlem Renaissance* (Ramparts Press, 1973, p. 368 - 369).

According to Hurleyites, the Aquarian Age would mean the end of white Protestantism and the end of segregation and of big men ruling over little men (Baer, p. 92 - 93).

Hurley's so-called prophethood to god head was gradual, but it reflected a Fardian pattern; furthermore, his lesson on minor prophets continuing the work of his major and final prophethood reflected Fardian messianic preachments. Hurley taught his congregation that the spirit of God is embedded in each man (consider the Nation of Islam dictum that Allah came in the person of Master Farad Muhammad). Hurley preached that as the "major god" he brought the "true light into this age," and his believers in that true light were the minor gods and goddesses (consider Elijah Muhammad's pronouncement that "whenever you see a black man, you are looking at God"). Hurley, like Farad, and later Elijah taught that heaven and hell are "right here on earth within every man and woman;" heaven is a state of peace, joy, happiness and success which is a satisfied mind on earth." Farad and Elijah specifically stated that hell was being the victim of white oppression; therefore, since the white man was (is) the source of hell, then he was the most likely candidate to be the devil. Of course, Hurley did not go to this extreme. Actually, hell for Hurley and his followers was a condition of hatred, Jim-Crowism, and prejudice created by racist white Christian enslavers.

Hurley passionately argued that European forces forced the Ethiopian people to join their churches during slavery and then psychologically persuaded them to accept a "white god, a white Jesus, white prophets, and white prophetesses."

Moreover, Hurley, like Farad and Elijah considered the traditional Christian concepts of the afterlife as an instrument for oppressing blacks with a pie-in-the-sky doctrine. Furthermore, he was very similar to Farad and Elijah insofar as his forceful criticism of white Christian racism was concerned. He like Farad -- the only difference was Farad attached his philosophy to Islam -- contested the white man's form of Christianity (Protestantism) among blacks as a weapon of propaganda devised to divide and conquer the Ethiopian people (Baer, p. 95). Thus a new form of Christianity must be ushered into existence, or a recapturing of the lost form of African Christianity. This is what prompted Hurley to establish the Universal Hagar Church and to fuse it with black spiritualism.

Hurley, Farad and Elijah contended that the white race all over the world assigned the black race to a position of inferiority; their use of derogatory names such as nigger, negress, coon, and sambo contributed to the debasement of people of African descent. Therefore,

48

unlike Garvey who clung to the word Negro, Drew Ali, Hurley, Farad and Elijah stressed that the term Negro must be eliminated from use, eradicated by law, and replaced by "black" in Farad and Elijah's case, Ethiopian in Hurley's case, and Moor or Asiatic in Drew's case. Hurley taught that Ethiopians were the first people in the world, the original Hebrew nation, God's chosen ones, the speakers of the original language of Arabic, the most industrious people on the earth, and the creators of civilization and hieroglyphics. According to Hurley, the first religion was the Coptic Ethiopian religion. All of the Old Testament prophets and patriarchs were Ethiopians.

The dissimilarities between Farad and Hurley was that for Farad and later Elijah a racial generalization was utilized as opposed to a racial specificity. By that I mean they taught the Black Man was original, in other words, the Black Man all over Africa was the original man and the Father of civilization. And for them, Islam was the original religion.

Father Hurley argued that whereas blacks or Ethiopians were the first people; whites therefore are the offspring of Cain, who had been cursed with a pale color because of leprosy. Farad expanded this theory by stating that the black man is the original man and the white man is a hybrid or a grafted man. Both of these preachers of race redemption and race salvation said to the world or anybody who listened that the black race had not been cursed, and that it had once reigned supreme and was bound to reign again.

The other major dissimilarity between Hurley and Farad was Hurley's belief in the American political system and his support for capitalism. In this instance, he was more aligned with Father Divine and Noble Drew Ali. The major similarity was that Hurley and Farad both declared that God throughout the ages had appeared in the form of black men and that all great religious prophets of history had been black.

The dissimilarity was that unlike Divine, Drew, Garvey and Elijah, Hurley did not provide his followers with an extensive economic base. He did not advocate the necessity for establishing self-help programs. Nor did he try to emulate the economic programs of Father Divine. He obviously did not, as did Garvey and Farad, promote or promulgate a back to Africa or separatist policy.

While there are specific differences among the doctrines that Drew, Garvey, Farad , Divine and Hurley espoused, their respective preachments contained profound life -saving similarities:

49

1. They taught that blacks have a glorious past.
2. The black man was (is) the original man.
3. The black man was god and all of the prophets were (are) black.
4. Blacks should renounce Christianity, or at least the white man's version of Christianity.
5. Blacks would again rise to their rightful place in the world.
6. Each preacher of salvation proclaimed himself to be a messenger, prophet and god.

Garvey was a masterful visionary in his fusing Christianity with political nationalism -- something that Elijah Muhammad would do later with Islam. Garvey's pragmatic approach to religion was based on the argument that Christianity preached that man was made in the image and likeness of God; therefore, black men should depict a God in their own image and likeness, which conclusively would be black.[4] The black god concept for Garvey was incontrovertibly enmeshed with economic and political autonomy for the black masses. It was also a means of dismantling the European image of God which psychologically impaired an impoverished mentally dead people. He insisted that if Negroes are in God's image and Negroes are black, then God must in some way be black.

> "If the white man has the idea of a white God, let him worship his god as he desires. . .We, as Negroes, have found a new ideal. Whilst our God has no color, yet it is human to see everything through one's own spectacles, we have only now started out (late though it be) to see our God through our own spectacles. . .We Negroes believe in the God of Ethiopia, the everlasting God -- God the Father, God the Son and God the Holy Ghost, the one God of all ages. That is the God in whom we believe but we shall worship Him through the spectacles of Ethiopia."

Understandably, Garvey strongly disagreed with Father Divine who proclaimed himself to be god. I surmise that there were possibly three reasons for this: 1. Garvey was still sympathetic to unadulterated Christianity, 2. He was becoming acquainted with the pristine theology of Islam through his association with Duse Muhammad Ali, and 3. He saw Father Divine as an aberrant competitor for the souls of the black masses. It must be remembered that Garvey loudly announced in Harlem that "A black god is coming.

50

Be ready when he cometh." Interestingly, Garvey's enunciation of a black god placed him in a religio-nationalist tradition that extended from Bishop Henry McNeal Turner to Elijah Muhammad's position that the black man was god.

Bishop Henry McNeal Turner, more will be said about him later, uttered his now famous dictum, "God is a Negro," as a protest against God's alleged whiteness. He extended the protest by proclaiming that, "'The devil is white and never black." As we can see, Farad was not the first to utter such preachments.

Garvey was a master eclectician, but Divine was a clever tactician. Divine, unlike Garvey, Drew Ali and Elijah Muhammad, sought to reconcile Christianity with Black America. He was able to do that because he modified the racial rhetoric of Garvey and Drew and thereby managed to integrate into a suburban environment that was replete with material success. These materialistic trappings, so to speak, cultivated his optimism in America and Christianity. In fact, he found in Christianity a source of inner strength for eliminating black oppression. In essence, Divine did not employ Garvey's program totally; however, he took segments of Garvey's program and vision and transformed them into a practical reality.

In the last analysis, Robert Weisbrot makes an interesting point about these mass organizations also called cults, and that is that the social and political climate contributed greatly to their radical or passive preachments. Garvey, Drew, and Elijah appeared on the scene during World War I at the height of extreme racist oppression. Contrarily, Divine's Peace Mission emerged on the scene after 1932 which was after the advent of Franklin D. Roosevelt's New Deal, a rejuvenated Black Christian activism, and a new heightened civil rights interest.[5]

Divine also differed with Garvey on two other issues; first, Divine urged his followers to register and vote in political elections. He and his followers established a "Righteous Government" Movement with several planks in its platform: eight focused on racial matters and three on economics, education, and politics. The second difference he had with Garvey and Elijah Muhammad for that matter was his cordial relationship with Anglo-Communists. He made the following statement to justify his position:

> "I stand for anything that will deal justly between man and man. The communists stand for social equality and for justice in every issue and this is the principle for which I stand. I am not especially representing religion. I am representing God on

earth among men and I will co-operate with any organization that will stand for the right and will deal justly."

Divine's encompassing economic, educational, and employment programs profoundly endeared his followers to him in an incalculable manner. It is worth mentioning that many of his followers were former Garveyites. Divine built an economic empire within the so-called ghettos of the United States; Garvey spoke passionately to all people of African descent; Divine through pragmatism and mysticism elevated people of both races. In fact, Divine had white men and women submitting to his self proclaimed deification.[6]

Garvey had long-range domestic programs; on the other hand, Divine gained immediate loyalties by feeding and sheltering people at the time of need. Garvey, encouraged more traditional policies like fraternal orders, which drew from members dues to assure certain sums of money to their families in a time of financial crisis.[7] Divine believed in offering enough security and well being so that the possibility of future illness would not conjure up feelings of helplessness.

Historically, the UNIA under Garvey was the culmination of a synthesis of previous messianic-nationalist organizations. This unique combination of economic, political, and racial nationalism produced an organizational structure that so impressed Divine that he in turn selectively utilized aspects of the UNIA and other messianic-nationalist groups to augment his Peace Mission. His cleverness rested on the fact that he structured his organization on policies that rendered immediate tangible results.

Divine was, by today's definition a conservative. He believed in the capitalist system; ironically, so did Garvey, Drew and Elijah, but with Divine it was capitalism and Christianity. Despite his flirtation with the white communist party, he was a staunch American. The profound similarities among those groups was their advocacy of the Protestant work-ethic, self-support, savings, investments, and the sanctity of private property.

On a final note, it is worth mentioning that Garveyism was an important influence on interest in Ethiopia. Thus Ethiopianism or the reverence for Ethiopia as an ancestral homeland played a major role in nourishing racial pride among Black Americans. As writer and poet Claude McKay so aptly put it, the Ethiopia of today was (is) the "wonderful Ethiopia of the Bible."

NOBLE DREW ALI:
A FORGOTTEN AND MISUNDERSTOOD LEADER

Noble Drew Ali (Timothy Drew) started teaching around 1913 in Newark, New Jersey about the Moorish (North Africa) identity of blacks. Drew was born in Simpsonbuck County, North Carolina, among the Cherokee Indian tribe on January 8, 1886. He traveled extensively in the East and in Africa, and concluded that blacks were not Ethiopians as proclaimed by early black nationalists, but that they were Asiatics, specifically Moors from Morocco. He believed that the Continental Congress stripped American blacks of their nationality and placed them in the menial role of slave. According to the movement's historical records, he was allegedly taught by Egyptian masters and earned the title "Egyptian Adept," thereby becoming a master in his own right. In Egypt he had the opportunity to visit the universities and travel through the inner chambers of the pyramids, by being in Egypt, he could see for himself that the black man had laws, science, math, art, and Godly-esteem. Afterwards, according to the movement's accounts, he traveled to Mecca and received his ancient birthright title as Ali from Sultan Abdul Aziz Ibn Saud, which allegedly gave him the authority to teach true Islam to the lost tribes of Israel in the North, South, and Central Americas.

Needless to say, he did not teach pristine Islam, I believe, because he did not know the vastness of Islam, the scriptural purity of the Quran, nor did he know Quranic Arabic. Certainly, one does not need to know Arabic or the Quran to teach Islam, for Islam stands on its own merit. However, in Drew's case, his lack of knowledge in these areas contributed to his mixing masonry, esotericism, and garveyism with marginal Islam. My point of contention is if it is true that he was sanctioned by Ibn Saud then why did not Saud properly prepare him for his mission? Furthermore, Ali can not be charged for his misguided errors in Islam -- nor can Elijah Muhammad -- simply because they lacked complete knowledge of the religion of Islam.

The purpose and goals of the Moorish Movement were enunciated by Drew Ali in the September 14, 1928 edition of *The Moorish Guide* --

1. Dispense charity and provide for the mutual assistance of its members in times of distress.
2. Aid in the improvement of health and encourage the ownership of better homes.
3. Find employment for members.

4. Teach those fundamental principles which are desired for our civilization, such as obedience to law, loyalty to government, tolerance and unity.

It has also been said by members of the Moorish communities that Noble Drew Ali also traveled extensively in India and perhaps studied among the Ahmadiya. Therefore, it may not be a circumstantial coincidence that the Ahmadiya were desperately trying to proselytize in the UNIA and in the Moorish temples after the death of Drew Ali. As I indicated earlier, Drew Ali synthesized esotericism, Sufism, Christianity, and he accepted and applied some customs and symbols of the Eastern Masonic Lodge. Noble Drew Ali published his alleged Holy Koran of the Moorish Science Temple of America, now known to members of the movement as the Holy Koran of the Moorish Science Temple Circle Seven, and he published a pamphlet and a collection of Moorish Science beliefs, conceived possibly from *The Aquarian Gospel of Jesus Christ*, a book received through the writings by spiritualist, Levi Dowling, in the 1890's. Ali's alleged Koran consisted of Garvey's teachings, Biblical passages, esoteric or theosophical philosophy, numerology, and Masonic teachings. One point must be stressed here and that is that Drew Ali's so-called Koran was very similar in verses to *The Aquarian Gospel of Jesus Christ* by Levi Dowling. Ali seemingly embraced segments of Dowling's teachings because they dealt with aspects of esotericism.[8] One of Ali's perceptions of eastern philosophy was described according to what he taught his followers. He taught his followers of the two-selves -- the higher self and the lower self.

It is said by some of his followers that his journey to Egypt was to prove himself by passing the severe test of the Egyptian priesthood. The test involved the pyramids of Egypt, in which Drew underwent the initiation into illumination. It is also said that he received a mission from the King of Morocco to teach Africans in America. Whether he was commissioned by Ibn Saud or the King of Morocco, my contentious question still stands.

There are two selves; the higher and lower self. The higher self is human spirit clothed with soul, made in the form of Allah. The lower self, the carnal self, the body desires, is a reflection of the higher self, distorted by murky ethers of the flesh.

54

This dualistic concept bespeaks Zoroasterianism and Manicheanism which, to a great degree, are Eastern precursors to Gnosticism and Christianity.

Returning to the subject of Drew Ali's Koran, I think it is safe to conclude that he had very little if any knowledge about the true Holy Quran. There were no Holy Qurans in wide circulation during his era. Furthermore, one of the first major English translated Qurans was by Maulana Muhammad Ali, and it did not get published until around 1917; additionally, it was not widely disseminated until years later. There were some Orientalist translations in the Library of Congress, but it is doubtful that he reviewed them for theological clarity. It is therefore my conjecture that his lack of knowledge of the Quran was somewhat eclipsed by his acquaintance with masonry and esotericism. Thus he devised a Koran, which I think, collectivized the best of those philosophies that appealed to him at that time, and that he considered germane for his mission.

Drew Ali's belief in Islam, as limited as that might have been, was never really subordinate to masonry or esotericism. He presented six principles that are obviously Islamic in nature:

1. Know thyself and thy Father, God Allah.
2. Islam is a very simple faith. It requires man to recognize his duties toward God Allah, his Creator and his fellow creatures.
3. The cardinal doctrine of Islam is the unity of the Father -- Allah.
4. To the one who is Supreme, Most Wise and Beneficent, and to Him Alone, belongs worship, adoration, thanksgiving and praise.
5. True Wisdom is less presuming than folly. The wise man doubteth often and changeth his mind; the fool is obstinate and doubteth not; he knoweth all things, but his own ignorance.
6. The fallen sons and daughters of the Asiatic nation of North America need to learn to love instead of hate; and to know their higher and lower self.

Contrarily, Drew's Koran consisted of some chapters taken from Levi Dowling's *The Aquarian Gospel of Jesus The Christ*. Levi Dowling or Levi was born May 18, 1844, at Belleville, Ohio. His father was of Scotch-Welsh origin and was a pioneer preacher among Disciples of Christ. Levi was a consistent student of the deeper meaning of life; thus he began preaching at the age of sixteen, and at the age of eighteen was pastor of a small church. As a young boy, he had a vision in which he was told that he was to "build a white city." This vision was repeated three times with years intervening. The building of the "white city" was the "The Aquarian gospel of Jesus Christ." Many people thought that he was a practitioner of witchcraft. However, this thought gradually changed, and gave way to the belief that Levi's son was the Messiah who had come to save the world.

Paradoxically, Levi's son was born on February 26, the symbolic day, but not the same year as Master Farad Muhammad. His son was his complete and final inspiration for the writing of the Aquarian Gospel. The Aquarian Gospel consists of eastern philosophy that supposedly was lessons and teachings that Jesus imparted to the world. People who read this book are seeking a deeper spiritual awakening. Therefore, it is no surprise to me why Noble Drew Ali was probably influenced by Dowling. Dowling, supposedly placed Jesus' teachings all over the world, especially in India and Egypt where Drew supposedly studied and developed as an initiate.[9]

The Aquarian Gospel of Jesus The Christ, The Philosophical and Practical Basis of the Religion of The Aquarian Age of the World by Levi (transcribed from the Akashuie Records (DeVoress and Co., Publishers, Marina Del Rey, California, 90294-0550, 1935 and 1964) p. 2, 39, 58 and 73.

THE NEXT FEW PAGES WILL DISPLAY THE UNDOUBTFUL SIMILARITIES BETWEEN DREW ALI'S KORAN AND LEVI DOWLING'S AQUARIAN GOSPEL.

CHAPTER X

JESUS SPOKE ON THE UNITY OF ALLAH AND MAN TO THE HINDUS

1. Benares is the sacred city of the Brahms, and in Benares, Jesus taught; Udraka was His host.
2. Udraka made a feast in honor of his guests, and many high born Hindu priests and scribes were there.
3. And Jesus said to them, with much delight: "I speak to you concerning life -- the brotherhood of life.
4. The universal Allah is one, yet He is more than one; all things are one.
5. By the sweet breath of Allah all life is bound in one; so if you touch a fiber of a living thing you send a thrill from center to the outer bounds of life.
6. And when you crush beneath your foot the meanest worm, you shake the throne of Allah and cause the sword of life to tremble in its sheath.
7. The bird sings out its song for men, and men vibrate in unison to help it sing.
8. The ant constructs its home, the bee its sheltering comb, the spider weaves her web and flowers breathe to them a spirit in their sweet perfume that gives them strength to toil.
9. Now, men and birds and beasts and creeping things are deities, made flesh; and how dare you kill anything?
10. It is cruelty that makes the world awry, when men have learned that when they harm a living thing, they harm themselves, they surely will not kill, nor cause a thing that Allah has made to suffer pain.
11. A lawyer said: "I pray to Jesus, tell who is this Allah you speak about; where are His priests, His temples and His shrines?"
12. And Jesus said: "The Allah I speak about is everywhere; He cannot be compassed with walls, nor hedged about with bounds of any kind."
13. All people worship Allah, the One; but all the people see Him not alike.
14. This universal Allah is wisdom, will and love.
15. All men see not the Triune Allah. One sees Him as Allah of might, another as Allah of thought, another as Allah of love.
16. A man's ideal is his God and so, as man unfolds, his God unfolds. Man's god today, tomorrow is not God.

17. *The nations of the earth see Allah from different points of view, and so He does not seem the same to every one.*

18. *Man names the part of Allah he sees, and this to him is all of Allah; and every nation sees a part of Allah he sees, and this to him is all of Allah; and every nation sees a part of Allah, and every nation has a name for Allah.*

19. *You Brahmans call Him Parabrahm, in Egypt He is Thoth, and Zeus is His name in Greece, Jehovah is His Hebrew name, but everywhere He is the causeless cause, the rootless root from which all things have grown.*

20. *When men are afraid of Allah and take Him for a foe, they dress up other men in fancy garbs and call them priests.*

21. *And charge them to restrain the wrath of Allah by prayers and when they fail to win His favor by their prayers, to buy Him off with sacrifice of animals or birds.*

22. *When man sees Allah as one with him, as Father Allah he needs no middle man, no priest to intercede.*

23. *He goes straight up to Him and says: "My Father God, Allah!" And then he lays his hands in Allah's own hand, and all is well.*

24. *And this is Allah. You are, each one, a priest, just for yourself; and sacrifice of blood Allah does not want.*

25. *Just give your life in sacrificial service to the all of life and Allah is pleased."*

26. *When Jesus had thus said He stood aside; the people were amazed, but strove among themselves.*

27. *Some said: "He is inspired by Holy Brahm" and other said: "He is insane," and others said: "He is obsessed; He speaks as devils speak."*

28. *But Jesus tarried not. Among the guests was one, a tiller of the soil, a generous soul, a seeker after truth, who loved the words that Jesus spoke, and Jesus went with him and in his home abode.*

CHAPTER XI

JESUS AND BARATA -- TOGETHER THEY READ THE SACRED BOOKS

1. *Among the Buddhist priests was one who saw a lofty wisdom in the words that Jesus spoke. It was Barato Arabo.*

2. *Together Jesus and Barato read the Jewish Psalms and prophets, read the Vedas, the Avesta and the wisdom of Guatama.*

3. *And as they read and talked about the possibilities of man, Barata said: " Man is the marvel of the universe. He is part of everything, for he has been a living thing on every plan of life.*

5. *Time was when man was not, and then he was a bit of formless substance in the molds of time, and then a protoplast.*

6. *By universal law, all things tend upward to a state of perfectness. The protoplast evolved, becoming worm, then reptile, bird and beast, and then at last it reached the form of man.*

7. *Now, man himself is mind, and mind is here to gain perfection by experience; and mind is often manifest in fleshy form, and in the form best suited to its growth. So mind may manifest as worm, or bird or beast or man.*

8. *The time will come when everything of life will be evolved unto the state of perfect man.*

9. *And after man is man in perfectness, he will evolve to higher forms of life."*

10. *And Jesus said: "Barata Arabo, who told you this, that mind which is man, may manifest in flesh of beast or bird or creeping thing?"*

11. *Barata said: "From time which man remembers not our priests have told us so, and so we know."*

12. *And Jesus said: "Enlightened Arabo, are you a master mind and do not know that man knows naught by being told?*

13. *Man may believe what others say, but thus he never knows. If man would know, he must, himself, be what he knows.*

14. *Do you remember, Arabo, when you were ape, or bird, or worm?*

15. *Now, if you have not better proving of your plea than that the priests have told you so, you do not know; you simply guess.*

16. *Regard not, then, what any man has said; let us forget the flesh and go with mind into the land of fleshless things; mind never does forget.*

17. *And backward through the ages master minds can trace themselves; and thus they know.*

18. *Time never was when man was not.*

19. *That which begins will have an end. If man was not, the time will come when he will not exist.*

20. *From Allah's own record book we read: The Triune Allah breathed forth, and stood seven spirits before His face. The Hebrews call these seven spirits Elohim.*

21. *And these are they who, in their boundless power, created everything that is, or was.*

22. *These spirits of the Triune Allah moved on the face of boundless space and seven others were and every other had its form of life.*

23. *These forms of life were but the thought of Allah, clothed in the substance of their ether planes.*

24. *Men call these ether planes, the planes of protoplast, of earth, of plant, of beast, of man, of angel and cherubim.*

25. *These planes with all their teeming thoughts of Allah are never seen by eyes of man in flesh; they are composed of substance far too fine for fleshy eyes to see, and still they constitute the soul of things.*

26. *And with the eyes of soul all creatures see these ether planes, and all the forms of life.*

27. *Because all forms of life on every plane are thoughts of Allah, all creatures think, and every creature is possessed of will, and in its measure, has the power to choose.*

28. *And in their native planes all creatures are supplied with nourishment from the ethers of their planes.*

29. *And so it was with every living thing until the will became a sluggish will, and then the ethers of the protoplast, the earth, the plant, the beast, the man, began to vibrate very slow.*

30. *The ethers became more dense, and all the creatures of these planes were clothed with coarser garbs of flesh, which man can see; and thus the coarser manifest, which man call physical, appeared.*

31. *And this is what is called the fall of man; but man fell not alone for protoplast, and earth, and plant and beast were all included in the fall.*

32. *The angels and the cherubim fell not; their will were never strong, and so they held the ethers of their planes in harmony with Allah.*

FROM THE HOLY PROPHET

33. *Now, when the ether reached the rate of atmosphere, and all the creatures of these planes must get their food from atmosphere, the conflict came; and then that which the finite man called survival of the best, became a law.*

34. *The stronger ate the bodies of the weaker manifests; and here is where the carnal of evolution had its rise.*

35. *And now man, in his utter shamelessness, strikes down and eats the beasts, the beasts consume the plant, the plant thrives on the earth, the earth absorbs the protoplast.*

36. *In yonder kingdom of the soul this carnal evolution is not known, and the great work of master minds is to restore the heritage of man,*

to bring him back to his estate that he had lost, when he again will live upon the ethers of his native plan.

37. The thoughts of Allah change not; the manifests of life on every plane unfolds into perfection of their kind; and as the thought of Allah can never die, there is not death to any being of the seven ethers of the seven spirits of the Triune Allah.

38. And so an earth is never plant; a beast or bird, or creeping thing is never man, and man is not, and cannot be, a beast, or bird, or creeping thing.

39. The time will come when all these seven manifests will be absorbed, and man and beast and plant and earth and protoplast will be redeemed.

40. Barata was amazed; the wisdom of the Jewish sage was revelation unto him.

41. Now Vidyapati, wisest of the Indian sages, chief of the temple Kapavistu, heard Barata speak to Jesus of the origin of man, and heard the answer of the Hebrew prophet, and he said:

42. "You priests of Kapavistu, hear me speak; we stand today upon a crest of time. Six time ago a master soul was born who gave a glorious light to man, and now a master sage stands in the temple of Kapavistu."

43. The Hebrew prophet is the rising star of wisdom, deified, He brings to us a knowledge of the secret things of Allah; and all the world will hear his words, and glorify his name.

44. You priests of temple Kapavistu, stay; be still and listen when he speaks; he is the living "Oracle of Allah."

45. And all the priests gave thanks, and praised the Buddha of enlightenment.

CHAPTER 28

BENARES is the sacred city of the Brahms, and in Benares Jesus taught; Udraka was his host.

2. Udraka made a feast in honour of his guest, and many high born Hindu priests and scribes were there.

3. And Jesus said to them, With much delight I speak to you concerning life -- the brotherhood of life.

4. The universal God is one, yet he is more than one; all things are God; all things are one.

Udraka gives a feast in Jesus' honour. Jesus speaks on the unity of God and the brotherhood of life. Criticizes the priesthood. Becomes the guest of a farmer.

5. By the sweet breaths of God all life is bound in one; so if you touch a fiber of a living thing you send a thrill from centre to the outer bounds of life.

6. And when you crush beneath your foot the meanest worm, you shake the throne of God, and cause the sword of right to tremble in its sheath.

7. The bird sings out its song for men, and men vibrate in unison to help it sing.

8. The ant constructs her home, the bee its sheltering comb, the spider weaves her web, and flowers breathe to them a spirit in their sweet perfumes that gives them strength to toil.

9. Now, men and birds and beasts and creeping things are deities, made flesh; and how dare men kill anything?

10. 'Tis cruelty that makes the world awry. When men have learned that when they harm a living thing they harm themselves, they surely will not kill, nor cause a thing that God has made to suffer pain.

11. A lawyer said, I pray you, Jesus, tell who is this God you speak about; where are his priests, his temples and his shrines?

12. And Jesus said, The God I speak about is everywhere; he cannot be compassed with walls, nor hedged about with bounds of any kind.

13. All people worship God, the One; but all the people see him not alike.

14. This universal God is wisdom, will and love.

15. All men see not the Triune God. One sees him as the God of might; another as the God of thought; another as the God of love.

16. A man's ideal is his God, and so, as man unfolds, his God unfolds. Man's God today, tomorrow is not God.

17. The nations of earth see God from different points of view, and so he does not seem the same to everyone.

18. Man names the part of God he sees, and this to him is all of God; and every nation sees a part of God, and every nation has a name for God.

19. You Brahmans call him Parabrahm; in Egypt he is Thoth; and Zeus is his name in Greece; Jehovah is his Hebrew name; but everywhere he is the causeless Cause, the rootless Root from which all things have grown.

20. When men become afraid of God, and take him for a foe, they dress up other men in fancy garbs and call them priests.

21. And charge them to restrain the wrath of God by prayers; and when they fail to win his favour by their prayers, to buy him off with sacrifice of animal, or bird.

22. When man sees God as one with him, as Father-God, he needs no middle man, no priest to intercede;

23. He goes straight up to him and says, My Father-God! and then he lays his hand in God's own hand, and all is well.

24. And this is God. You are, each one, a priest, just for yourself; and sacrifice of blood God does not want.

25. Just give your life in sacrificial service to the all of life, and God is pleased.

26. When Jesus had thus said he stood aside; the people were amazed, but strove among themselves.

27. Some said, He is inspired by Holy Brahm; and others said, He is insane; and others said, He is obsessed; he speaks as devils speak.

28. But Jesus tarried not. Among the guests was one, a tiller of the soil, a generous soul, a seeker after truth, who loved the words that Jesus spoke, and Jesus went with him, and in his home abode.

CHAPTER 32

AMONG the Buddhist priests was one who saw a lofty wisdom in the words that Jesus spoke. It was Barata Arabo.

2. Together Jesus and Barata read the Jewish Psalms and Prophets; read the Vedas, the Avesta and the wisdom of Gautama.

3. And as they read and talked about the possibilities of man, Barata said,

4. Man is the marvel of the universe. He is part of everything for he has been a living thing on every plane of life.

5. Time was when man was not; and then he was a bit of formless substance in the moulds of time; and them a protoplast.

6. By universal law all things tend upward to a state of perfectness. The protoplast evolved, becoming worm, then reptile, bird and beast, and then at last it reached the form of man.

7. Now, man himself is mind, and mind is her to gain perfection by experience; and mind is often manifest in fleshy form, and in the form best suited to its growth. So mind may manifest as worm, or bird, or beast, or man.

8. The time will come when everything of life will be evolved unto the state of perfect man.

9. And after man is man in perfectness, he will evolve to higher forms of life.

10. And Jesus said, Barata Arabo, who taught you this, that mind, which is the man, may manifest in flesh of beast, or bird, or creeping thing?

11. Barata said, From times which man remembers not our priests have told us so, and so we know.

12. And Jesus said, Enlightened Arabo, are you a master mind and do not know that man knows naught by being told?

13. Man may believe what others say; but thus he never knows. If man would know, he must himself be what he knows.

14. Do you remember, Arabo, when you were ape, or bird, or worm?

15. Now, if you have no better proving of plea than that the priests have told you so, you do not know; you simply guess.

16. Regard not, then, what any man has said; let us forget the flesh, and go with mind into the land of fleshless things; mind never does forget.

17. And backward through the ages master minds can trace themselves; and thus they know.

18. Time never was when man was not.

19. That which begins will have an end. If man was not, the time will come when he will not exist.

20. From God's own Record Book we read: The Triune God breathed forth, and seven Spirits stood before his face. (The Hebrews call these seven Spirits *Elohim*.)

21. And these are they who, in their boundless power, created everything that is, or was.

22. These Spritis of the Triune God moved on the face of boundless space and seven ethers were, and every ether had its form of life.

23. These forms of life were but the thoughts of God, clothed in the sbustance of their ether planes.

24. Men call these ether planes the planes of protoplast, of earth, of plant, of beast, of man, of angel and of cherubim.

25. These planes with all their teeming thoughts of God, are never seen by eyes of man in flesh; they are composed of substance far too fine for fleshly eyes to see, and still they constitute the soul of things;

26. And with the eyes of soul all creatures see these ether planes, and all the forms of life.

27. Because all forms of life on every plane are thoughts of God, all creatures think, and every creature is possessed of will, and, in its measure, has the power to choose.

28. And in their native planes all creatures are supplied with nourishment from the ethers of their planes.

29. And so it was with every living thing until the will became a sluggish will, and then the ethers of the protoplast, the earth, the plant, the beast, the man, began to vibrate very slowly.

30. The ethers all became more dense, and all the creatures of these planes were clothed with coarser garbs, the garbs of flesh, which men can see; and thus this coarser manifest, which men call physical, appeared.

31. And this is what is called the fall of man; but man fell not alone, for protoplast, and earth, and plant and beast were all included in the fall.

32. The angels and the cherubim fell not; their will were ever strong, and so they held the ethers of their planes in harmony with God.

33. Now, when the ethers reached the rate of atmosphere, and all the creatures of these planes must get their good from atmosphere, the conflict came; and then that which the finite man has called survival of the best, became a law.

34. The stronger ate the bodies of the weaker manifests; and here is where the carnal law of evolution had its rise.

35. And now man, in his utter shamelessness, strikes down and eats the beasts, the beast consumes the plant, the plant thrives on the earth, the earth absorbs the protoplast.

36. In yonder kingdom of the soul, this carnal evolution is not known, and the great work of master minds is to restore the heritage of man, to bring him back to his estate that he has lost, when he again will upon the ethers of his native plane.

37. The thoughts of God change not; the manifests of life on every plan unfold into perfection of their kind; and as the thoughts of God can never die, there is no death to any being of the seven ethers of the seven Spirits of the Truine God.

38. And so an earth is never plant; a beast, or bird, or creeping thing is never man, and man is not, and cannot be, a beast, or bird, or creeping thing.

39. The time will come when all these seven manifests will be absorbed, and man, and beast, and plan, and earth and protoplast will be redeemed.

40. Barata was amazed; the wisdom of the Jewish sage was revelation unto him.

41. Now, Vidyapati, wisest of the Indian sages, chief of temple Kapavistu, heard Barata speak to Jesus of the origin of man, and heard the answer of the Hebrew prophet, and he said.

42. You priests of Kapavistu, hear me speak: We stand today upon a crest of time. Six times ago a master soul was born who gave a

glory light to man, and now a master sage stands here in temple Kapavistu.

43. This Hebrew prophet is the rising star of wisdom, deified. he brings to us a knowledge of the secret things of God; and all the world will hear his words, will heed his words, and glorify his name.

44. You priests of temple Kapavistu, stay! be still and listen when he speaks; he is the living Oracle of God.

45. And all the priests gave thanks, and praised the Buddha of enlightenment.

Noble Drew Ali gave special consideration to the Masonic teaching of the number seven and it can be concluded that the circle seven on his Koran (numerology) refers to the book of seven seals in the book of Revelation in the Bible. On the other hand, the seven breaths or planes of Allah is how Ali explained his perception of ultimate reality:

> The Triune Allah breathed forth, and stood seven spirits before his face . . .

> These forms of life were but the thought of Allah, clothed in the substance of their ether planes.[10]

> Notice that despite Ali's unconscious pollution of Islam, he still places the creator, Allah, at the center of his preachments.

The Masonic teachings of the number seven state that the seven degrees allude to the process of ascension upwards to the light. Seven is a number which represents completion or wholeness. The *Masonic Encyclopedia* states "the word seven signifies full or complete." The York Rite Order symbolizes or represents seven as the complete ascension of man or the complete man, the model human being. The complete man or total human being is a man of rational behavior and spiritual knowledge. In essence, he is a balanced human being.

Continuing with this aspect of Masonic teaching, Ali taught his followers that seven is the number which centers around universal ideas, such as: there are seven days in a week, seven days in creation, and seven days in a circle; moreover, he bestowed the title E1 on his followers which stands for Elohim is at various times called the seven eyes of God.[11]

Drew's use of the number seven also had spiritual significance. Consider, for example, the Seven Salaams: there are seven instances in the Holy Quran where the word Salaam (peace) is used in the sense of blessing either upon the blessed or upon Allah's Prophets (Surahs: 36:59, 87:79, 37:109, 37:120, 37:130, 37:181, and 97:5). These Surahs are recited in times of distress or upon auspicious occasions. The Seven Speeches or "Seven Scripts" mean that a Hadith states that the Quran is revealed in Seven Speeches, readings, scripts, or versions. The best interpretation for the Seven Speeches is that of "Seven Levels of Meaning." The Seventh Heaven marks the end of supraformal creation, and, in the symbolism of the seven directions of space, is the center. Furthermore, according to Dr. Seyyed Hossein Nasr, the Holy Quran speaks of the seven earths as well as seven heavens, of the Divine Pedestal (Kursi) and Throne (arsh), which became important elements of Islamic cosmology.

The secret sects that sprang from the Shiah movement -- some of them masonic in nature -- placed emphasis on the number seven.

The Moorish Scientists believe that Drew Ali was a prophet and Marcus Garvey was John the Baptist. John the Baptist was the forerunner of Jesus, and he was to warn and stir up the nation and prepare them to receive the Divine creed which was to be taught by Jesus. Interestingly, Drew discussed Jesus' alleged travels in India which, I believe, he adopted from the Ahmadis. The Ahmadis believe that Jesus taught in India and did not die on the cross, but escaped to India where he continued to teach until his natural death.

As I mentioned earlier, Drew seemingly embraced certain customs and symbols from the Masonic Order primarily because he was supposedly a mason of high degree and a Shriner. His uniform, for example, the names EL, Bey, and Noble are Masonic in content.

In addition, Ali's form of dress, particularly, his wearing the turban and the fez also bespeaks Masonic and Eastern influences. Interestingly, the Honorable Elijah Muhammad and his followers wore a fez and a turban in the early days of the Nation of Islam movement. Ali's perceived incorporation of Masonic customs and mannerisms into his movement were seemingly transferred from the Ancient Arabic Order of the Nobles of the Mystic Shrine to the Moorish Science Temple. I believe his unconscious admixture of Masonry with Islam stemmed from the direct or indirect influence of Masonry, and the philosophies he learned from his travels to Egypt, Morocco and India which assisted him in giving theosophical formation to the Moorish Science Philosophy or teaching.

Considering the above information, I think it is befitting at this time to take a brief historical look at the development of some alleged Masonic influences in Orthodox Islam and the probable impact they had on Drew Ali. After the death of Prophet Muhammad (Peace Be Upon Him), a number of sects, some were called secret socie-

Seyyed Hossein Nasr, *Science and Civilization in Islam*, 1968, p. 95 and 99.

ties, were formed by Muslims who believed that there was (is) a deeper, higher meaning to the Holy Quran than can be comprehended by the average believer.[13] Unfortunately, this belief later underwent grave philosophical distortion based on divergent interpretations.

Each one of those sects, however, was not shrouding itself in secrecy for the purpose of utilizing its knowledge to willfully manipulate or control. On the contrary, each sect was in its own peculiar way responding to its cultural and historical comprehension of Islam. With the exception of the Druze, those sects did not deviate drastically from the fundamental tenets of Islam. This fact will be demonstrated and reiterated because of its relevance.

Other secret organizations were formed for the purpose of military warfare interests. Another important event that took place after the Prophet's death was the schism in the once unified Muslim community. The community divided into two major sects (Sunni and Shiah) over the rightful successors of Prophet Muhammad. Interestingly, the Shiah, despite strong criticism from the Sunni community, did not deviate from the fundamental tenets of Islam. However, various secret societies emerged out of the Shiah, and some of these groups deviated from Islam by way of interpretation. The major groups that emerged out of the Shiah were the following:

1. The Druzes
2. The Qarmatians
3. The Fatimids
4. The Assassins, they were also called the Hashishin
5. The Ismaillis

It is important to point out that some of these societies were indeed known for their wisdom, knowledge, understanding, and high regard for the Holy Quran.[15] Another point that I must state is that I believe a brief historical acquaintance with these groups or sects will

Various studies attribute the origin of the Ancient Arabic Order of the Noble of the Mystic Shrine to Caliph Ali, who was also the cousin of Prophet Muhammad. There is no valid documentation for this claim.

For the Masons, the fez (tashboosh) is a symbol of knowledge and scholarship. It became a symbol of learning because students of intellectual repute wore the fez in Fas, Morocco.

assist us in better understanding and perhaps excusing Noble Drew Ali -- Drew in particular -- and the Honorable Elijah Muhammad because they were in one way or another effected by these secret organizations and their offshoots.

It must be stated that Elijah Muhammad was not emotionally or conceptually attached to masonry as was Noble Drew Ali.

The Qarmatians (Carmathians) were an early offshoot of the Seveners, which was a kind of resurgent Gnosticism that emerged in Islamic disguise after the death of Isma'il, the son of Ja'far As-Sadiq. The Qarmatians are named after Hamdan Qarmat, a peasant who was their insurrectionary. The Qarmatians combined secret religious doctrines with revolution and a program of social justice and redistribution of wealth.

They represented a peasant sect that engaged in uprisings against the orthodox establishment and they attempted to usurp power from the establishment by way of rebellion, but also by way of conspiracy. The Qarmatians social philosophy was a kind of pristine egalitarianism. The ideology of the Qarmatians like that of the Isma'ilis was a Gnostic Dualism which sees evil as having a reality and substance of its own, as the good has.

On a different note, Leila Ahmed, Muslim scholar and feminist, states that the Qarmatian movement diverged in their interpretation of Islam in that they emphasized the ethical, spiritual, and social

The Assassins were also known as Hahishin because they allegedly used hashish or marijuana to achieve an exotic, mystical state. They occupied mountain fortresses in what is now Syria and Lebanon until they had achieved what amounted to a mini-state in the mountainous region between Muslim Hama and Christian Latakia. The Hashishin were not randomly vicious; however, their struggle was more against the Sunni Muslims than against the Crusaders. Again, the Hashishin were Shiah. Whenever someone joined this esoteric sect, each of the Hashishin made a hijra to their seemingly inaccessible mountain fortresses, withdrawing from the world. There they practiced a form of mysticism, which introduced the initiate to secret knowledge of what they claimed was true Islam.

As stated above, despite the five factions cited above that emanated from the Shiahs, no body or branch of the Shiahs had ever deviated from the fundamental tenets of Islam. It was claimed that these factions had been handed down through a different line from that of the Sunnis.

teachings of Islam as its essential message and viewed the practices of Prophet Muhammad and the regulations that he put into effect as ephemeral aspects of Islam relevant primarily to a particular society at a certain stage in its history. Professor Ahmed also informs us that the Qarmatians rejected concubinage and the marriage of nine-year old girls, and they banned polygamy and the veil. She points out that Sufi ideas implicitly challenged the way Sunni Islam conceptualized gender, as is suggested by the fact that they permitted women to give a central place in their lives to their spiritual vocation; thereby affirming the paramountcy of the spiritual over the biological.

Nesta Webster also informs us that Abdullah Maimun's advocacy of Ismail was nothing more than a smoke screen designed to conceal his materialistic motives. He, in turn, founded a sect known as the Batinis with seven degrees of initiation. The Batine is a doctrine which is esoteric, secret, and initiatic. The central tradition among the Batinis is an Ismaili one. Most of the splinter groups associated with it included the Qaramates, the Musta'lis, the Nizaris, and the Druze, which deserves and will get some attention. These groups are basically secret in nature; they share a common heritage of religious and theosophical ideas which set them apart from the orthodox tenets of Islam.[18]

The Batini order contained some rather ingenious routes for linking their cosmology with human history. They extracted from Pythagorean, Babylonian and Chaldean traditions; they also became fascinated with number analogies, mystic numerals and letters, which they incorporated into a complicated hero-history of prophetic emanations. For the Batini, each age had a prophet who was accompanied by an "Asas" or "silent one," who understood the inner meanings of revelation. Moses had Aaron, Jesus had Peter, Mohammed had Ali . . . .[19]

I do not want to spend too much more time on these secret orders; however, I do think that a brief elaboration on the Druze is

---

Al-Ghazali rendered a conclusive argument that the mystics -- the Sufis -- were the heirs of the Prophet Muhammad. They alone walked the path of direct knowledge and they were the decisive authorities on doctrine. At the same time, he affirmed the indispensable need for the esoteric framework to make that possible. He strongly refuted the teachings of the Isma'ilis (Ia'Limiyyah), they were active as the Assassin sect during that time and their enticements of "secret teachings" and "hidden master."

important because they are extremely removed from mainstream Islam, and it is suggested by Imam Alauddin Shabazz, noted Islamic scholar, that Farad Muhammad might have been an ideological Druze. From the outset, opposition to the prevailing currents in Islam centered on the person of Ali, the Prophet's cousin and husband of his daughter Fatima. Afterwards, the Shiah doctrine maintained that the Prophet explicitly designated him as his successor at a place called Ghadir Khumm, on their return from the Farewell Pilgrimage. Of course, Sunni Muslims vehemently reject this on the basis that the Prophet merely urged the Muslims to hold Ali in high esteem. To reiterate, the Shiahs even split over the question of Ali's successors into four factions, the fourth divided into two further sects. Both of these retained their allegiance to the descendants of Ali, in this case, Ja'far as-Sadiq. But Sadiq did not have an interest in leading a movement. His eldest son Ismail would have inherited Ja'Jar's authority had he not died prematurely. Without a figurehead, the Shiah's looked to Ja'far's next son, Abd Allah, but he too died, lastly they looked to the next son, Musaal-Kazim, who was the eldest as the legitimate successor.

Isma-ilism, historically began as an offshoot from what was generally characterized as Twelver-Imam. However, it is possible to view Twelver-Imam as an offshoot of Isma-ilism, or rather as the result of fusing political shiahism with someone to champion political justice who should be of the descent of Ali. Thus, Shiah believe certain successive descendants of Ali to be intermediaries between man and God.

It is imperative to point out that the Sunnis also divided into splinter groups within 100 years after the death of Prophet Muhammad. Thus, the 72 different sects that exist in Islam today did not stem only from the Shiah sect.

The Shiahs believe in 12 Imams, whom they consider to be immaculate and sinless. All kinds of attributes are given to these Imams which the Quran does not allow even for the Messengers of Allah. Therefore, the Sunni find this to be bordering on Shirk, a major sin in Islam. Additionally, the Shiahs believe in the Mahdi, the Twelfth Imam who will supposedly return. The Mahdi, say the Shiahs, disappeared as a child and has been in "occultation" for all these centuries. Again, this is in sharp contrast to the Holy Quran, and it is probably borrowed from the Christian belief about the return of the Messiah, Jesus, son of Mary. The Sunnis, therefore, reject the Shiahs because they are a sect that have incorporated some teachings into their belief system which are not to be found in the Quran or in the Hadith.

Furthermore, the followers of the Isma-ili held a concept of the Imam that was more absolute than that of the other Shiah offshoots, in that for them the Imam was no mere intermediary, but the essence of Divinity. The followers of the Isma-ili sect came to be called the Seveners because they declared that Ismail was the embodiment of the seventh Imam, and that, with the number seven, a cycle had now been completed, heralding a new beginning and a new doctrine.

According to Nesta H. Webster, an intriguer of cunning character would usurp the Isma-ili movement, which would cease to be schismatic and would become subversive not only to the pristine tenets of Islam, but to religion in general.

The mysterious man was Abdullah Ibn Maimun, the son of a learned and free thinking doctor in Southern Persia, who was brought up in the doctrines of Gnostic dualism and profoundly versed in all religions and was in fact a materialist. By proclaiming knowledge of the Isma-ilis' creed, he succeeded in placing himself at the head of the Isma-ilis.

Fundamental to Gnosticism is the belief in a transcendent God, merciful and good. He is God the Father, who belongs to the upper world of light, but is utterly remote from our cosmos, and is indeed a stranger to it. Associated with him is his Son, the Logos. The cosmos itself is intrinsically evil, and is not the work of the true God, but of an opposing entity known as the demiurge, or creator. Gnosticism is comprised of a hierarchy of celestial beings, which are divided into two classes: good angels, working for the upper world of light, and evil archons working for the inferior world in which we live.

Man is involved in the primordial duality that pervades the universe. He fell from the world of light where he had his origin, and is now entrapped in matter and in the clutches of the demiurge. Salvation from this predicament has nothing to do with morality, good works or faith, but depends on a kind of transcendent knowledge (gnosis) of God's redemptive purpose through the Logos.

Religiously, the Shiahs have supplied Islam with saints, intercessors, mysteries, belief in atonement, and a spirit of high cult. Similarly, the Isma-ilis introduced esoteric mysteries around the number seven, namely because Ismail was considered the seventh Imam.

Islam like Christianity and other religions received its share of Gnostic elements. Long before the birth of Prophet Muhammad, Christian communities had already been established in the Hejaz in the west by missionaries of the Abyssinian (Ethiopian) church, in the Yemen in the east and along the Persian Gulf by missionaries from India, and in the north on the borders of Iraq by missionaries from the Byzantine Empire.

The Christianity that was being propagated was not that of western Christendom, but one or other of the many schismatic forms, especially those with a strong Nestorian or Gnostic bias, and it was these that exercised their influence on the newly emerging faith of Islam. Therefore, when Islam spread to Iraq it became colored by various Gnostic influences prevailing there. The influence of the Gnostic is of course most conspicuously seen in Sufism. Islam itself was opposed to monasticism, and the Sufi orders were therefore not regarded as being in the true Islamic tradition, and were long proscribed by the orthodox theologians. One of the earliest Sufi mystics, Ibrahim Bin Adham was instructed by a Christian anchorite, Father Simeon, in the means of acquiring gnosis (Arabic, Maarifa). This prepared the way for the Sufi mystics who followed, leading ultimately to the un-Islamic Logos doctrine in which the Logos is made incarnated in Prophet Muhammad.

It is noteworthy to mention that Medieval Christian scholars did not look upon Muslims as members of an alien or non-Christian faith, but rather as those who had broken away from a fundamentally Christian doctrine.

Gnosticism reached its fruition in the Christian era. It evolved out of a disaffected and heterodox Judaism and perhaps expressed the failure of Jewish hopes. Some of the early Gnostic schools had distinct Jewish roots and many prominent Gnostics were Jews who had renounced Judaism. They denied Jehovah, the Old Testament and the Mosaic law, and therefore propounded an inverse form of Judaism.

Benjamin Walker, *Gnosticism Its History and Influence*, Acquarian Press, 1983, p. 165 and 166.

As I mentioned above, the Druze are far removed from the orthodox tenets of Islam. They are also an offshoot of the Isma-ili order, and they have carried their belief in the Divine Imamate to the point where they constitute a separate religious philosophy. The order originated during the reign of the third Fatimid Caliph, Hakim, who as an Isma-ili Imam held a position in his community corresponding to the cosmic intellect. He was an eccentric and a cruel autocrat that became obsessed with power. He contributed his share to disorder and rancor when he accursed the first three Caliphs.

Paradoxically, a small group of his followers saw in his power wielding and eccentricities, a manifestation of the Divine. Encouraged by two devout followers, Ismail Darazi, a Turk, and Hamza Ali, a Persian, these religious intellectuals began to propagate the doctrine that Hakim was not merely the Imam, but was an actual personification of the Highest Cosmic Intellect -- in other words, God Himself.[20]

Interestingly, the Druzes are named after Hamza and Darazi; other points of information are once they secured some mountain areas they tore down all the Masjids and established their own systems of law. They do not observe Ramadan or make the Hajj.[21]

Considering the above, it is now important to look at what Webster has to say about the Druze and their Masonic structure. The Druze, according to Webster, as a secret society present several analogies with the Masonic Order. For example, instead of the nine degrees instituted by the Lodge of Cairo, the Druzes are divided into only three -- Profanes, Aspirants, and Wise -- to whom their doctrines are gradually unfolded under a seal of the strictest secrecy to ensure

Hakim was murdered because of his viciousness. It is said that his sister was the leader of the group that supposedly murdered him and concealed his body. As a result of the concealment, his loyal followers declared that the Divinity had merely vanished in order to test the faith of the believers, but would reappear in time and punish the apostates. Thus, it was complete, Hakim became the God-head of the Druze Order.

Furthermore, the Druze practice endogamy, insisting on equal treatment for men and women in marriage, and, with rare exceptions, they refuse converts.

Further, the Druze believe that emanations of Divine principles are made incarnated, or act through, functionaries or representatives of Hakim. Because of their Isma-ili origins, Druze beliefs are characteristically dualist or Gnostic.

which signs and passwords are employed in the manner of Free Masonry.[22]

The similarity between the Druze and the Grand Orient Freemasonry is more than obvious.[23] Webster contends that the Druze have modes of recognition which are common to Freemasonry, and the taking of oaths and the swearing to secrecy are points of irrefutable affinity.

The Druzes are, in all likelihood, the Freemasons of the East. Their organization resembles that of the Craft Degrees in Western Masonry, and such is their power that few if any European Masons have ever succeeded in discovering the essence of their doctrines. Their power and influence over the political affairs of the Middle East is more persuasive than that of the Grand Orient over the political affairs of Europe.[24]

In practice there are several different degrees of initiation which along with Druze precepts are designed to promote obedience, group cohesiveness, and solidarity in the face of pressure from outside. The process of initiation begins at the age of eighteen. The guidance given to the Druzes is represented as being the will of Hakim expressed through his "ministers."

Research suggests that the Druze philosophy had more of a theoretical influence on Farad Muhammad than it did on Noble Drew Ali. Morroe Berger wrote a highly informative article titled "The

In a simplified version of the Isma-ili hierarchy, which distinguishes between the unenlightened leadership around the Imam and the masses for whom the truth is dangerous, the Druzes are divided into two ranks, the 'Aquils (Sages) and Jahils (Ignorant ones). The 'Aquils, who may include women, are initiated into the inner secrets of the faith after passing a series of spiritual tests. They are required to live extremely devout lives. The Jahils, on the other hand, are allowed more personal freedom than the Aquils, but it is assumed that the Jahils will be denied spiritual growth. They may, however, have a chance of initiation in a future life. The Druzes, like the Hindus and Gnostics believe in the transmigration of the soul.
Equally important, the Druze can be an extremely ethnocentric clan.

Another thought provoking feature of the Isma-ili and Druze belief system is the concept of Taqiyya or dissimulation, whereby a persecuted believer may hide his or her religion and even profess another faith. This concept Taqiyya, and the Druze ban on proselytizing and intermarriage, have made the Druze a close and tight-knit group which brooks little interference with its way of life.

Black Muslims" (Horizon magazine, Winter 1964, p. 61) in which he brings the Druze, Farad subject to closer scrutiny. Berger's argument follows in this manner: The Druze philosophy which comprises secrecy, revelation of the doctrine only to initiates and then in stages, belief in a succession of incarnations of God, cycles of history, and great emphasis upon the coming of a savior is comparatively similar to the philosophy of Farad Muhammad. Berger also argues that the Black Muslims shared with the Druzes and Isma-ilis an interest in the occult sciences and the magic of numbers. Farad placed great emphasis on numbers. Each of these features can be found in other medieval religions as well, and even in some contemporary ones; however, this unique synthesis of disparate elements suggests to Berger that Farad, more so than Drew, might have been a Druze or an Isma-ili. Furthermore, when Farad was organizing the Temple people in Detroit in the early 1930's, there were hundreds of Druzes there who had come from Syria.

The following comments from Elijah Muhammad show the similarity between the Druzes and the Black Muslims' concepts on the cycles of history and a succession of gods which are based in mathematics:

> In discussing the Black Man as the original man. Elijah Muhammad said: "We make history once every twenty-five thousand years. When such history is written, it is done by twenty-four of our scientists . . . There is a significance to the number 24 scientists and the 25,000 years." The significance he pointed out is that there are twenty-four hours in the day and approximately twenty-five thousand miles in the circumference of the earth. Furthermore, he said that Allah taught him that every twenty-five thousand years each God coming after the other God would make a new civilization. His belief, teaching, and theology were different from the other God who preceded him who made a beautiful change in the history of the wisdom of man.

As I indicated previously, the adherents of the Isma-ili sect were called the seveners primarily because they declared that Ismaili was the seventh Imam, and that, with the number seven the cycle had been completed. Moreover, the various sevener movements were in fact, to become a secret insurrectionary movement with underground branches all over the Muslim world, and they sought to overthrow the Abbasids, the dynasty that followed the Umayads.

The Fatimids was one Isma-ili sect that successfully conquered Egypt and became the Fatimid dynasty. Another Isma-ili sect, which I discussed earlier, was the Qarmatians who successfully conquered East Arabia, Bahrain, and at one point briefly occupied Mecca. Here are two points of importance that I failed to mention earlier about the Qarmatians as well as the Fatimids: The first Isma-ili movement to make an important impact on the Islamic world was started by the Qarmatians in the latter part of the ninth century. In the tenth century the Qarmatians founded a dynastic state based in Bahrain which achieved notoriety in 969 when its leader, Hamdan Qarmat, occupied Mecca and carried away the Black Stone.

Furthermore, the most far-reaching dynasty created by the Isma-ili sect was that of the Fatimids, so-called because they legitimized themselves in North Africa in 909 and conquered Egypt sixty years later. At its height, Fatimid power extended from the Atlas mountains to Sind. They ruled in Tunisia, Egypt, Syria, the Hejaz, Yemen and Omam at a time when, under its overlords, the Abbasid Caliphate was confined to Mesopotamia and the Persian (Iranian) plateau.[25]

Another informative point is that the Isma-ilis were very active in spreading their doctrine. They were not only in Egypt, Syria, and Persia, but they also infiltrated India. All of the Isma-ili missionaries in India were astute enough to adapt Isma-ilism to Hinduism and vice-a-versa.

Masonry is also known as Free Masonry; it consists of doctrines and practices of the Fraternal Order of Free and Accepted Masons.   It

Leila Ahmed, *Women and Gender in Islam*, Yale University Press, New Haven 1992, p. 66 and 95.

According to historical accounts, when the Qarmatians stole the Black Stone it was in three pieces and smaller fragments. It is now in seven pieces. It is surmised that they broke it into seven to bring the number of pieces in line with the new age represented by the seventh Imam.

supposedly evolved from the stone mason guilds of the Middle Ages. Webster also states that one of the founders of this group, Dr. Walter M. Fleming, claimed the Mystic Shrines, who are Masons of the highest degrees, was founded by Ali, the son-in-law of Prophet Muhammad. Fleming did not present any source for his claim.

It is doubtful whether Ali was founder of the Mystic Shrines. It can be argued with some degree of certainty that the disputatious conflict between the Sunnis and the Shiahs, as well as the subsequent divisions that developed within the Shiahs gave birth to the Mystic Shrines.

Ali, according to Islamic history, was revered by the Sufis as the fountainhead of esoteric doctrine; more generally, he is remembered for his religious piety, nobility, and knowledge. He was also a warrior on the battlefield during Islam's struggle against the Meccans; he is a model of chivalry, as well as generosity and Quranic Learning.

It has been proved that Ali's personal relationship to Prophet Muhammad was special. Prophet Muhammad referred to him at least twice as "my brother" and three times as "my heir." The Prophet of Allah blessed the marriage union of Ali and Fatimah in an extraordinary manner by anointing them both on their marriage night. As far as is known, the Prophet did this for no one else.

With the above information, a plausible conjecture can very easily be made that because of Ali's piety, his position with the Sufis, the political divisions that erupted between the Kharijites (the first sect to secede) and Muawiyah, Caliph Utman's cousin, and Ali's military prowess he founded the Masons or the Mystic Shrines. Ali was first and foremost a Muslim.

Mustafa El-Amin points out that Freemasonry is un-Islamic in most respects; however, there is one common, positive feature between Islam and the Shriners . . . El-Amin states this: Freemasonry has been defined as a "system of morality veiled in allegory." If there is any compatibility between Freemasonry and Al-Islam, it is at the level of the Shrines, although Freemasonry emphasizes seeking knowledge, light and wisdom throughout each degree, that is by far its most positive injunction. Muslims can appreciate and respect that because we are commanded to do the same.[26]

Comprehending all of the above information pertaining to the various orders that emerged out of the Shiah and Isma-ili sects, I think it behooves us to return to Noble Drew Ali and the Moorish Science Temple. Noble Drew Ali was undoubtedly the first quasi-Islamic pioneer in the United States; he signed the first charter making the Moorish Science Temple of America a legally incorporated movement.

He, depending on how you assess him, skillfully synthesized conceptual and philosophical disparities into a compact organizational unit. His very name, Noble, was of Masonic content. It is a title bestowed on members of the Shriners upon initiation into the lodge. Remember, Drew was supposedly an Egyptian Adept. Conjecturally speaking, he embraced the name Ali because it was the name of the fourth Caliph who was also the cousin of Prophet Muhammad (Peace Be Upon Him). As I mentioned earlier, Caliph Ali supposedly instituted the order of the Shriners.

Despite his Masonic leanings, Drew Ali was by strict definition of the word a Muslim. His character and behavior reflected an Islamic consciousness.

Drew's use of the name Moorish Science Temple has some Masonic origins -- science and temple are the two words open for immediate discussion. Most knowledgeable people know the name Moor is related to the BlackaMoors, the African conquerors of Spain, from North Africa. The most famous was General Tarik who defeated King Roderick.

As I just stated, Drew's use of the name Noble is also Masonic in nature. The parallels are clear in the Shriners' question and answer initiation:

Question: Are you a Noble of the Mystic Shrine?
Answer: I have traveled the Arabic Path.
Question: You are a Noble then, I presume?
Answer: I am so accepted by all men of Noble Birth.

On a subjective note, I think Noble befitted his philosophy and his character. The following bears testimony:

"I urge you to remember there is work enough for all to do in helping to build a better world. The problems of life are largely social and economic. In a profound sense, they are moral and spiritual. Have lofty conceptions of your duties to your country and fellowman in general and especially those with whom you deal. This includes such honesty and righteousness as will cause you to put yourself in the other fellow's place. Look for the best in others and give them the best that is in you. Have a deeper appreciation for womanhood. Brighten the hopes of our youth in order that their courage be increased to dare and do wondrous things. Adhere at all times to the principles of love, truth, peace, freedom and justice. I am your affectionate leader. I shall continue to labor day and night, both in public and private, for your good, thereby contributing to the welfare of our country and its people as a whole."

Moors from the Latin Maurus, which is derived from the Greek Mauros, which means "dark complexioned."

Ali's use of the word Temple -- Elijah also used the word -- might have come from the Knight of Templars. The Templars were influenced by the Order of the Assassins. The Templars emerged victorious nineteen years after the first crusade had ended with the defeat of the Muslims, the capture of Antioch and Jerusalem, and the installment of Godefroi de Bouillon as King of Jerusalem, and a group of nine French soldiers led by Hugues de Payens and Godefroi de Saint-Omer, established an order for the protection of pilgrims to the Holy Sepulcher. Baldwin I succeeded to the throne of Jerusalem some time later and presented them with a house near the site of the Temple of Solomon; thus the name Knights of Templar is the origin of the name for which they were to become famous.[27] In other words, the Knights Templar got their name from the building of King Solomon's Temple. Hence, the word Temple denotes wisdom which stems from the frontal-lobe or forehead, and a place to worship.

Furthermore, the Knights Templars disseminated much of the knowledge they acquired from the East in Europe, and that is manifested in the higher degrees of masonry. From the Muslims, the Templars derived certain concepts that they fused into their own order and introduced into Europe on their return, which made them the creators or at least the inventors of the higher degrees in the Masonic Order.[28]

Elijah Muhammad stated that Temple means a "Nation" a righteous nation that would be built in the "Northwest Hemisphere" America. It would be built with people who were in mud, naked, rejected by everyone. This referred to black people in North America.

It is difficult to ascertain the origin of the name Drew other than the fact that it is a past tense verb that means "to take or pull out, to pull toward one."

The building of King Solomon's Temple was the beginning of masonry. Thus it can be deduced that the Canaanites (Africans) were the authors of masonry. Interestingly, Noble Drew Ali did name his first Temple the Canaanite Temple.

I have embraced conjectures pertaining to his use of the word science. The first is the belief that everything finds its root in mathematics; that is the sum total of knowledge in the universe is 360 degrees. The second is connected to the Brotherhood of Purity which was a secret society in Basra (Mesopotamia). They published fifty-one tracts known as the Rosa'il ikhwan as-safa (The Treatises of the Brotherhood of Purity) which consisted of an encyclopedia of knowledge in theology, philosophy, metaphysics, cosmology, and all of the natural sciences. They were thought to have flowed from the Ismailis. The ethical foundation of their creed was linked with self-knowledge and the emancipation of the soul from materialism leading to a return to God.

It is possible that Drew Ali utilized the word in accord with the essence of the Brotherhood in mind, or he could have, based on his travels in Africa and India, applied the word science to denote the knowledge of high science that people of color possessed in their establishment of civilization.

The last three aspects of Drew Ali's Masonic incorporation were his standing position. The position of Drew Ali's stance is known in masonry as "standing on a square." What is interesting is that the Honorable Elijah Muhammad's lessons talked about being on the square.

Although Elijah Muhammad issued his followers lessons that discussed some aspects of Masonry, he was adamantly opposed to Masonry -- especially the intermixing of Masonry with Islam. He said this: "To begin with, Masonry is the fraternity of the brotherhood of mankind (the white race). It is suppose to succeed in uniting men where a religion fails." He added this: "Islam is the father of truth, the whole truth . . . Masonry is only a very small fraction of Islam

Afterwards, Ali and Elijah -- especially Elijah -- used the word Mosque.

As mentioned above, the Templars had been founded by nine French noblemen who had made their way to the Holy Land in AD 1119 -- twenty years after Jerusalem had been captured and occupied by Europeans. The most distinguished of the nine were Godfrey de St. Omer and Hugh de Payens. Hugh de Payens was in fact the first Grand Master of the Order.

and it is taught to the Negro, but it is a front . . . It is used to rob them and still keep them in darkness." He continued: "Freemasonry itself does not take you any further than Australia and into Europe, but Islam will take you all over the Earth. I want you to wake up and know yourself to be the people of the First Order, not of the Last Order."

Elijah Muhammad often admitted that he too was a mason. He skillfully related the masonic symbolism to the black man and his severe condition in North America. He paid particular attention to the Temple Lesson on Hiram Abiff. His comments on this subject is as follows:

"The Masonic Order is founded on robbery, kidnapping and murder. The entire program was derived from the symbolic Hiram Abiff, the widow's son from the land Tyre, a master builder of the Universe. This Asiatic Black Man is described in the Bible as the builder of King Solomon's Temple. The so-called Negro is segregated as a Mason and he is symbolically 'buried' in the North corner of 'King Solomon's Temple.' The Holy Quran speaks of those who have fabricated against the kingdom of Solomon; the Masons have lied on Solomon who was a righteous Muslim. The Order's ritual is derived from the three thieves who attacked Hiram to rob him of his knowledge which consists of 360 degrees of wisdom, knowledge and understanding. During the attack Hiram was hit in the head and killed without uttering the secrets of the universe which is free to all black men who accept Islam and submit to the One God, Allah. Hiram was hit in the head at high noon, dragged from East to West and was buried in a shallow grave (ignorance) with an evergreen tree planted on his grave. The hitting in the head three times means the so-called Negro was hit with first, slave chains, second, wine, and third, Christianity. After they killed Hiram, they said, now we will never find out the secret of the Universe, we will use a substitute until future generations learn better. They have killed him at high noon meaning at a high period of the blackman's civilization, for there would have been no need of capturing savages for a savage with no knowledge of mathematics, agriculture cannot build homes, roads or plant and harvest crops no matter how much you whip him. The evergreen tree shows life, meaning the Blackman was physically alive and mentally dead. Hiram Abiff represents the so-called Negroes of America."

Elijah Muhammad stated his position on masonry in this manner:

"I will not go into the history of the Masons since I was a Mason myself once and I swore, too, not to reveal the secrets. Masons who have reached such degrees as 32nd and 33rd are not called Masons. They are called Moslem Shriners.They are reaching up to us. When you take the 33rd degree you are taught to greet each other; "As-Salaam-Alaikum." You are taught Islam from then on because you become a Muslim when that degree is conferred on you. At least you are supposed to be a believer in Islam. They teach you, almost from the start, to turn your face to the East. In the East, they tell you is the true Masonry. But this (white man's) Masonry carries you no further than Australia, America, England and Europe."

Now, the square as it is explained by the Masonic Order is an angle of 90 degrees and it forms the fourth part of a circle. Furthermore, every Masonic Lodge has a square and compass on its alter. It represents virtue, reason, and right thinking. Study the Masonic questionnaire:

"Are you a Fellow Craft Mason?" "I am, try me." "How will you be tried?" "By the Square." "Why by the Square?" "Because it is an emblem of morality, and one of the working tools of a fellow Craft Mason."

On the next page, it will be interesting comparing the Mason's questionnaire with the Temple lesson of Elijah Muhammad.

Another important point of information is the feet position that was adopted by the members of the Moorish Science Temple and the members of the Nation of Islam, in their early days, while performing their prayers. The given feet position is in fact the Muslim prayer position.

The third and last point is the apron, which is known as a "Badge of Dignity" in masonry. Noble Drew Ali wore his apron like that of a Shriner, on the side, as opposed to wearing it in the front as worn by

Temple Lesson No. 39, "The Mystery of Hiram," and "Masonic Order."

The Theology of Time by Elijah Muhammad, p. 282, (United Brothers and United Sisters Communications Systems, Hampton, Virginia, 1992

the masons. This was an indication that he had become a Moslem Shriner. Thus he had reached his 32nd or 33rd degree.

Elijah Muhammad enhanced the Masonic explanation of the 90 degree angle. We must remember that Muhammad was not in favor of Masonry for black men. He said this: "Knowledge is suppose to raise you from a dead level of ignorance and make you upright perpendicular on the square (90) degrees. But Masonry teaches 33 degrees in a counterfitted degree 57 degrees short of perpendicular on the square 90 degrees. Water freezes at 32 degrees and since knowledge is measured in degrees a man with 32 degrees is at a dead level, he is dependent on some one else for his livelihood and the necessities of life."

The following is a questionnaire from the Temple lessons of Elijah Muhammad. The similarity to the masonry questionnaire is strikingly obvious:

Who are you?
How do you ask?
On the square.
And how am I to know that you are on the square?
I am the square.
I am a Muslim Brother.

The following is also from Elijah Muhammad's Temple lessons on the Masonic Order that addresses the subject of Hiram Abiff, master builder of King Solomon's Temple, who was slain at high noon. This lesson symbolically refers to the Lost and Found Black Man:

His brother looked for him in the East, they searched for him in the North and South. But they found him in the West buried two feet underground a shrew of evergreen covering his grave there they raised him from a dead level to a living perpendicular on the **Square**:
Have you seen Hiram?
How do you ask me that?
On the **Square**.
How do I know that you are on the **Square**?
I'm the **Square**.
Hiram who?
Hiram Abiff.
He's around.
Around where?
I'm He.

Temple Lesson Number 39, "Knowledge on Masonry."

Another aspect of Drew's masonic carryover was his hand position. His right hand was usually on his chest or near his heart. In masonry, one of the two officers, who presides over the initiates for the twenty-eight degrees, teaches the candidate the sign of a knight of the sun. The first sign is made by placing the right hand flat upon the heart, the thumb separated, so as to form a square. The answer sign is made by raising the right hand, and with the index finger pointing to the sky. This is to clearly demonstrate that there is but one God, the source of all living and nonliving truth. In the Muslim prayer (Salat) performance, the index finger is raised acknowledging the oneness of Allah. Additionally, many Muslims place their right hand on their heart as an affectionate greeting.

In concluding this chapter, I feel compelled to say that Noble Drew Ali, like Elijah Muhammed, was an uneducated man who learned enough about Islam to consider it the key that would be later called black liberation. At the core of his teachings was the remembrance of Allah. The Moorish American prayer goes as follows: Allah the Father of the universe, the Father of Love, Truth, Peace, Freedom and Justice. Allah is my protector, my Guide, and my Salvation by night and by day, through his Holy Prophet, Drew Ali (Amen).

Drew Ali's man-made Koran discusses Islam and Prophet Muhammad, and in Chapter Thirty-Five he expounds on the compassion, mercy, and power of Allah.

For Drew Ali Islam was the religion of the Moors, the black warriors and conquerors from Africa who overran a part of Europe and educated a backward country in Europe, Spain. How could anyone with such a proud and noble history suffer the degradation which was the general situation of blacks in America.

Thus he understood that there is a definite relationship between what you are called and how you are perceived and treated. "It is in the name," he concluded. The black man's problems began when he accepted a pejorative nomenclature. He therefore gave himself and his followers names that reflected their proud African-Islamic heritage. Each one of his followers (Moors) was issued an appropriate name and an identity card indicating his or her religious and political status in a society where "Negroes" were constantly debased.

All of this research information has compelled me to declare that Noble Drew Ali should be exonerated from the charge of "religious shirk" (idolatry or association) because his intentions were obviously good. What must be noted is that Drew never presented his teachings or his movement beyond or outside of the realm of Allah (God consciousness). In fact, he maintained the "Divine Spirit" concept of God. He did not associate a partner with Allah, nor did he claim to be God. His actions were based on sincerity and a lack of knowledge of the pristine doctrine of Islam. His sincerity was echoed in this statement: "This Moorish Science Temple of America . . . (derives) its power and authority from the Great Koran of Muhammad to propagate the faith and extend the learning truth of the Great Prophet of Ali in America it is to appoint and consecrate missionaries of the Prophet to establish the faith of Muhammad in America."

Drew Ali, undoubtedly, continued the legacy of Marcus Garvey, but the major exception, aside from a religious one, was Drew Ali's support or advocacy of American citizenship for his followers. He believed in the constitution of the United States and I think this stemmed from the fact that the Moroccan nation was the first in the world to recognize the continental government of the United States. Morocco signed the first international treaty with the United States in 1787; I find this ironic in that this country was, at the time, still engaged in the heinous practice of slavery. Be that as it may, the Moorish-Americans always flew their flag beside the American flag as a reminder of their shared dual heritage.

Interestingly, Noble Drew Ali and the Honorable Elijah Muhammad encouraged their followers to respect the laws of the United States. Unlike Drew, Elijah Muhammad saw the American flag as a symbol of black oppression.

Another manifestation of Drew Ali's advocacy for the principles of the United States government was his endorsement for political candidates such as Oscar DePriest who ran for and successfully won the United States Congressional seat in 1928. He was the first African American to serve in the United States House of Representatives. As a result of Drew Ali's urging his followers to cast their votes for DePriest, a number of state, city, and national politicians gave praise and honor to Noble Drew Ali for political foresight. This, I think, was the main deviation from Garveyism. Of course, Elijah Muhammad took an extremely different position -- he eschewed politics because he believed that it rendered non-tangible results for black people. However, he did believe that Muslims would make the best politicians. Drew was an advocate of economic self-help; he founded the Moorish Manufacturing Corporation which produced a number of health remedies. He also encouraged his followers -- Farad Muhammad and Father Divine probably used his example -- to establish independent businesses such as grocery stores clothing stores, furniture stores, and restaurants. Noble Drew Ali was adamant with these words: "We shall be secure in nothing until we have economic power. A beggar people cannot develop the highest in them, nor can they attain to a genuine enjoyment of the spiritualities of life."

He was also one of the first leaders to encourage the establishment of athletic clubs for children and a young people's league. He always displayed his love and dedication to young people and their great potential: "It takes sympathy, patience, interest and the trained eyes of men, well versed in the training and handling of young men to see the hidden beauty beneath the rough exterior." "Remember that better boys make better men," and better men will make better husbands for our daughters."

Another important organizational practice that Drew inherited from Garvey and the pioneer black abolitionists was the use and development of a news organ. Garvey had the *Negro World*, Drew had the *Moorish Guide*, and Elijah had the *Muhammad Speaks*. Garvey utilized his paper for propaganda purposes; according to Tony Martin, it was an ideological tool designed to uplift the "Negro race and the good of humanity." The Negro World was translated into scores of dialects and served as a gospel for black people throughout the world. It was a nationalist and anticolonialist paper.

The Moorish Guide under Nobel Drew Ali reflected the same principles insofar as the uplift of the race. The difference was the Moorish Guide was directed toward universalism as well as racial uplift. Its concept of race independence was stated as follows:

> *The Moorish Guide* feels that the greatest weapon in the hands of our group today in America is our press. The truth will never be told about a disadvantaged minority by the general press of any country, whether that minority be racial, political, or religious. Unless we express ourselves through papers of our own the truth about us will not be told. Many of our accomplishments, many of the beautiful things, many of the hopeful things and the events which mark the progress of our group, would go under-recorded were it not for papers of our own.

Drew also used a red flag with a green star. It was similar to the red, black and green flag of the Universal Negro Improvement Association (UNIA) of Marcus Garvey.

Our papers are our hope of shoveling ourselves out from under the avalanche of lies that are annually let loose upon us. "A strong free press is the best possible safeguard of the liberties and general promotion and defense of the interests of a strong free people."

As a gesture of good will and reinforcement of their belief in America. *The Moorish Guide* declared:

> *The Moorish Guide* enters the field of journalism with "malice toward none and charity to all." It is not its purpose to disregard the work of other splendid journals; it is not our purpose to fail to give due attention and space to all American citizens, individuals, and organizations alike, who are working in their chosen fields of endeavor for the progress and development of all American citizens and of all institutions. We hope to cooperate with them in the intensive and grueling battle for universal justice.

Before concluding this chapter, I think Chapter XLVIII (p. 59) of Noble Drew Ali's Koran clearly demonstrates that he and his followers were convinced he had been chosen for the deliverance of his people. They compared his so-called prophethood to Garvey's mission, and considered Garvey as did Garvey's followers to have been John the Baptist. The language and content of the following passages are undeniably similar to the Nation of Islam's teachings pertaining to Farad Muhammad and Elijah Muhammad:

1. The last Prophet in these days is Noble Drew Ali, who was prepared divinely in due time by Allah to redeem men from their sinful ways; and to warn them of the great wrath which is sure to come upon the earth.
2. John the Baptist was the forerunner of Jesus in those days, to warn and stir up the nation and prepare them to receive the divine creed which was to be taught by Jesus.
3. In these modern days there came a forerunner, who was divinely prepared by the great God-Allah and his name is Marcus Garvey, who did teach and warn the nations of the earth to prepare to meet the coming Prophet; who was to bring the true and divine Creed of Islam, and his name is Noble Drew Ali: who was prepared and sent to this earth

by Allah, to teach the old time religion and the everlasting gospel to the sons of men. That every nation shall and must worship under their own vine and fig tree, and return to their own and be one with their Father God-Allah.

Now, it is important to analyze some of the language that Farad used in his cultural and spiritual teachings. I should again mention that Noble Drew Ali used the terms Moor, Asiatic, and colored. Similarly, Farad used these terms as identity catchphrases. The black man was not a Negro for Farad; he was from the tribe of Shabazz a noble tribe that came with the earth. Drew Ali stated that the black man was from Morocco and therefore a Moor. Notice that Farad, in the interest of mobilizing the Temple People around Islam, Eastern and African culture, did not mention the slave trade, and the part that Arab and African Muslims played; instead, he used the words tricked and stolen.

Farad's lessons' equated mathematics with Islam and vice-a-versa; he also equated culture with astronomy and mathematics. Throughout some of his lessons, there is an emphatic mention of mathematics. Hence, the Honorable Elijah Muhammad always stressed the importance of studying science and math. I am convinced that this part of Farad's teachings helped reinforce the Temple People's interest in the literacy classes they were required to take.

Farad wrote two manuals: *The Secret Ritual of the Nation of Islam,* which was to be memorized, and *Teaching for the Lost-Found Nation of Islam in a Mathematical Way.* Both employed a lot of symbolic Masonic language -- especially the latter (The second manual was also called the problem book).

I think it is important, before discussing Master Farad Muhammad, to scrutinize the programmatic similarities between the Moorish Science Temple and the Nation of Islam:

	Moorish Science Temple And	Nation of Islam
Nationality	Moorish Americans	Asiatic-Black Man
Prophet	Noble Drew Ali	Farad Muhammad and Elijah Muhammad as Messenger
Religion	Islam, without Authentic Quran	Islam with genuine Quran
God	Allah	Allah and Allah in the person of Master Farad Muhammad
Race	Asiatics	Asiatic Blacks (Tribe of Shabazz)
Place of Worship	Temple	Temple and Mosque
Heaven and Hell	In the Mind	States of conditions on earth
Separation of Sexes	Yes	Yes
Names	Bey and El	X and Shabazz
Sacred Text	Koran by Drew Ali	Holy Quran & Bible
Citizenship	United States and Morroco	Nation within a Nation
Land	No desire for separate state	Separate state within the U.S. or elsewhere
Flag	Red Flag with green star	Red Flag with star and crescent
Language	Arabic/English greeting Peace and Islam	Arabic greeting: As Salaam Alaikum
Independent Businesses	Yes/national	Yes/national and international
Newspaper	Moorish Guide	Muhammad Speaks

MASTER W.D. FARD MUHAMMAD

MASTER FARAD MUHAMMAD
The Enigmatic, Eclectic Savior

MASTER FARAD MUHAMMAD:
THE ENIGMATIC, ECLECTIC SAVIOR

According to some historical accounts, Farad Muhammad was a follower of Noble Drew Ali and claimed to be the reincarnation of Drew. Understandably, some people will object strongly to this claim. However, it is an established fact that Farad appealed to many southern born African American migrants, as did Drew and Garvey. Drew Ali mysteriously died in 1929 at the beginning of the Great Depression; Farad Muhammad made his appearance known in Detroit in 1930.

Imam Warith Deen Mohammad has declared that he doubted whether Farad was ever in the Moorish Science Temple. He stated that Farad was a very wise man in Islamic Studies and Comparative religion, and he was very wise in religious symbolism. Imam Mohammad believes that Farad studied Noble Drew Ali's approach to introducing the Holy Quran and Islam to the black community and he therefore developed his own programmatic methodology.

Farad familiarized himself with the misery of black people by subjecting himself to the same type of harsh physical persecution. He did this in the hope of proving to them how venal Europeans could be when it involved their justified right to human dignity. His explanation for this scenario went like this: If they (caucasians) can mistreat me and I am the Mahdi in person then their mistreatment of you will continue unabated. Thus Farad developed his program based on his and black peoples' experiences in white America.

Therefore, the mystic, exotic looking Farad offered the suffering blacks with whom he came in contact a renewed hope. One of his alluring snares was his explanation for their economic, and especially their physical hardships. These black migrants were unaccustomed to the harsh, cold northern winter climates. As a result, they contracted a number of body ailments. It was these physical illnesses caused by the environment that Farad capitalized on to convey his teachings. Farad

There was (is) a belief in the Nation of Islam that because Farad had difficulties with the laws of the united States and the oppression of black people, he willfully disappeared in 1933.

Imam Muhammad contends that Farad's mysterious disappearance was predicated on his introducing himself as a Christ figure to displace the caucasian Christ. Therefore, he disappeared in order to create a mystery about himself.

was also a skillful eclectic; he fused the teachings of Garvey, Drew Ali and some early black nationalists. Interestingly, he encouraged his followers to study the writings of Judge Rutherford of the Jehovah's Witnesses, and he encouraged the study of masonry and its symbolism. I will say more about these points later.

He stressed the importance of these black migrants to study their historical roots by reading works such as James Henry Breasted's *Conquest of Civilization* and Hendrik Van Loon's *Story of Mankind*. Farad initiated literacy classes so that they could read, at least sparingly, these recommended historical words. All of his early followers were called Temple People, and all of them were directed to convert their homes into schools. Thus basic English and mathematics were taught as a means of alleviating illiteracy. Farad's other exhortation was the development of a general welfare system; Temple People were not allowed to accept government assistance (We see the same philosophy in the Peace Mission). Instead, they were encouraged to develop independent business ventures.

Farad's eclecticism contributed greatly to the systematic structure of his teachings and budding movement. He synthesized factual history with symbolism, mythological history, and he advanced the belief that in order for his followers to be Muslim scientists again they must change their bad eating habits. His teaching was in essence as follows:

> "The Black man in North America is not a 'Negro,' but a member of the lost tribe of Shabazz, tricked by traders 379 years ago into leaving their homes 9,000 miles across the ocean. The prophet came to North America to find and bring back to life his long lost brethren from who the Caucasians had taken their language, their nation, and their religion. Here, in North America, they must learn that they are the original people, noblest of the nations of the earth. The Caucasians are the colored people, and have been grafted away from their original color which was black. The original people must regain their religion, which is Islam, their language which is Arabic, and their culture, which is astronomy and higher mathematics, especially calculus. They must live according to the law of Allah, avoiding all meat of poison animals, hogs, ducks, geese, possums, and catfish. They must give up completely, the use of stimulants, especially liquor. They must clean themselves up -- both their bodies and their houses. If in

94

this way they obeyed Allah, he would take them back to the paradise from which they had been stolen -- the Holy City of Mecca."

Farad's intimate involvement with his followers in Detroit compelled him to address their lowly physical condition. Notice in the above teaching, he admonishes them to live according to the will of Allah, which meant, in part, that they should discard their sloughfulness and despair for better eating habits, and abstinence from alcohol. Notice again that he states if they obey Allah regarding these concerns they would be taken back to paradise. As I indicated, many of the black migrants suffered tremendous body ailments from the cold, damp, crowded tenements they were forced to reside in. And they had a very difficult time getting adjusted to the climatic conditions of the north. They ate what they were accustomed to eating in the south as poor sharecroppers; therefore, the living conditions, the climate, and the bad food exacted its toll. This grave situation prompted Farad to state the following in his lessons:

> The wife of Mr. W. D. Farad's uncle, in the wilderness of North America were other than herself; therefore she has rheumatism, headaches, pains in all joints, and cannot walk up to the store. She is troubled frequently with high blood pressure and registers more than thirty-two; her pulse is nearly eighty times per minute, and she died at the age of forty-seven.[29]

The noun, uncle, refers to the black nation to whom Farad was sent to awaken.

Elijah Muhammad stated that Farad's use of the word Caucasian coincided with some Arab scholars definition, "one whose evil effect is not confined to one's self alone, but affects others."

Contrary to that definition, is Johann Friedrich Blumenbach who coined the word Caucasian to describe the white race. This word is based upon a single skull in Blumenbach's collection which came from the Caucasus region of Russia. Blumenbach found strong resemblances between this skull and the crania of the Germans. He, therefore, surmised that possibly the Caucasus regions may have been the original home of the Europeans.

Imam Mohammed points out that these mathematical lessons were designed to compel the believers to exercise their mental muscles. So without having the believers go to school and learn science, chemistry, physics, and math, these problems (lesson) were forcing the believers' minds to wake up to scientific knowledge. More about these lessons will be discussed later.

Farad continues describing, through the use of mathematical language, the deplorable condition of his followers or black people with whom he had contact:

> The uncle of Mr. W. D. Farad lives in the wilderness of North America, and he is living other than himself; therefore, he weighs more than his height and his blood pressure registers more than thirty-one. This killed him at the age of forty-four years.[30]

He continues the mathematical game pertaining to the health problems of black people:

> The second uncle of Mr. W. D. Farad, in the wilderness of North America, lived other than himself, and therefore his blood pressure registered over thirty-two; he had fever, headaches, chills, grippe, hay fever, regular fever, rheumatism also pains in all joints. He was disturbed with foot ailment and toothaches. His pulse beat more than eighty-eight times per minute; therefore, he goes to the doctor every day and gets medicine for every day in the year; one after each meal and three times a day, also one at bed time.[31] Farad was obviously very clever in attacking the socioeconomic problems of black people. His ability to synthesize mythology, masonry, aspects of Drew Ali's esotericism, and segments of black nationalism was indeed a tactic that Mr. Mohammed successfully extended.
>
> The lesson's of Farad were incorporated and expanded -- even the deification of Farad -- according to Mr. Mohammad's understanding of Farad's mission (more will be said about this later).
>
> Take for example the subject of bad food, under Mr. Muhammad's leadership certain foods such as pork, corn bread, collard greens, etc. were forbidden, for they were a "slow death" for those who ate them. Most foods that were common to the diet of southern blacks were not to be eaten, since they constituted a "slave diet."

In keeping with Farad's lessons, liquor and even tobacco were forbidden, and Muslims were criticized for overeating -- a habit that developed during slavery. Moreover, one meal a day was considered sufficient, for such discipline eliminated mental and physical lethargy and allowed more time for self-help ventures.

Allah (God) has taught me, in the Person of Master Farad Muhammad, how to eat to live, so that I also may teach you. He desires to extend our lives from a short span, averaging 62 years, to a span of one thousand (1,000) years -- or for as long as we desire to live. He said there is no set time for us to die. We kill ourselves daily by means of what we think, what we eat and what we drink. (*How To Eat To Live I*, by Elijah Mohammed, page 57.)

Another part of Farad's lesson deals with grafting. Mr. Muhammad never wavered from this part of Farad's teachings; as a matter of fact, he used it quite frequently to explain the social, political, economic, physical, and moral debasement of black people. Psychologically speaking, this teaching, as abstract or non-foundational as it might appear, extricated black people from their sense of genetic self-worthlessness. It answered their questions; why is the white man so full of hate for me? Elijah Muhammad answered the question by stating that the nature of the white man (Caucasian) had been grafted out of the original black man. Therefore, his aberrant malicious behavior was attributable to his hybrid nature or abnormal genetic structure. Racism, capitalism, rapacious plundering, deception, and mendaciousness were practices of a people with a grafted nature. Thus, on a fundamental and physiological level, the "salvation" of white people would lie in grafting them back to originality. That is, back into the nature of original black people.[32]

As Muslim scholar and teacher, Dr. Dorothy Fardan points out the teaching of grafting back into originality and wholeness was not in the strict sense of the word black supremacy in reverse. That teaching did not advocate domination, control, violation, or elimination of other groups. It was, in actuality, an axiology of separation, reclamation, and a reunion of people who were interfered with on every level of life by white racists.[33]

Undoubtedly, Farad's instructions provided efficacious results. According to a report in the 1930's by Erdman Beynon these rejected and despised migrants transformed themselves in a relatively short time.

At the time of their first contact with the prophet, practically all of the members of the cult were recipients of public welfare, unemployment, and living in the most deteriorated areas of Negro settlement in Detroit.[34]

That was in the early 1930's; by 1937, Beynon reported:

At the present time, there is no known case of unemployment among these people. Practically all of them are working in the automobile and other factories. They live no longer in the slum section . . . but rent homes in some of the best economic areas in which Negroes have settled. They tend to purchase more expensive furniture, automobiles, and clothes then do their neighbors even in these areas of high-class residence.[35]

For lack of a better word, Farad politely borrowed some of Drew's organizational concepts. Farad's knowledge of black America extended only to a superficial level. Thus he was compelled to study the examples of those successful "race leaders" who came before him. It is in this category that he should be assessed. According to the literature on Drew Ali, he separated the men and women during temple services; his reason(s) is not fully known. However, Farad instituted the same practice and Elijah Muhammad consistently enforced it. His reason was based on the natural attraction that both sexes have for each other. Therefore, sitting together would lead to distractions and contribute to a disregard for the instructions that were being offered. Sex separation was the best method to avoid this strong possibility.

Drew Ali exhorted his followers to adhere to a dress code that properly identified who they were and what they believed. The standard dress code was long dresses or loose pants for women, and no makeup. The men were encouraged to wear suits and ties, and they were to always wear a red fez with a black tassel. The women were only permitted to wear a turban with a long dress.

Farad employed the same type of dress code for his followers. The exceptions were the wearing of a turban and pants for women. Later, Mr. Muhammad would design and encourage the wearing of Fruit of Islam (FOI) uniforms for the men and he modified the dress code for the women. This is one of a few things that Mr. Muhammad transformed. He wanted his followers to dress according to modern times. After awhile, one could see Muslims in various styles of dress -- especially the women -- that reflected both their religion and the era.

The 1970's was a rather liberal period for the dress code; everyone was permitted to dress stylishly as long as he or she remained properly covered and respectful.

Noble Drew Ali and Master Farad Muhammad called themselves "prophet" which for them probably meant the thought of Allah manifested in the flesh to save nations from the chastisement of Allah. Obviously Drew did not know or understand the Arabic meaning for prophet or its Arabic spiritual essence. I am somewhat certain that he took this lofty title from examples in Black American history, and from the English definition. And maybe he truly felt that Allah had chosen him to deliver black people. As I just said, there were lots of examples of black men and women that called themselves prophet and prophetess. Noble Drew Ali, at some time, from what I understand, did read an English translated Holy Quran. Therefore, I think, he came into a more complete realization that in the Arabic sense of the word and from an Islamic sense, Prophet Muhammad was the last and final prophet. Moreover, I go so far as to say that he always knew Prophet Muhammad was the seal of prophethood. Here again, his use of the word prophet was indicative of the black historical experience. I heartily accept the argument espoused by comparative religion scholar, Dr. Alauddin Shabazz, that Ali embraced the English definition of prophet as it related to his mission and the black historical definition of the word.

The English definition for prophet is one who is gifted with more than ordinary spiritual and moral insight. One who tells the future. An effective or leading spokesman for a cause, doctrine or group.

It is this definition that Drew Ali and Farad Muhammad probably considered. As a reputed Mason of high order, and as one who had supposedly studied the Egyptian Mystery System as well as aspects of Islam, Drew believed that his experiences qualified him to take the lofty title of prophet. At least, this is my contention. After all, a number of black country preachers called themselves prophet and god, and most did nothing to uplift the black nation.

On the other hand, Farad knew and understood the Arabic (Nabi) meaning for prophet, and I am sure that he also knew and understood the historical significance of the word prophet as it related to the African and African American struggle. However, I think Farad fused the English definition with some aspects of the Arabic translation. Here is what I mean, the Quran says that there is no people to whom a prophet has not been sent (10:48) and the Hadith puts the number at one hundred and twenty-four thousand; that is, a number so large that humanity can not claim it was not adequately warned of Allah's Judgment.

Now black people in America were an enslaved, transplanted group that had been severed from their religio-cultural roots. According to some scholars such as Alan Austin and Sulayman Nyang only about fifteen percent of these transplanted slaves were Muslims. Thus, a large percentage of these African slaves were believers in traditional African religions. This means that they had to be taught Islam and especially about God's judgment. Therefore, Farad presented himself as being one of those twenty-four thousand warners (prophets) to the lost and found so-called Negroes.

The title of prophet sufficed until he was elevated to the level of God by his religiously ignorant followers.

Farad utilized -- as did his most trusted follower, Elijah Muhammad -- the scripture in the Bible (Genesis 15:16-16) to rationalize his claim as prophet and supreme ruler. This particular scripture or verse is usually thought to refer to the Israelites; however, upon careful reading of the Torah (five Books of Moses) Exodus 12:40, it was not the Israelites who were in bondage for 400 years. It was the black people in America who best fit that scriptural description. On the contrary, the Egyptians held the Israelites in bondage for 430 years as the book of Exodus indicates. This was the rationale that Farad and Muhammad employed.

For Mr. Muhammad, a prophet was also a scientist, and the duty of a prophet is to uplift fallen humanity. Thus a new civilization begins with prophets.

Farad used several names such as Mr. Farad Muhammad, Mr. W. D. Farad, Mr. F. Muhammad Ali, and Wali Farad Muhammad. He was also known as Professor Ford. A number of legends emerged as to the true origin of this mysterious individual. One such legend was that Farad was a Jamaican black of mixed ancestry. Another described him as a Palestinian Arab who had been engaged in racial agitations in India, South Africa and London before coming to Detroit. Some of his followers believed him to be the son of wealthy parents of the tribe of Koreish or Quarish -- the tribe of Prophet Muhammad (Peace be Upon Him).[36]

Farad, however, claimed to be the "Supreme Ruler of the Universe," and some of his followers especially Mr. Muhammad -- considered him to be the expected Messiah of the Christians and the Mahdi of the Muslims. At the other extreme, and I will say more about this shortly, is the investigation by the *New Crusader*, a Chicago newspaper, and *Insight*, a *Washington Times* magazine out of Washington, D.C., which refers to Farad as "a Turkish-born Nazi agent who worked for Hitler in World War II."[37] This article in the *New Crusader also states that Farad claimed he was white.[38]*

According to the *Insight* article, Farad told blacks that he was a "light-skinned Negro," but the records show that in three arrests between 1918 and 1926, all in California, Farad whose so-called real name was Ford (Wallace Dodd Ford) listed himself as white. He listed himself white on a September 1930 birth certificate in Los Angeles for his son, Wallace Max Ford. He listed himself as an Arab on a May 1933 booking slip in Detroit. However, fingerprints taken by the FBI of Wallace Fard Muhammad in Detroit in May 1933, when he told his followers he was "a light-skinned Negro" matched those of the "white" Wallace Dodd Ford taken in 1926 at San Quentin.[39]

Farad or Ford told the Detroit police his cult was "strictly a racket" he had dreamed up in July 1930, about a year after his release from San Quentin Prison in California, where he had served three years for selling heroin. Ford confided he was using the cult (that was the initial pejorative term) to get "all the money out of it he could."[40]

He used 18 aliases, claimed to be from Mecca, Saudi Arabia, he also said he was of British and Polynesian descent; he also listed his birthplace as Portland, Oregon. His followers knew little else about him. He had this to say in 1930: "More about myself I will not tell you yet, for the time has not yet come." "I am your brother. You have not seen me in my royal robes."[41]

In 1962, the Federal Bureau of Investigation (FBI) formulated a policy that was designed to discredit and disrupt the Nation of Islam. The method utilized to accomplish this goal was the fabrication of news stories planted in the Hearst newspaper syndicate. It was also in 1962, that the Chicago field office Special Agent-in-Charge (SAC) acknowledged that the FBI was unable to adequately identify the background of W. D. Fard or Farad Muhammad. As a result, the Bureau decided to accelerate its "dirty tricks" campaign. Thus the W. D. Farad hoax took form. This scheme was calculatingly directed at destroying the Nation through slander. Ed Montgomery, a journalist was given doctored mug-shot photographs, fake files and fake birth certificates of the subject, W. D. Fard. With all of this fabricated material at his disposal, Montgomery wrote his concocted story in July of 1963, titled "Black Muslim Founder Exposed as White." Montgomery claimed that W. D. Farad was a white man named Wallace Dodd Ford, a convicted heroin dealer, who deserted his white girlfriend and illegitimate infant son in Los Angles in 1929 before going to Detroit and founding the Nation of Islam in 1930.

The FBI knew full well that W. D. Fard was not a European American because they had authentic files, photographs and fingerprints that were processed by the Detroit Police Department when Farad was arrested on May 25, 1933. No official charge was made against Fard. It was an investigation in which Farad was photographed, fingerprinted, held overnight, and ordered out of Detroit the next day.

The fake mug-shot photos were provided by the San Francisco Field Office and the trumped-up charge of drug dealing by the Los Angeles Field Office. Furthermore, the white woman, mentioned by Montgomery, who was the alleged mother of W. D. Farad's son, did in fact have a son by one Wallace D. Ford. This Wallace D. Ford was a movie actor in the 1930's. His name conveniently came up as a lead when the FBI was looking for the real W. D. Farad under the alias Wallace D. Ford in Immigration and Naturalization Service (INS) records. The actor, Wallace Ford, dropped the Dodd and immigrated to the United States from Australia. (Excerpts taken from "FBI Plot against the N.O.I. in 1960's failed: Photo Hoax Proven." by Prince-A-Cuba, *The Commentator* Newspaper, March 1992.)

Imam As Sayyid Isa Al Haadi Al Mahdi, former leader of the Ansaaru Allah community, initially argued by way of the so-called FBI report that Wallace Douglas (Dodd) Ford (Fard) was an imposter. According to Isa -- he has retracted this claim -- Abdul Wali Farad Muhammad Ali was the one who instituted the Nation of Islam building process. The shallow scenario went like this: Farad Muhammad Ali was arrested and subsequently murdered because he was raising black consciousness; as a result, he was replaced by the imposter Wallace Douglas (Dodd) Ford, who was supposedly recruited by the Communist Party to introduce communism to black people.

Upon careful analysis, one can easily see that this allegation is full of ideological contradictions. The allegation stated that Dodd (Ford) was both a Nazi-agent and a communist; moreover, the allegation included that Dodd was a member of the Henry Ford Foundation which was communist affiliated, and that Dodd was a Jew.

An outstanding refutation to the allegations that the Nation of Islam, or as they were called at that time, the Temple People, were never aligned with the communists or any other "subversive group" is conveyed by Erdmann D. Benyon in his "The Voodoo Cult Among Negro Migrants in Detroit," American Journal of Sociology, XLIII No. 6, May, 1938 (p. 904):

> The solidarity and cultural isolation of the Moslems have rendered ineffectual the various attempts made by interested parties to redirect the activities of the cult in order to further their own particular purposes. The first of these efforts was made by the communists in 1932, but the cult members rebuffed their appeal. Then came Major Takahashi, a reserve Japanese officer, who sought to lead the Moslems to swear allegiances to the Mikado. Only a small minority of the members followed him into the new movement he organized -- The Development of Our Own. With his deportation, this schismatic movement came to naught. An Ethiopian, Wyxzewixard S. J. Challaoueliziczese, sought in June, 1934, to reorganize the movement as a means of sending financial support to Ethiopia. This too, was unsuccessful.

Any elementary student of history knows that these allegations are not only contradictory, but invalid at best. I am happy that Isa retracted these baseless claims. It has been established by the Honorable Elijah Muhammad and Imam Warith Deen Muhammad that Master Farad Muhammad was indeed a deliverer for black people. Furthermore, a disgruntled follower gave momentum to this hoax, which the caucasian press gladly capitalized on.

Let me briefly discuss the meaning of Fard's name. In *Message to the Black Man* (p. 141) by the Honorable Elijah Muhammad he tells us that Fard means the morning obligatory prayer and it is a name that

The aforementioned information is thought provoking in that the FBI obviously initiated this campaign in 1959 and heightened it in 1962-3.

corresponds with the time of his coming -- which is in the early days (or years) of the seventh thousand years. The early morning is the first part of the seventh thousand years and the year under the name Millennium (which the Christians say means the 1,000 years Christ will reign on the earth). Mr. Muhammad continues on page 142 of *Message to the Black Man* "Fard is a name many of the scholars have said is not one of the 99 attributes, but still it is a name that is self-independent, and one which means that the Believers are obligated to obey. We can see clearly why he took this Name (Fard) for himself."

Hakim Shabazz (Cosby) wrote an interesting book, *The Life & Teachings Of Master Farad*, in which he contends that Farad Muhammad was probably a Sufi. He connects Farad's title Master, and his name, Wali, to a Sufi definition. Master is synonymous with the Sufi title Khawaja:

> The word Khawaja means wise man or master, and is best rendered Master of Wisdom. It is an historical fact that a major role in the (spiritual) transformation of Central Asia was played by a society or brotherhood of wise men known as the Khwajagans or Masters. [42]

Master, is indicative of brotherhood of spirituality, and it refers to a mental state, or Divine mind. It is also known in Masonry as a title of high order. Additionally, it means teacher or one who has knowledge.

Wali refers to a function within the hierarchy of mystical saints. According to Sufi philosophy, there is a hierarchy of saints at all times in the world, through which God manifests himself. [43] Wali also refers to the spiritual initiation of the people of God. [44] Wali means saint , or more properly Wali-Allah, the friend of God. Wali means a governor, and Wali Allah is the heir apparent to a ruler.

In essence, according to Hakim Shabazz's analysis, Wali has three distinctly unique meanings which actually enhance one another:

1. A high degree of righteousness of saintliness.
2. Spirituality or spiritual functions.
3. The spiritual initiation of the people of God. [45]

Fard also means the obligations God places upon man, such as witnessing the truth, prayer, and fasting. It is synonymous with duty and exceptional destiny - Fard represents uniqueness, the time of his work, and the stage of the black man's development.

With regard to the Henry Ford, Communist Party idea, I think this idea stemmed from the "conspiratorial view of History" as opposed to the traditional view, which is called the "accidental view of history."

To reiterate, Wali means someone who is under special protection, "friend", it is the attribute given by the Shiahs to Ali, the fourth Caliph, the Wali Allah par excellence. The word is, both active and passive: a Wali is one whose affairs are led (tuwulliya) by God and who performs (tawalla) worship and obedience. The auliya Allah, the 'friends of God," are mentioned in the Holy Quran several times, the most famous occasion being Sura 10:63: "Verily, the friends of Allah, no fear is upon them nor are they sad."

Elijah Muhammad often wrote and stated this about Farad: "I asked Him: "'Who are you, and what is your real name?'" He said: "I am the one the world has been looking for to come for the past two thousand years." I said to him again: "What is your name?" He said, "My name is Mahdi, I am God, I came to guide you into the right path..." For Muslims Mahdi means the one who is rightly guided by God, and the one who will come at the end of days to right all wrongs on earth.

What is most interesting is that Tynetta Muhammad addresses the title Mahdi from a Mathematical standpoint. Interestingly, as pointed out earlier, Farad issued a lesson in mathematical problems; more will be said about that shortly. Now, according to Tynetta's analysis, the name Mahdi has mathematical as well as etymological significance. She writes:

> The name, Mahdi, that was given to the Honorable Elijah Muhammad to identify Master W. F. Muhammad is a name or title that conceals the presence of God in the word, AHD. By prefixing the letter M in front of the word AHD and the letter I, at the end, we then derive the name Mahdi which is a cover name or title for the presence of God who suddenly appears in the world, coming out of hiding, at the end of the Devil's rule. [46]

Master Farad Muhammad was the embodiment of inscrutability. [47] The following lesson issued by the Nation of Islam titled "The God Head" somewhat explains why there was external and internal consternation surrounding his true identity. One thing is for sure, he must always be understood within the context of black peoples' condition at that time. He was referred to as a Prophet, the Mahdi, the Son of Man, Our Savior, and since he referred to black people as

Imam Warith Deen Muhammad bestowed the title Master on the Honorable Elijah Muhammad after he passed in 1975.
Anne Marie Schimmel, <u>Mystical Dimensions of Islam</u>, The University Press of North Carolina, Chapel Hill, 1975, p. 199.

his uncle that meant that he was their nephew. Each one of these titles were designed to instill hope and confidence in the suffering masses. To say that black people were his uncle was a lofty gesture. This title also denoted that black people were once advisers and leaders because an uncle is one who is supposed to encourage and assist. This title reflected the historical African personality.

The part of the lesson which states "His uncle could not talk his own language, and did not know his true identify" meant, I believe, that black people did not know the language of Islam and the Holy Quran; nor did they know their African and universal history.

> The various Hadith about the Mahdi, which may therefore be late inventions to support political causes, state that he will be a descendent of the Prophet and have the same name, Muhammad, possibly in one of its other forms, such as Ahmad.

On the next page titled the God Head, a contradictory description of Master Farad Muhammad is presented.

THE GOD HEAD

Prophet W.D. Fard, whose activities among the so called American Negroes in the wilderness of north America, have already been described. He is the God of our people, because his body was created and prepared in the holy city of Mecca, he carries the god head.

That is why he is referred to as Allah, God; in the person of Master W.F. Muhammad, to whom all praise are due. The great Mahdi or Messiah, as the christians say. He is also the son of man and our savior. According to our teachings, Allah came to us from the holy city of Mecca, Arabia, on July 4, 1930. The messenger describes him as one who spoke with authority and independence.

Prophet Fard came to North America by himself. His Uncle was brought here by the slave trader 379 years ago (so called American negroes). His uncle could not talk his own language, and did not know his true identify.

The Honorable Mr. Elijah Muhammad teaches us that he came from Mecca to the United States in 1930. He is the Mahdi, the only Mahdi. He is a man and yet not man, in the ordinary sense. His knowledge is unlimited. He is pure, holy and undefiled. White people in authority knew the Mahdi quite well (Herbert Hoover and son). But he had difficulties with the laws of this country, and was deported in 1933. He suffered persecution because he sought redemption of the so called negroes, who he has chosen as his beloved children.

It is within the above that Muhammad Ahmad Ibn Sayyid Abd Allah declared himself to be the Mahdi of the Sudan, the Divinely guided leader predicted by the Hadith.

Logically speaking, the Sudanese have no right to criticize followers of Elijah Muhammad who affectionately refer to him as "Messenger." The argument can be raised as to their referring affectionately to Muhammad Ahmad as "Mahdi."

Another part of the lesson refers to black people as his "beloved children". This undoubtedly considered the child-like mental state that slavery imposed on black people in the United States. Slavery and race hatred gave birth to feelings of insecurity which lead to modes of behavior characteristic of childishness. Adult behavior is manifested in part, by self-independence, self-evaluation, self-love, self-discipline, self-organized behavior and originality.

Tynetta Muhammad's book title is taken from Chapter 86 of the Holy Quran, Muhammad Ali translation.

Black people who are victims of a severe lack of self knowledge manifest the opposite modes of behavior. They are dependent, intemperate, they lack self confidence, and they are guided by childish thought patterns. [49]

It is within the above context that I think the plural pronoun "children" belong. Furthermore, one could very easily equate Fard to a mother who has the responsibility of providing for and taking care of her children. The mother carries out God's will by nurturing the child into the knowledge of himself or herself and into the knowledge of God and his laws.

He is also the Son of Man and Our Savior. The first part of this was obviously based on the racial philosophy of the Nation, and the second part intertwines and becomes cataclysmic. "Who is the original Man? The Asiatic black man, the maker, the owner, the cream of the planet earth, God of the universe." Elijah Muhammad said that Farad's mother was Caucasian and his father was black (original man); therefore, by saying that he was the son of man he was symbolically saying that he too was of the original black nation. More importantly, he was saying that a so-called black God was on a mission to the United States to save (savior) black people from destruction. What is extremely important to note is that many of these lessons were contradictory and removed from logic. There is no doubt that they were formulated as a symbolic weapon to battle white supremacy and black inferiority.

Allah is a Divine spirit, not a Supreme Being, because a Being denotes the qualities that constitute an existing thing, something or someone conceivable; essence or a living personality. Thus the part of the lesson which said Fard was 'a man and yet not a man, in the ordinary sense,' is interestingly contradictory. Here, he fulfills the saying, "God in the person of Master Fard Muhammad," if that meant that he carried the spirit, or the breath of life of Allah to an infant people.

Then, I do not think that poses much of an argument. So, the rationale goes as such: Master Fard Muhammad came to America

That part of the lesson which states that Fard came to America from Mecca meant, from a symbolic standpoint, that he had the mind set of spirituality, righteousness, or Islam. Also, since the masons use the names Mecca and Medina for their temples, Farad's use of Mecca possibly could have represented his knowledge and understanding.
Furthermore, Mecca means blessed; the Quran says: "The first sanctuary appointed for mankind was that at Bakkah (original name of Mecca), a blessed place, a guidance for the peoples" (3:96).

with the spirit, and the vital-life force of Allah within him, but he was not and could not have been the all encompassing Lord of the universe because the Lord or King (Malik) of the world is incalculable, or infinitesimal.

It is befitting to look at the racial philosophy pertaining to this subject. Elijah Muhammad stated that the Nation of Islam believed in a succession of Gods who followed the first Black God, the Supreme Being who created the universe seventy-six trillion years ago. He has had successors, but no equal. W.D. Fard, is the latest God, or Allah. Sixty-six trillion years ago, stated Mr. Muhammad, the moon separated from the earth: Then came the black race of men and women, the original and first human beings, whose religion was Islam, and who founded the Holy city of Mecca.

Elijah Muhammad in his <u>Our Savior Has Arrived</u> (page 182 and 183) is very specific and poignant on the question of the Son of Man and who he was:

"The son of man is the son of a man. He is not a spirit as to the ignorant are prone to believe. He is the son of Original Man, the Black Man.

The Bible does not teach you that he is the son of mankind. Mankind is the made-man, the white man. The Great Mahdi is the son of the original man, the Black Man.

The son of mankind is the made man, the white man whom the original man, the Black Man drove out of the Garden of Eden.

"The son of man, spoken of as coming in the Last Days, is the son of original man. Therefore, they have it right when they say he is the son of man...that is the original man, the Black man."

"The Great Mahdi, the God and Judge who is now present in the World, Master Fard Muhammad, to whom praises are due forever, taught me that his father was a real Black Man. His Father went up into the mountains (governments of the Caucasians) picking out a white woman to marry so that she would give birth to a son looking white but yet the father is Black."

The above teaching regarding the succession of Gods, again, manifests the similarity between the philosophies of the Druze and the Black Muslims.

Undoubtedly, this idea contradicts traditional Islam which believes in one God for all time and in only one messenger of God. Furthermore, Elijah Muhammad contradicts this teaching himself in The Supreme Wisdom Volume Two (pages 9, 11 and 53). He states some of the following:

"A Muslim is one who believes in one God, Allah. it is forbidden by Allah for us to believe in or serve anyone other than him as God." Elijah then refers to the Holy Quran (112:1-4) on this matter.

He continues:

"Allah has clearly warned us not to set up an equal with Him, as he was one in the beginning from which everything had its beginning, and will be the one God from which everything will end."

"It is the worst of ignorance for us to choose a God or attempt to make something as an equal to Allah. Foolish people all over the world have been trying for the past 5,000 years to make an equal to such one Allah who had no beginning and for whom there is no end."

These words demonstrate unequivocally that Mr. Muhammad projected the black God concept for the purpose of restoring black people to a mentally free and dignified position in Northern America. I also think that he was temporarily mesmerized by Farad's language and courage in the face of heinous racism; thus out of blind ignorance and literal interpretation of the Bible which states that the savior (Messiah) would come like a thief in the night he concluded that Master Farad fulfilled that prophecy. Later he evolved into the truth, but he could not reveal it in total because black people were still babies in Islam.

Kersey Graves discusses at length how foolish or ignorant people have ascribed kinship, partners and especially human form to God. He addresses three major areas:

1. God must come down to suffer and sympathize with the people.

The people then demanding a God of sympathy and suffering, their credulous imagination would not be long in finding one. Let a man rise up in society endowed with an extraordinary degree of spirituality and sympathy for human suffering: Let him visit the poor, console their sorrows, and labor to mitigate their griefs, and in performing such acts of love, kindness, and benevolence, he soon would command the homage of a God. [50]

2. The people must and would have an external God they could see, hear, and talk to. That the practice of promoting men to the God head originated with minds on the external plane, and evinces a want of "The Nineteenth Century," a christian writer tells us "The idea of the primitive ages were wholly sensuous, and the masses did not believe in anything except that which they could touch, see, hear and taste." [51]

3. Men were deified on account of mental and moral superiority. The ancient nations, in their entire ignorance of the philosophy of the human mind, and the laws controlling its actions, always accounted for the appearance of great men amongst them by supposing them to be Gods. Every country occasionally produced a man, who, by virtue of natural superiority, rose so high in the scale of moral and intellectual greatness as to fill the ideal of the people with respect to the characteristics of a God. [52]

Godfrey Higgins in his mammoth two volume work Anacalypsis informs us that "men of brilliant intellects and high moral attainments, and great healers (this includes Jesus) were almost certain to be deified."

After pondering over the above information, it becomes even clearer why Fard was transformed into a deity. He brought, including Mohammed, those oppressed and rejected black people hope, love, respect, dignity, and peace of mind amid turmoil. For many of them, the spirit God in the Bible had either betrayed them or abandoned them. Thus Fard conveniently filled the void. Furthermore, Fard knew and the Euro-American Christians knew that his claim to be God was the same as their projection of a human Europeanized Jesus. After all,

The information from Supreme Wisdom shows that Elijah Muhammad had an understanding of orthodox Islam and the oneness of God. Furthermore, he periodically said that he fully understood why the Arabs and other orthodox Muslims were angry at him for his brand of Islam, however, he felt he had to teach Islam according to his peoples' condition in America.

111

The portrait on the wall is the only known portrait of Master Fard. The young man standing next to Mr. Muhammad holding the Holy Qur'an is his son, W. D. Muhammad.

St. John was the first writer that taught the doctrine of the 'word becoming flesh", and that Jesus made his appearance on earth. Therefore, Elijah Muhammad and Farad said and did no more than the Christians.

It is important to reiterate and retain that Farad and Elijah taught in a manner to transform the total condition of black people. Therefore, the lessons should be interpreted and understood within that context. Farad established a University of Islam (it was not in actuality a university) to teach general subjects, especially mathematics. He encouraged his followers to appreciate math by telling them that this could be used as a weapon against the white man's "tricknology". He invented mathematical riddles and parables (problem book) stated as mathematical problems which were no more than mental calisthenics. Let us analyze problem number 31:

A lion, in a cage, walks back and forth sixty feet per minute, seeking a way out of the cage. It took him nearly four centuries to find the door. Now, with modern equipment, he is walking three thousand feet per minute and he has three miles by two miles to go yet.

How long will it take him to cover this territory of said three thousand by two thousand miles at the above walking rate? Five thousand two hundred and eighty feet equal one mile. He also has seventeen million keys, which he turns at the rate of sixteen and seventeen one hundredths per minute.

How long will it take him to turn the whole seventeen million? Sixty minutes equals one hour, twenty-four hours equals one day, three hundred and sixty-five days equals one year. The above figures do not include rusty locks. It has been said by the labors of Islam, for allowing extra time to oil the locks rusty locks is insufficient.

See and understand the skillfulness of Farad with language. University of Islam was only a primary and secondary school . Yet he knew the significance of applying language in the superlative, and expressing hyperbole when it applied to the situation. He wanted black people to think big and to do big things.

This symbolism is obviously formulated to make the student get enough self-confidence in him and herself as well as pride in the black nation to start dealing with symbolism and mathematical problems. The caged lion in this problem represented the black man or original man, Elijah often said that the black man was a sleeping lion, and the four centuries represented the four hundred years that the original man has been enslaved. The seventeen million represented the approximate number of black people in America at that time. The question, how long will it take him to turn the whole seventeen million refers to the time it will take the Muslim laborer to convert the seventeen million so-called Negroes to Islam. The modern equipment meant the teachings of Islam, and the rusty locks meant the so-called Negroes who were resisting Islam.

Farad's purpose was to bring the black man's mind back to life (mental resurrection) so that he could stand firm and confront his slavemaster using a superior mind. In essence, these lessons were designed to make the black (man) people stop loving and fearing caucasians. Imam Warith Deen Muhammad expressed the following sentiment with regard to Master Fard Muhammad and the lessons he constructed:

> "Fard Muhammad was truly a master. W e have heard that he went to different schools but he was not a college man; he just was a man with natural genius. It is because Master Fard was not a product of the colleges of the world that he was able to manifest his natural genius for had that been the case, the college would have produced a different man who would have been unable to do the job. So he just threw out and rejected all of their principles and formulas and used something entirely new to their college knowledge. However, it was not new to religion for it's the same method that has been used all along in religion. He just put it in a new language and made better use of it."

(This excerpt is taken from a Minister's Meeting that occurred August 15, 1975, p.61)

Fard Muhammad was also a master teacher because no Eastern Muslims (scholars) took an interest in the hapless condition of black people to challenge his unorthodox philosophy. The rejection and resentment on the part of most Eastern Muslims for African Americans (this still exists) opened the door of ideological opportunity for Fard. Eastern Muslims did not, with the exception of the Ahmadis and African Nationalist, Duse Muhammad Ali, who assisted Garvey, stand in protest with African Americans in the 1930's, 1940's, 1950's and especially during the Civil Rights era. Surprisingly, a Hindu, Mahatma Gandhi, and some of his adherents, particularly Lala Lajpat

Rai were more supportive (verbal) of the African American struggle than were Eastern Muslims.

These so-called universal or color-blind Muslims who still passionately attack the Nation of Islam under the leadership of Minister Louis Farrakhan as being racist should engage in introspective assessment, and thereby redirect their passion rectifying their shameful Islamic deportment. For it is sheer hypocrisy to preach what you do not practice.

Imam Warith Deen Muhammad continues to acknowledge the genius of Master Farad Muhammad by informing us that Farad introduced the authentic text of the Holy Quran to Elijah Muhammad and the Nation of Islam. However, he introduced the Quran using the same racial-nationalist approach as Drew Ali. Drew identified caucasians as the embodiment of evil; Farad identified them as devils. Drew said that caucasians (white people) were the rider of the horse-- he extracted that out of the Bible to identify the white man as the pale horse, whose rider is death.

According to Imam Muhammad, Drew did not use the word devil, but he did say the angel of death riding a pale horse is disguised as the devil. Farad was smart enough to decipher that to mean that the caucasian race was the embodiment of evil. In other words, Farad was not elusive he stated in clear language that the caucasian race is a race of devils.

Elijah Muhammad, out of loyalty to Farad, continued to teach this aspect of Farad's philosophy until the last two or three years of his leadership. More will be said about this when we analyze Elijah Muhammad's "last Sermon."

Sudarshan Kapur, Raising Up A Prophet The African American Encounter with Gandhi (Beacon Press, Boston, 1992) pp. 7, 8, and 14.

This aspect of Farad's philosophy will be repeated throughout the text for the purpose of informational clarity.

For Farad Muhammad and Elijah Muhammad, the categorization of caucasians as the embodiment of evil, the collective Devil, was Christian in biblical and historical content. In Christianity the word Devil or Satan represents a monstrous or evil figure. Satan is irredeemable and irreformable. In Islam, however, the Devil is Iblis or Shaitan, one who refused to submit to Allah (God). He represents arrogance, pride, falsehood, deceit and defiance. Interestingly, Shaitan is more manageable in Islam, and will be forgiven on the last day.

The Moorish Science Temple
OF AMERICA
UNITY

The Divine Constitution and By-Laws

ACT 1.—The Grand Sheik and the chairman of the Moorish Science Temple of America is in power to make law and enforce laws with the assistance of the Prophet and the Grand Body of the Moorish Science Temple of America. The assistant Grand Sheik is to assist the Grand Sheik in all affairs if he lives according to Love, Truth, Peace, Freedom and Justice, and it is known before the members of the Moorish Science Temple of America.

ACT 2.—All meetings are to be opened and closed promptly according to the circle seven and Love, Truth, Peace, Freedom and Justice. Friday is our Holy Day of rest, because on a Friday the first man was formed in flesh and on a Friday the first man departed out of flesh and ascended unto his father God Allah, for that cause Friday is the Holy Day for all Moslems all over the world.

ACT 3.—Love, Truth, Peace, Freedom and Justice must be proclaimed and practiced by all members of the Moorish Science Temple of America. No member is to put in danger or accuse falsely his brother or sister on any occasion at all that may harm his brother or sister, because Allah is Love.

ACT 4.—All members must preserve these Holy and Divine laws, and all members must obey the laws of the government, because by being a Moorish American, you are a part and partial of the government, and must live the life accordingly.

ACT 5.—This organization of the Moorish Science Temple of America is not to cause any confusion or to overthrow the laws and constitution of the said government but to obey hereby.

ACT 6.—With us all members must proclaim their nationality and we are teaching our people their nationality and their Divine Creed that they may know that they are a part and a partial of this said government, and know that they are not Negroes, Colored Folks, Black People or Ethiopians, because these names were given to slaves by slave holders in 1779 and lasted until 1865 during the time of slavery, but this is a new era of time now, and all men now must proclaim their free national name to be recognized by the government in which they live and the nations of the earth, this is the reason why Allah the Great God of the universe ordained Noble Drew Ali, the Prophet to redeem his people from their sinful ways. The Moorish Americans are the descendants of the ancient Moabites whom inhabited the North Western and South Western shores of Africa.

ACT 7.—All members must promptly attend their meetings and become a part and a partial of all uplifting acts of the Moorish Science Temple of America. Members must pay their dues and keep in line with all necessities of the Moorish Science Temple of America, then you are entitled to the name of, "Faithful". Husband, you must support your wife and children; wife you must obey your husband and take care of your children and look after the duties of your household. Sons and daughters must obey father and mother and be industrious and become a part of the uplifting of fallen humanity. All Moorish Americans must keep their hearts and minds pure with love, and their bodies clean with water. This Divine Covenant is from your Holy Prophet Noble Drew Ali, thru the guidance of his Father God Allah.

NOBLE DREW ALI
Founder

MOORISH AMERICAN PRAYER
Allah the Father of the universe, the Father of Love, Truth, Peace, Freedom and Justice. Allah is my protector, my guide and my salvation by night and by day, thru his Holy Prophet Drew Ali. "Amen."

THE MOORISH SCIENCE TEMPLE OF AMERICA
SALVATION
Home Office of Noble Drew Ali: Chicago, Ill., U.S.A.

Noble Drew Ali & the Moorish Science Temple were forerunners of The Honorable Elijah Muhammad and the Nation of Islam.

Fard Muhammad was an astute student and observer of black American history. He paid close attention to pioneer Christian nationalists such as Bishop Henry McNeal Turner, Reverend Henry Highland Garnet, Edward Wilmot Blyden and Alexander Crummell, political nationalist, Martin Delaney; they exposed a "get-re-acquainted with the African personality" and emigration program. The racial, social and economic themes that permeated the nineteenth century black movement inspired Fard to extract the best from these movements, and fuse them into an organizational structure that paid special attention to the need, wants, and aspirations of indigent, black migrants.

The social, racial, and economic situation for black people in the nineteenth century compelled them to develop and maintain three primary related political themes that inspired groups such as the Christian nationalist, the Universal Negro Improvement Association, the Moorish American movement, and the Nation of Islam. These themes included the struggle for equality and human dignity, the interest in African repatriation and the desire for an unfettered connection to some land. The struggle for equality and human dignity failed miserably as the country turned more vicious after Reconstruction, and as it moved toward industrial and geographical expansion.

The interest in African repatriation (separation) was sustained by only a few writers and leaders such as the ones mentioned earlier. As an idea, it never materialized. However, the passion of ex-slaves for land gained impressive momentum, but like the other two yearnings declined after the Reconstruction period.

The land issue was discussed on a political level. As early as 1825 a member of congress proposed that the Federal Government should buy Indian lands west of the Rockies where "Negroes" could settle. Needless to say, the government callously failed to even consider such a proposal (Abraham Lincoln tried to resettle blacks for emotional and political reasons).

The desire for land and its connection to freedom prompted Benjamin Pap Singleton, a former slave, to assume the role of a Prophet Moses of the Colored exodus. Singleton was sparked by the belief that God had given him the mission of taking black people to the "promised land." In this case, the "promised land" was Kansas. He spoke about his mission and proposed movement in this manner:

> "My people, for want of land--we needed land for our children--and their disadvantages--that caused my heart to grieve and sorrow; pity for my race, sir, that was coming down, instead, of going up--that caused me to go to work for them. I set out to Kansas perhaps in 66--perhaps so; or in 65, any way--my memory don't recollect which; and they brought back tolerable favorable reports; then I jacked up three or four hundred, and went into Southern Kansas, and I formed a colony there, and bought about a thousand acres of ground--the colony did-- for my people."

It is common knowledge that Southern caucasians did not take heed to Singleton's spiritual mission. As a matter fact, the Exodus of 1879 came to a dramatic end because of the external pressure against it. He led thousands of black people to Kansas where they subsequently founded several rural colonies. Unfortunately, lack of government assistance and economic hardships contributed to the failure of this noble venture.

The Old Testament theme of a promised land enveloped blacks in their legitimate quest for freedom and human dignity. It has already been shown that many blacks who sincerely had the interest of their people at heart assumed the role of self-styled prophets. In Philadelphia, for example, Prophet F.S. Cherry would often vehemently attack the caucasian image of Jesus. One interesting point about Cherry is that he not only insisted that Jesus and God were black, but that the original man on the earth was also black. As we can see, this original black man concept was not introduced by Master Farad Muhammad. Adding to this fact, Bishop Henry McNeal Turner in articulative protest against a white deity vigorously affirmed his ontological belief in God's blackness. Turner's preachments, upon scrutiny, resemble, in a unique kind of way, Farad and Elijah's preachments on the original man. Turner presented the following argument:

Before God created light, God must have been
"shrouded in darkness, so far as human comprehension
is able to grasp the situation" for countless numbers of
years.

Turner added clarity to his position with this declaration:
"God's blackness was coordinate with the original
blackness of humanity."

Turner strongly believed that the first human beings were black-
skinned people who had lived in Africa, and that white people had
been created by a bleaching process that occurred among those
humans who moved in northerly directions.

It is imperative to delineate some more facets of history that
pertain to this matter concerning the original man, or the African
origin of humanity. Charles Darwin in his Descent of Man (1871)
debunked the prevailing theory at the time that Asia was the
birthplace of the human race, and therefore Asia was the first
civilization.

On the contrary, Darwin strongly suggested that Africa was most
likely to have been the cradle of mankind. He wrote the following:
"We are naturally led to enquire, where was the
birthplace of man ... In each great region of the world
the living mammals are closely related to the extinct
species of the same region. It is therefore probable that
Africa was formerly inhabited by extinct apes closely
allied to the gorilla and chimpanzee, and as these two
species are now man's nearest allies, it is somewhat
more probable that our early progenitors lived on the
African continent than elsewhere." (Descent of Man,
pg. 520)

Excluding what appears to be a racist comparison, Darwin
surprisingly, was intellectually veracious insofar as Africa was
concerned.

Another honest European scholar was Dr. Albert Churchward who
postulated that the earliest members of the human species appeared in
Central Africa two million years go. As early as 1921, Churchward
was vigorously asserting that the original African man emerged from
the Great Lakes region and spread out over the entire African
continent. According to Churchward, certain groups of these early
Africans wandered down the Nile Valley, settled in Egypt, and then
spread out and colonized the entire world. As these Africans wandered
over the world, they differentiated into the various human subspecies
that now inhabit the globe. Africans who remained in the tropics and

119

the equatorial regions retained their dark complexions. Those who settled in temperate zones lost some of their pigmentation and developed a fairer skin.

Churchward boldly argued the above points in his highly thought provoking work The Origin and Evolution of the Human Race.

Martin R. Delaney, black nationalist and medical physician, declared in The Origin of Races and Color (1879) that color or dark complexion and human kind originated in Africa. Delaney wrote in opposition to the developing distortions of Darwin's thesis "The Survival of Fittest," which some racists utilized to justify so-called African inferiority. He looked at world history and saw Africa as its spiritual and intellectual foundation. He synthesized biblical history and scripture, archaeology and anthropology to dispel the myth of African inferiority. He presented clear evidence to the open-minded inquirer that Africa was not only the birthplace of the human being, but it was also the continent that produced the builders of the pyramids, the sculptors of the sphinxes, and the original God-Kings. This radical information laid the groundwork for contemporary scholars, and especially for would-be prophets who saw the importance in adopting this knowledge to advance their movements and the cause for black liberation and survival.

One can conclude, based on the preceding information, whatever one thinks is appropriate about Master Farad Muhammad. One thing is for certain, he was a well-read scholar who fully understood the dialectical process, he was obviously a non-biased Muslim insofar as black people were concerned, and he had a heartfelt concern for the plight of black people.

Dr. Alauddin Shabazz makes the following irrefutable point regarding Farad Muhammad:

> "The Nation of Islam was/is an indictment on so-called "Orthodox Eastern Muslims," with few exceptions. There would not have been a need for the Moorish Science Temple or the Nation of Islam, if "Orthodox Eastern Muslims were true to their Islamic claims of brotherhood, color blindness....There would not have been room for Farad Muhammad, an Eastern Muslim, to concoct a doctrine amalgamated with myths and actual truths under the caption of Islam."

NATIONALISM AND NATIONAL IDENTITY

The subject of land (separation), African repatriation and human dignity were inseparable issues for the pioneer black nationalists. African repatriation or a separate land base was rooted in the legitimate quest for human dignity and racial assertiveness. The Universal Negro Improvement Association advanced that cause very well. In fact, Garvey's UNIA was the only organization that actualized the nationalist ideology in a concretized manner. His objective was the redemption of Africa for Africans at home and abroad. He believed that if Africans in the United States were economically viable and independent they would be able to redeem the African continent and establish a world wide confraternity of African people. More importantly, he believed that Africans of the world once united by the consciousness of race and nationality, could become a great and powerful people once again. Even though Garveyites continued to use the term "Negro" they passionately identified with their African origins. Garvey frequently used Ethiopian as a symbolic term for all of black Africa.

Racial redemption was an important conjunct of black nationalism. Without a national identify, however, there could be no genuine love for Africa, or a struggle for African independence. Every nationalist, including the above mentioned Christian nationalists, wrestled with the crucial concerns of racial redemption and racial identification. Noble Drew Ali, for instance, postulated a more anthropological explanation for the origin of Africans and Europeans. His position on the origin of black and white was obviously adopted to a great extent by Farad Muhammad. Drew's discourse on the subject was as follows:

> The original man was born or rather formed in a climate most suitable for his existence. This climate was in the tropics. All persons who live in the tropics for any length of time are of an olive color, what is generally called dark. The people who live in such climates are very prolific and the multiplicity of the first men made living hard. The law, of the survival of the fittest was brought to bare on these people to such an extent that the weaker were forced to leave in order to sustain life. They left the tropical regions of Amexem, now known as Africa, and went into the land of colder climates. Here these people had to work for their living very different to the land from which they were forced. The conditions surrounding their stay in these colder regions brought about a change in their complexions. They were made paler. Their brothers who remained in their original home of course maintained their original color.
>
> The terms White and Black are altogether wrong. There are no white men nor any "black men. This word black comes from the comparison of the races who take their standards from the "European and when he calls himself white, which he says is an emblem of purity, he then names those whose hue is more olive than his, and more beautiful also black which he says is of evil. This is his psychology to create an inferiority complex in every one who is not his hue.
>
> That the forefathers of the Asiatics, who are branded"Negroes", were the masters of the first civilized of the world, is a fact which has been disputed, but it remains the fact just the same.
>
> There are no white and black. There are only Moorish Americans and European Americans. SO LET IT BE.[53]

Drew's racial nationalism went a step further than Garvey's in that Drew taught that the people termed "Negroes" in the United States were "Asiatics" and, specifically, that they were Moors whose forbearers inhabited Morocco before they were enslaved in North America. In making this racial declaration, Drew was actually denying the affinity, etc., of blacks to the white power structure. In addition, he successfully differentiated blacks from their "Negro-ness" and from their subculture. He insisted that "so-called Negroes" must know their national origin and refuse to be called Negroes, black folk, colored people, or Ethiopians. They must call themselves Asiatics, Moors, or Moorish Americans. He believed that before a people can have a God they must have a nationality, and the Moorish Nation was (is) Morocco. According to Drew the word " Ethiopian" signified division, "Negro" (black) meant death, and "colored" signified something that was painted. He argued that the name Moor is all meaningful. For by stripping him of his Asiatic name and calling him Negro, black, colored, or Ethiopian, the European robbed the Moor of his power, his authority, his God, and every other worthwhile possession. Christianity, he said, is for the European (white), and Islam is for the Asiatics (olive-skinned persons). He also believed that until each group has its own peculiar religion there will be no peace on this earth.

If one scrutinizes Drew's racial-nationalist philosophy, one can clearly see the contradiction that it displays. He rightly rejected terms such as "Negro", "black", "colored", and "Ethiopian". However, in his passionate endeavor to replace these terms, he presented other terms that added to the racial-nationalist or identification confusion. He stated that blacks were Moors who came from Morocco (North Africa); on the other hand, he stated that blacks were Asiatics with olive skin . Thus the Asiatic nation constituted the Moors who were also the ancient Moabites (Egyptians). Notice that Drew does not mention Africa in terms of its historio-cultural connection to Islam. This task would be undertaken by Farad and expanded by Elijah.

Farad and Elijah adopted and slightly resolved the Drewian contradiction by postulating that the whole earth was once called Asia, and the original man on earth was the Asiatic black-man the maker, the owner, the cream of the planet earth, the god of the universe.

Therefore, the Asiatic black man was god. Contrary to Drew, they did mention Africa in terms of its cultural affinity to Islam. Also, Muhammad during the last ten years of his mission directed Africans all over the world toward each other. And he always preached that Islam was the black man's religion, or natural way of life.

Elijah Muhammad's early position on separation was one that was ambiguous in content. It was a position that slightly deviated from the concept of the Asiatic black man; he claimed that the black man (so-called negroes) had their home in Arabia and that they founded the city of Mecca; therefore Saudi Arabia was a more likely and logical homeland. He also argued that the Nile Valley in Egypt was the last known settlement before black people were brought to North America. I think Muhammad was addressing the importance of the Muslims in America establishing a religious-cultural link to Islamic countries in the Middle East. His preference and advocacy for the Arabic-speaking countries in the Middle East and later in Africa demonstrated that he was motivated more by his Islamic interests than by his nationalist sentiments.As stated above, Farad and Elijah not only utilized the Drewian concept of nationality or national identity, but they also resolved the contradiction and expanded its message. The methodology that was employed involved members of the Nation of Islam referring to their nationality as Asiatics--descendants of the original black nation of Asia, of the Great Asiatic nation, from the continent of Africa.

Here we see Asia and Africa as a geo-cultural unit; therefore, Asia and Africa were the foundation of black civilization.

Restating what was discussed earlier, Farad and Elijah included Egypt and Saudi Arabia in their teachings in such a way that advanced Drew Ali's teachings holistically. They offered this logical scenario: Within the Asiatic nation is a group known as the "Tribe of Shabazz," which originated in Africa when a great explosion divided the earth from the moon some 66 trillion years ago. The Tribe of Shabazz discovered the best part of our planet to live on (The Tribe of Shabazz were the forefathers of black Americans), the rich Nile Valley of Egypt and the present seat of the Holy City, Mecca.

Thus Farad and Elijah's Tribe of Shabazz was an attempt to provide Black Americans with an African-Asian and Islamic identity. They assisted, through skillful discourse, their followers to believe the glorious history of Black Afro-Asia and Saudi Arabia. Notice that Noble Drew Ali's teachings are respectfully retained.

> Master Farad Muhammad taught his early followers that they were Black Asiatics and Noble Drew Ali taught his followers that they were descendants from a great Islamic Kingdom and Drew Ali taught his followers the same.

Unlike Noble Drew Ali, Farad and Elijah gave the term black genetical, historical, anthropological and racial significance. As was stated earlier, Ali dismissed the terms black and white as meaningless with regard to racial identifies. Farad, and especially Elijah, equated black with supremeness or godliness and white with debaseness and diabolism. His ideas on the subject are as follows:

124

The Black man, for the first time since he has been in the Western Hemisphere, is accepting himself as a Black man and not as a colored man.

Although the Black man has been colored--now the Black man has learned that the coloring was false and that the coloring came from a robber (the devil).

After he (the devil himself) had put our Black fathers asleep to the knowledge of their Black selves, the white man pretty nearly destroyed all of the original color of us; and he has added in his own color. Never have we, the Black man, been so happy to be called Black. And the book (Bible) teaches us that God will come one day and God will choose us, the Black people, to be his people.[54]

We did not know anything about the false color part that God had in mind to remove from us; and He is teaching us the knowledge of our color; and we love our own Black color.

And now we have learned that the color or our enemy has almost destroyed our original Black; we are now waking up to the knowledge that Black is the first color and the last color, (if there be a last).

And now that we have learned that Black is a better color, we want to be Black. You just do not have a better color than Black. Black looks good all of the time. The beautiful part of Black if that we love Black.

God has declared us, the Black man, to be the righteous and God makes it plain to see why we are the righteous. We are from the righteous Black people by nature. We, the Black man, are righteous by creation, and we can not be other than righteous. The Black man, is the best of the people![55]

The legitimate search for a proper identify was synonymous with the justified quest for an independent homeland. It was this passionate yearning which led to the Ethiopian and Abyssinian movement. The Ethiopian movement or tradition emanated from shared political and religious experiences of African nationalists during the late eighteenth and early nineteenth centuries. It found expressive reverberations in the slave narratives and in the preachments of rebellious slave preachers such as Henry Highland Garnet, Danial Alexander Payne, Robert Hamilton, Alexander Crummell.....From a literary standpoint, it was used in sermons and appeared in political tracts of the urban and politically conscious elite such as W.E.B. DuBois. The name Ethiopianism traditionally spoke to the psycho-historical and cultural needs of inferiorized black people.

125

Consider the Biblical passage, "Princes shall come out of Egypt, Ethiopia shall soon stretch out her hands unto God" (Psalms 68:31), this verse was seen as an inspiring prophecy that Africa would soon be saved from the darkness of heathenism. This idea was presented by black-Anglo oriented Christian missionaries such as Crummell who really did not know and understand how to historically and culturally assess Africa.

The verse also was interpreted to mean a promise that Africa would soon experience a dramatic political, industrial and economic renaissance. Others, such as some American black nationalists, argued that the true meaning of the verse is that some day the black man will rule the world.

The Ethiopian and Abyssinian movements were both semi-religious and nationalistic in scope and content. These movements were an ideological effort on the part of English-speaking African and black American nationalists to assess their enslavement and cultural dependency in terms of the larger history of African civilization. It reminded them that the technological civilization of Europe and America would decline like all previous empires. The Ethiopian and Abyssinian ideology expressed the belief that the tragic racial experience of Africans all over the world has historical value--that it has endowed the people of African descent with moral, psychological and cultural superiority and made them worldly seers.

Ethiopia and Abyssinia became symbols of black sovereignty to eighteenth and nineteenth century black nationalists throughout the world. When black nationalists, and Ethiopianists quoted the Psalm, "Princes shall come out of Egypt and Ethoiopia shall soon stretch forth her hand unto God", several interpretations were presented. Couched in the verse was a vision of what they called "the redemption of Africa", a concept that in its non-religious import meant eventual release from domination by European colonial powers and, perhaps, the restoration of the glories of ancient Egypt and Ethiopia. Insofar as Ethiopia was a symbol or metaphor for "black men everywhere," it also meant the elimination of slavery and racism. For the idealistic black nationalists, Ethiopia meant a return to "the Motherland", an ingathering of the exiles. For all devout Revolutionary black Christians it meant that the entire continent would eventually be converted to a form of Christian nationalism.

DuBois' interest in the Ethiopian tradition stemmed not only from his knowledge of black Christian nationalism but also from Greek and

Egyptian literature. He saw the connection between land and identify, culture and history and the psychological redemptive power of Ethiopianism. Throughout the Ethiopian and Abyssinian tradition, Ethiopia always included all of Africa and its people.

DuBois' interest in the Ethiopian movement as a unique vehicle for the resurrection of an African identity, the source of civilization, and a means for black Americans to avoid the pejorative label "Negro" with all its connotations of inferiority was stated with full literary force in such poems as "Star of Ethiopia":

> Hear ye, hear ye! All them that come to know the truth and listen to the tale of the Wisest and Gentlest of the Races of Men whose faces be Black. Hear ye, hear ye! And learn the ancient Glory of Ethiopia. All-Mother of men, whose wonders men forgot. See how beneath the Mountains of the alike in the Valley of Father Nile and in ancient Negro-land and Atlantis the Black Race ruled and strove and fought and sought the Star of Faith and Freedom even as other races did and do. Fathers of Men and Sires of Children golden black and brown, keep silence and hear this mighty word.[56]

Whether it was the Ethiopian or Abyssinian movement or the Black nationalists, all of these movements attempted to deal with the problem of black or ethnic identity by strongly insisting that what black people needed was complete separation from the white majority and the establishment of a national homeland. The Ethiopianists, Abyssinianists and black nationalists stressed and maintained that a positive identification with their African-ness and with their ancestral homeland was a prerequisite to both personal dignity and effective social action. It is important to point out that the issue of what their ethnicity or race should be called produced a measure of disagreement. Some, such as T. Thomas Fortune who did not fall into the category of a nationalist of any sort preferred "Afro-Americans" or "African Americans". Others preferred "Africans abroad" "Persons of African Descent, " "Asiatics", or "black people". As stated earlier, the Moors under Drew Ali initiated the term Asiatic" and rejected Ethiopian, black and Negro. Similarly, the Muslims (Nation of Islam) under Farad and Elijah Muhammad very rarely used the term Negro; however, when the word was used it was prefaced or qualified by so-called or used contemptuously to differentiate "Negroes" from conscious black people. Farad and Elijah also removed themselves from the use of the word "race" simply because they believed that black people constituted a "nation".

The Honorable Elijah Muhammad added more to this issue by stating:

> You can't pinpoint a Negro because there is no such thing as a Negro. This is a slang term given to our fathers by the white devils, the slavemasters. They called us all kinds of slang. Never do you find a good name which they gave our parents. Nor even today do we find them giving us good names. Even after the coming of God and God calling you by his name they (the slavemasters) still don't want to call you by the name Allah gives to us, we being his people.

Table Talks With Muhammad: Question and Answer Session, p.2.

The history of this subject would not be complete or enhanced without properly ascertaining the reason(s) why the Honorable Elijah Muhammad used black as a term for ethnic identification. The rationale is actually rooted in distorted Biblical and Quranic verses and historical derogation of black as a symbol. The historical aspect includes the evidence presented by historians that show the word black in a specific language which has numerous derogatory synonyms and referents. Some scholars such as Roger Bastide and Kenneth Gergen add a comparative feature by studying the meaning associated with black in a variety of contexts cross-culturally, contrasting these associations with those made with the word white. This symbolic dualism emanated from the Manichaean religion of ancient Persia (Iran) which presented a struggle between darkness and light. Therefore, the wanton misinterpretation of this religious view was transferred to or associated with the light and dark skin of human beings. As a result of the dialectics relating to color symbols, some people became convinced that not only was (is) there a universal dislike of darkness in abstract symbol systems but also that invidious distinctions are made everywhere between light and dark people. The Manichaean theory then emerged to account for the existence of derogation of blackness in symbol systems and the victimization of black people through these derogatory implications. Proponents of this theory assert that all people contrast night and day, darkness and light. They argue that because of unpleasant associations with the night, day is preferred to night. Therefore, the argument continues, people will associate night and darkness with sin, evil, and impurity; on the other hand, light or white is associated with saintliness, goodness, and purity. Furthermore, these symbolic attributes will become associated with dark skin and light skin of human beings. [57]

The distorted Biblical story that relates to black is the story of Prophet Noah. Noah becomes drunk with wine made from grapes he planted in a vineyard after spending forty days and nights in the ark. According to the King James version of the Bible, "Ham saw the nakedness of his father", who was lying uncovered within his tent. Ham told Shem and Japheth, his brothers, what he had seen. They showed respect for their father and "took a garment and laid it upon both their shoulders and went backwards and covered the nakedness of their father." When Noah was sober, he punished Ham for his act of filial disrespect by placing a curse on Canaan, his youngest son--not on Ham, nor on Misraim, Put, or Cush, his other sons: cursed be Canaan, a servant of servants shall he be unto his brethren, but blessed be the Lord God of Shem, and Canaan shall be his servant. 58

Professor St. Clair Drake in his highly scholarly Black Folk Here and There Vol II, expresses his understanding why the Jewish people in their origin myths, portrayed the sons of Canaan as cursed to be their servants, whereas no reference was made to any such curse being placed upon those of Ham"s sons who were specified as progenitors of Libyans, Egyptians, Sabeans, Babylonians, and Ethiopians. This curse on Canaan "legitimized" the Hebrew claim to the land they fought for and took after the so-called Exodus. Focusing the curse on Canaan exempted from condemnation potential black allies in the struggle against the Canaanites and other enemies.

The Biblical story of Noah's curse is directed at the Canaanites, worshipers of Baal, with whom the followers of Jehovah engaged in warfare for centuries. One rabbinic justification for taking the land of the Canaanites stated this, "What the slaves have belongs to the master."

Centuries later, some dastardly Muslims and Christians maliciously distorted the Noah story in a effort to substantiate a claim for exercising hegemony over Africans and enslaving them. They therefore utilized the myth of a Noaic curse to their advantage.59 The Biblical version, justified Canaanite slavery but not African slavery. As a matter of fact, the Biblical version makes no mention of skin color or facial features. 60 No version of the Biblical story speaks of any such curse being laid upon anyone other than Canaan.. 61 Nor is

Medieval scholars inherited from some of the early church Fathers a traditional interpretation of the skin color of Ethiopians as a symbol of sin. A Manichaean contrast between black and white was viewed as a metaphor for impurity versus purity. Ethiopians were considered a special missionary target. Along with the Manichaean black/white duality, the early Christian tradition transmitted the idea that Christianity could "wash an Ethiop as white as snow."

there any mention of dark skin color being the result of a curse by Noah. Christianity did not inherit any such tradition from the Bible; however, certain non-biblical Judaic versions of the Noah and Ham story have been used from time to time to derogate Africans, and by those seeking to justify the enslavement of Africans.

As indicated earlier, scholars such as Gergen and Bastide argued that people universally make negative associations with the color black and blackness. And positive associations are made with white and whiteness. The old Testament offers some ample evidence to the contrary. Incidentally, there are more references about Africa (Ethiopia) in the Bible than in the Quran. This is because the Quran is scripturally based on human behavior whereas the Bible inherited some of its stories from Jewish Folklore and the Talmud. Take for example, again, the story of Noah and his sons which made black skin a curse that was pronounced as a result of the breaking of various sexual taboos. Both the Babylonian Talmud and the Midrash include stories about black skin as a curse. However, these derogatory images of black people did not find their way into the Old Testament in the sense of a negative and positive symbolic color in duality. 62

> There are several passages in a ancient Jewish literature indicating the beauty of blackness. The well-known Song of Solomon verse (1:5) "I am comely, O'ye daughters of Jerusalem", On the other hand, white is associated with a curse, in Numbers 12:10 Moses' sister Miriam denounces his marriage to an Ethiopian woman, after which she is punished by God for this offense. The punishment was leprosy--"Behold, Miriam became leprous--white as snow".

As mentioned above, the Old Testament casts black and white as symbols in a psychological light: The word "black" is occasionally used to refer to depressed psychological states and to mourning attire, but there is no consistent presentation of white and black as polar opposites in the Old Testament. Much of the discussion about the presence of such a contrast in Biblical symbolism fails to distinguish between color--black and white--and brightness--light and dark. The former deals with color, the latter deals with degree of brightness. 63

Adding to this, in the Epistle of Barnabas, for example, (ca. 70-100 A.D.) the devil was referred to as the "Black One". European languages are corrupted by their connection to the symbolisms of "black"--its erroneous link to heathenism and slavery--and "white", which, in the English Bible, are most often written as "dark" and "light "and variations like "night" and "day". From the first chapter of Genesis (1:4), "And God saw the light, that it was good: and God divided the light from the darkness", to the last chapter of Revelation (22:5), "And there shall be no night there; and they need no candle, neither light of the sun; for the Lord God giveth them light; and they shall reign for ever and ever". There are dozens of verses in which darkness signifies evil , sin, death, failure, ignorance, and damnation, while light always means pure, virtuous, good, happy, clean, and salvation. "I am the light of the world," Christ said in John (8:12) "he that followeth me shall not walk in darkness, but shall have the light of life". On the other hand, it is extremely important to point out that there are twenty-one instances where the words black, blacker, or blackness appear in the Bible, only six refer to people, and then not to race but to mood, such as gloom. Twelve references might be interpreted as negative. Moreover, the word white is used a total of sixty-nine times; skin color is rarely a point of reference, and when it is the connotation is clearly negative: white is used to designate leprosy. Twenty-eight of the references to white are negative, compared to ten that are neutral. Of the thirty-one positive references that are mentioned, many refer to white garments as a symbol of cleanliness and purity. Thus, it is clear according to the above that Blackness is rarely used as a symbol of sin and evil.

Before the rise of Islam, local origin myths had been replaced in much of the Middle East by Hebrew stories that became part of the Christian Bible. In the Arabian peninsula, variations on these stores were blended with Midrashic legends and other Semitic lore. In the Hedjaz, for instance, racial diversity was explained by the myth that Allah had used several different colors of mud when he was creating mankind, not just "dust of the earth", as the Hebrews declared. It is dubious whether the Quran was the first to say that only black mud had been used, or whether this variation had appeared among Arabs in an earlier period.64 More will be said about this later.

The Holy Quran mentions Ibrahim (Abraham) and Noah, but says little about Nimrod or Cush, who predominated in Jewish folklore. However, Commentators of the Quran are familiar with some of the rabbinic material. They display acquaintance with some of the stories about Ham, who is not mentioned in the Quran. 65

It appears that Prophet Muhammad and the Muslims did not have any knowledge about the legend that descendants of Ham were cursed through his son Canaan to be servants of descendants of Shem and Japheth, the story that Hebrews found so useful in justifying their territorial battles with Canaanites. However, by the tenth century A.D., this story was known to intellectuals writing in Arabic and perhaps to a wider circle.

> I am compelled to concede, and I shall reiterate this during the course of this explanatory discourse, that the Quran nor the traditions of Prophet Muhammad contain statements prejudicial to Africans, although some comments have been wrongfully interpreted in this manner.

The rabbinic and Midrash stories that interpret black skin as a curse were apparently not part of early Arab traditions. However, they indeed became known after the Arab conquets, among scholars in Mesopotamia who were developing Islamic thought. By the eleventh century the black-skin-as-curse story was widely known and internalized. 66

Professor Bernard Lewis, Near Eastern Studies and orientalist scholar, suggests that the portrayal of blacks in Islamic literature began at an early date, and immediately found its way into a few stereotyped categories. Blacks usually were shown as slaves, and demons and monsters in Persian mythology, as the remote and exotic inhabitants of the land of the Zanj and other places, as for example the cannibals, islands of South and Southeast Asia. They appeared in the mythical adventures of Alexander, in Arabic called Iskandar. The romance of Alexander was a popular theme of Muslim writers, in both verse and prose. In the Persian legend, Alexander is the son of the mythical Darab, and the half-brother of King Darius, for whom he claimed his heritage.

> In pre-Islamic and early Islamic Arabia, there would have been no reason whatever for Arabs to regard Ethiopians as inferior or to regard Ethiopian ancestry as a mark of base origin. On the contrary, there is a good deal of evidence that Ethiopians were regarded with great respect as people on a level of civilization substantially higher than that of Arabs themselves. In fact, Ethiopians (Africans) contributed greatly to the ascent of Islam.

In one episode of the romance, the hero Iskandar goes to Egypt, which he delivers from the menace of the Zanj. In the course of his struggle against them, Iskandar invades the land of Zanj, emerges and defeats their army, and takes a number of captives. The adventures in Africa attributed to both Iskandar and his father, Darab.

Similar adventures are ascribed, in medieval popular romances in Arabic, such figured as the legendary Yemenite hero Sayf Ibn Dhi Yazan, who conquers and converts a variety of so-called pagan Africans.

There are only two passages in the Quran which have a direct bearing on ethnicity and ethnic attitudes. The first occurs in chapter XXX, verse XXII and reads as follows:

> Among God's signs are the creation of the heavens and of the earth and the diversity of your languages and of your colors. In this indeed are signs for those who know.

This is part of a larger section enumerating the signs and wonders of Allah (God). The diversity of languages and colors is adduced as another example of Allah's power and versatility.

The second passage is in chapter XLIX, verse XIII:

> O people! We have created you from a male and female and we have made you into nations and tribes so that you may come to know one another. The noblest among you in the eyes of Allah is the most pious, for Allah is omniscient and omnipotent.

It is clear that the Holy Quran expresses no racial or color prejudice. It only enjoins each ethnic group to respect one another as unique entitles. The two passages cited above show a consciousness of ethnic difference. The second of them insist that piety is more important than ethnicity or birth.

In the Quran, the subject of race or color is obviously not an issue. It became a burning issue in later times, as can be seen from the elaboration on these texts by subsequent commentators and collectors of tradition. Consider how chapter 3, verse 106 and chapter 39, verse 60 were maliciously distorted and willfully mis-interpreted:

> On the Day when Some faces will be (lit up with) white, and some faces will be (in the gloom of) black: To those whose faces Will be black (will be said): Did ye reject Faith After accepting

The Zanj were from that part of East Africa south of Ethiopia, and, more generally, of so-called Bantu-speaking Africans.

133

it? Taste then the Penalty For rejecting Faith.

On the Day of Judgment Wilt thou see those Who told lies against God: Their faces will be turned Black; is there not in Hell an abode For the Haughty?

The references in the Quran describing the darkening of the unbelievers faces on the day of the Resurrection is to their punishment and not to their original color. Thus blackness (Al-Sawad) is a description of a condition--rather than an inherent characteristic--of the countenance.

Opponents of color prejudice among some Arabs--Elijah Muhammad having been one of the staunch opponents --often quoted from the Maulana Muhammad Ali translation of the Qur'an; chapter 15; verse 26: "And Surely wherein Allah says We created man of dried clay, of black mud, fashioned him into shape, and we had before created the devil of bustle fire.' The Qur'an also says that when Iblis, the rebellious angel, said, "it is not fit that I should worship man whom thou hast created of dried clay, of black mud, "Allah said, "Get thee therefore hence...and a curse shall be on thee until the day of judgment."

This reference to human beings and the substance of black mud was omitted from Yusuf Ali's translation of the Qur'an, but clearly discussed in Muhammad Ali"s translation. Ali's translation is the one that Elijah Muhammad was partial to. More about this subject later.

As just stated, the Qur'an teaches that all people are made of one substance, black mud. Obviously there was no negative connotation to black as a color. In the early Islamic period there were nothing but positive associations with blackness, as for instance the kaba of pre-Islamic and present Islamic ritual, and the tradition that Prophet Muhammad's turban was black as were the banners carried by the believers of the Abbasid Caliphate.

To reiterate, there are no pejorative remarks about Ethiopians or other Africans in the Qur'an or in the Bible. The story of Ham was useful as a justification device for the enslavement of Africans.

The root denoting blackness occurs ten times in the Qur'an. Three times it has the meaning of Lordship (Al-Siyadah). Five times it describes a condition (al-Sawad). There remain two uses of the word, one of them a description of mountains. The last occurrence is in a description of night.

The Holy Qur'an Translation by A. Yusuf Ali

134

It should be clear that Elijah Muhammad's popularization of the term black was a masterful counterattack to the historical derogation of black. Color words in the western world and even in the non-western world were (are) used with chauvinistic overtones and hegemonistic feelings. Drew Ali and Elijah Muhammad passionately rejected the term Negro, I believe, because its Latin derivation "Niger" even though it means black was (is) synonymous to "nigger" and had no positive connection to Africa or Africans in the diaspora; additionally, it left the term black in a continual state of degradation. Furthermore, the English language had (has) a preponderance of sinister connotations relating to black: the outlook is black, blackball, blackguard, black death, blacklist, blackmail, black hand, black hearted, and a black cat represented bad luck. Before the rise of Farad and Elijah, African Americans or blacks in America had so internalized the negative aspects of black as a symbol that many of them would literally kill another black person if he invoked the term black in a provocative manner. In other words, black was a fighting, and even a killing word.

It was this pathological mentality, along with what created it, and the venal Muslims and Christians who also embraced the derisiveness of black that activated Farad and Elijah--especially Elijah--to give black esthetic and theological value.

The esthetic or theological quality that Elijah Muhammad assigned to blackness advanced the blackman to the position of "Father of Creation". He did this not by advocating an Afrocentric approach, but by advocating a concept that placed black people and especially the man, in a timeless, universal realm.

For Muhammad, Africa was significant, but it was not ethnically or culturally encompassing, in fact, he viewed Africa as being spiritually limited. He went far beyond the black nationalists, the Afrocentrists , and the Nile Valley civilizationists.

From a psychological standpoint, his philosophy or teaching on blackness transformed so-called lowly blacks (Malcolm X being the most famous) into moral, entrepreneurial, intellectual and spiritual giants. Utilizing a racial metaphysical methodology, this is how Muhammad psychologically removed blackness from a state of inferiorization:

Black was also associated with Africa, that is, black and Africa were synonymous with heathenism, bestiality, filth, sex, and demonology. "Black Africa "and the "Dark Continent" referred to a geographical area that was and is for Europeans and others bereft of civilization and cultural beauty.

The age of the Black man has not yet been determined. Deep in what many of you say are signs that you like to mix in the white's man tricknology with truth. You are being taught that the Black man is the first creature in the Sun.

You must realize that the Black man was the first to see the light after coming out of total darkness. He came out of total darkness and He was dark. He proved that He came out of darkness, because His own color corresponds with the conditions of what is now the Heavens and the Earth, that was nothing then Man came out of total darkness and you are not satisfied to learn that you were the first and the only powerful creature in darkness. 67

Here, Muhammad compels the black man to take his destiny into his own hands by way of a psychological rebirth. Thus the black man can extricate himself from Eurocentric thought and behavior through the acquisition of a renewed psycho-spiritual and genetically-cosmic affirmation.

Elijah Muhammad even gave a positive teaching for black people"s hair texture. He resented how much black people hated their so-called "nappy hair". Here is his explanation:

The origin of our kinky hair came from one of our dissatisfied scientists, fifty thousand years ago, who wanted to make all of us tough and hard in order to endure the life of the jungles of East Asia (Africa) and to overcome the beasts there. But he failed to get the others to agree with him. He took his family and moved into the jungle to prove to us that we could live and conquer the wild beasts and we have.

The Supreme Wisdom, Solution to the so-called Negroes Problems Vol. I by Elijah Muhammad

I think it is safe to say that Elijah Muhammad was not cognizant of what he was doing on a psychological level; his burning and uncontrollable desire for the termination of "white supremacy", was his motivating factor.

THE HOLY QUR'AN, THE BIBLE AND ELIJAH

Before I discuss the subject involving Muhammad's use of the Qur'an and Bible, I think it is befitting at this juncture to briefly elaborate on his varied positions regarding "orthodox Islam". Most Muslims and non-Muslims consider Muhammad to have been a religious imposter, or one who practiced shirk (associating anything with God). They almost always never scrutinize his historical background, or his teachings in total context. Reiterating what I said earlier, he often said that he understood why Arab Muslims were upset with him for teaching Islam in the manner in which he taught; however, he implored them to understand that he had to teach Islam according to black people's social , economic, moral, and ethnic situation. Ponder his words:

> "My brothers in the East were never subjected to conditions of slavery and systematic brainwashing by the slavemasters for as long a period of time as my people here were subjected. I cannot, therefore, blame them if they differ with me in certain interpretations of the Message of Islam. In fact, I do not even expect them to understand some of the things I say unto my people here". 67

Despite his religious unorthodoxy, he, at different times, presented a position that bespoke Islamic correctness, and even more to the point he made Umra (minor hajj) and extolled the profundity of that Islamic principle. His respect and appreciation for Al-Islam were consistently acknowledged; a unique case-in-point revolved around his (hajj) trip to Mecca in December 23, 1959. After he circles the Kaaba for the seventh and final time, he explained that highly noble experience in simple and captivating words:

> There were between five and ten thousand Muslims inside the court of the Mosque. Such a prayer service I have never witnessed before--being with these thousands of sincere worshipers of God, His religion, and Muhammad, His Prophet. On encircling it for the last time, the pilgrim makers are asked to Kiss the Black Stone. There before my eyes were many hands of pilgrims trying to reach for the stone.

"This I'll Never Forget." I will not ever forget Allah for blessing me to make the pilgrimage. 68

The Honorable Elijah Muhammad's position on orthodox Islam can be found in The Supreme Wisdom, Volumes I and II; these volumes were issued in 1957 and they were structured in a manner that coincided with the religious-nationalism of the Nation of Islam. I must add that both volumes are conspicuously repetitious. On the other hand, if one reads these volumes very carefully one can see the acknowledgement of Al-Islam, and the shift back to the doctrine of the Nation of Islam. I will concentrate at this time on his teachings pertaining to pristine Islam.

According to Elijah Muhammad, the aim of Islam for black people was the following:

1. To teach black people the truth.
2. To clean black people up and make them self-respecting and to unite them to their own kind.
3. To bring black people face to face with their God and to teach them to know their enemies. In essence, he argued "Islam is offered to our people (the so-called Negroes) as a Solution to their problems".

The Supreme Wisdom, Volume II, by the Honorable Elijah Muhammad, p. 61.

In the second volume of the Supreme Wisdom (page 53), Muhammad informs the reader that Islam's Number one principle is the belief in one God. "Allah, is the Number One principle teaching of Islam." "Muslims know and believe that Noah, Abraham, Moses and Jesus, and all the prophets of Allah also believed in the One God and taught this Truth". Regarding Allah and Prophet Muhammad, he stated the following in the second volume(page 54):

> We Muslims love all of Allah's prophets. But we will not pray for life to come to us from a dead prophet--not even Muhammad, who lived nearly 1,400 years ago. We pray in the name of Allah and mention the name of His Last Prophet in our prayer as an honor to him and as our thanks to God (Allah) for His last guide to us.

Here, it is crystal clear that the Honorable Elijah Muhammad recognized Prophet Muhammad as the seal of the prophets and not himself. He was given and accepted the title of Messenger which demands differentiation from prophet. Since he did not know Arabic, the title messenger beckons for an understanding within the English definition. Thus the religiously lofty title prophet (Nabi in Arabic) should not be an issue for further contention. He did not refer to himself as a prophet in the strict scriptural sense of that word. As a matter of fact, he initially responded to the title of "Chief Minister".

Surprising to most immigrant and idigneous Muslims, he did not, nor did he ever consider himself a prophet. Here, again is what he said about that touchy subject:

> "I don't represent myself as a prophet, because you don't need a prophet today. This is the end of prophets. The time that we are living in today is the end of prophets. There is no need for a prophet, after the coming of God! There is no need for a prophet at the end of the present worlds time. The prophets were before. And the prophets, they were sent throughout the 6,000 years of the Caucasian history on our planet. And there were three great ones; namely, Moses and Jesus and Muhammad the Last . Muhammad takes us up in the resurrection."

He also made this comment regarding the simplicity and power of Islam and its lack of ritualistic procession on the potential believer:

> "Just believe in Almighty God, Allah, and believe in his prophets, believe in the Scriptures that they brought and believe in the Resurrection and the Judgment of the world. It's easy to believe. It's easy to understand.

> The above comments are taken from a 1962 Radio Broadcast, titled 'The Tribe of Shabazz."

If and when he referred to himself as a prophet, it was in the sense of being a religious preacher, not in the sense of one who foretold the future, or one who received the scriptures of the Holy Qur'an. He was an inspired preacher, not a prophet of Allah in the scriptural sense.

Most Muslims, understandably, criticized and even condemned Muhammad for claiming that Farad Muhammad was Allah (Shirk). This is what he had to say in the second volume of Supreme Wisdom (page 10) regarding that contentious issue:

> Muhammad (May the peace and blessings of Allah be upon him) took hold of the Belief in one God (Allah) and he was successful. And fourteen hundred years later, we--- that is you and I who will not set up another God with Allah--are successful.

The above statement taken from the Supreme Wisdom shows, I think that the Honorable Elijah Muhammad instinctively knew, perhaps within a certain period of time, that Farad Muhammad was not Allah, the Divine Creator. He purposely deified Farad because black people in America were accustomed to worshiping a mortal man, in the form of a Caucasian looking Jesus, as the creator. Therefore Muhammad gave them a replacement for this image, and declared that he was a black god.

The above is just one major example of how Muhammad fused orthodox Islam with the Nation of Islam philosophy.

> "We read the Bible and Holy Qur'an. You want to make the Holy Qur'an something that is not worthy to be respected as the Bible. We make the Holy Qur'an more respected because the people who translated the Holy Qur'an were not liars. The people who translated the Bible added into the truth. Not that the Bible does not contain truth. It has plenty of it if you understand by putting the truth in symbolic language knowing that you cannot understand that which they have made symbolic."

This quote is taken from The Theology of Time (p.234)

The above quote demonstrates that the Honorable Elijah Muhammad considered the Bible to be comprised of half-truths. His referring to the Title as the 'poison book and the graveyard of my people" meant that, to him, the Bible was not, in total scripturally divine. He made this statement: "From the first day that the white race received the Divine Scripture they started tampering with its truth to make it to suit themselves and blind the black man.' "It has poisoned the very hearts and minds of the so-called Negroes so much that they can't agree with each other." Taken from Supreme Wisdom, Vol II (p.59)

Because he believed that the Bible had been used to put black people to sleep (mental), he also believed that it could be used to awaken them. It was his desire to raise his people from a dead state of being and release them from the "spooky" concept of the creator that held them captives and made them willing mental slaves. This is the major reason why he taught out of the Bible more than he taught out of the Holy Qur'an.

As I pointed out earlier, the Bible was actually dialectical in context. More about this later. It could be utilized for whatever reason or purpose an individual had in mind. In actuality, however, the Bible did not specifically address black people in a negative manner. But some evil-minded, pallid Christians distorted some aspects of biblical scripture to convince black people that they had been cursed 'black' by the creator and would actually turn 'white' in heaven.

The Bible was indeed the foundation of Christian beliefs and conduct; however, unlike the leaders of the Protestant Reformation, American Christians were inclined to interpret it "less according to

140

the norms of classical Christianity than through the presumed competence of private reason and individual experience.' 69 And reason and experience told both the slave holders and the abolitionists what each wanted to believe.

When David Brion Davis outlined the network of beliefs and associations regarding slavery shared by the nations of Western Europe, he listed the Bible first, followed by classical antiquity and experience with various kinds of servitude. 70

Professor Forrest G. Wood points out in his voluminously informative book, The Arrogance of Faith (p. 43) that the Bible has always been a source of controversy and the religious foundations of the proslavery argument had been laid in discussions, letters, and sermons far back in the colonial period; it was not until the second quarter of the nineteenth century that southern whites, largely in response to the attacks by abolitionists, began to invoke, in a distorted way, certain scriptures in literal defense of slavery.

To persuasively articulate that defense, it was necessary for Christian slave holders and defenders of slavery to resolve ambiguities over the definitions of certain English terms. For example, the word denoting servitude that appeared most frequently in the Authorized Version of the Bible was relatively benign "servant", but because of the contexts in which it was often used and the conditions that presumably existed in biblical times, many Christians simply assumed that 'servant' always meant 'slave.' There should be no doubt that such an assumption conveniently served the purposes of the American slave holders.

Referring to the biblical servant as slave may have been self-serving for Christian slavemasters, but it was closer to the original meaning of the term, as modern English and American translators of the Bible have agreed. At the same time, the Puritans apparently found a middle ground between the Jewish "servant" and the gentile "slave". A slav or slave in New England often lived close to his master's family, "in keeping with the custom of the Hebraic family," and was often called "servant," a term that, in fact applied to anyone who worked for someone else, slave or otherwise. Of course, the great majority of the black population was in the South, where differences over definitions had the most meaning. Almost as though anticipating the southern rationale, English scholars who prepared the authorized Version translated Paul's terms as "bond" and "servant", which to one who was looking for a moral justification of slavery, could not, or course, have meant anything other than "slave." Paul wrote this letter to the Ephesians:

141

> Servants, be obedient to them that are your masters according to the flesh, with fear and trembling, in singleness of your heart, as unto Christ; doing the will of God from the heart; with good will doing service, as to the Lord, and not to men: knowing that whatsoever good thing any man doeth, the same shall be received of the Lord, whether he be bond or free. 71

Once this passage from Paul was firmly established, it was not difficult for the American slaveowners to find any number of biblical examples of slavery and to conclude that God had indeed given the institution of slavery his sanction.

The Bible's dialectical or dualistic theme regarding bondage and color symbolism was ideally applicable to American slavery. As discussed in the previous chapter, Noah's curse (Ham) and the words servant or slave were not, initially, associated with race or color until after the ascent of the Bible."

Moreover , what was extremely insidious was the indirect terminology and the convoluted interpretation of the Bible that perverted the Euro-American Christian's attitude toward black people. As a result, Europeans and Euro-Americans were able to concoct an elaborate defense of human bondage out of three Old Testament verses (a total of fifty-one words in the Authorized Version), and that most of the Christian world failed to challenge that defense, is very difficult for the religiously conscious person to comprehend. Historically, the myth of Noah's curse had become a rationale for a theory of ethnocentric behavior before the first African ever arrived in an English colony. As early as 1521, a German scholar named Johan Boemus, surmised that all of the primitive and barbaric peoples of the earth were descendants of Ham while everyone else had descended from Shem and Japheth. 72

The dialectical or dualistic themes in the Bible were clearly manifested in the Euro-American slaveowners and the African slave's interpretation of the scriptures regarding bondage and freedom. What is important to note here is that the principle of dualism was uniquely suitable for slavery. Slaveowners realized that persuading the slave to accept his or her lot was much easier if he or she could expect 'eventual deliverance,' and there was plenty of biblical scripture that was available for them to contort. A unique case-in-point, for example, was Paul's letters to the Christians of Cornith, Colosse, and Ephesus which exhorted servants to be content with their condition, no matter how intolerable it might be, simply because God ultimately would reward their suffering in heaven.

Unfortunately, for most slaves, the contortion worked, and it worked well. Jupiter Hammon, who is credited with being the first American black poet, admonished his fellow slaves against insurrection in his thirty stanza of "A Dialogue Entitled the Kind Master and the Dutiful Servant."

> Come my servant, follow me,
> According to thy place;
>
> And surely God will be with thee.
> And sent thee heave'nly grace.
>
> Dear Master, I will follow thee,
> According to thy word
> And pray that God may be with me
> And save thee in the Lord. 73

Hammon was so-called humanely treated by his master; he received the rudiments of learning instruction in various manual skills, and intensive religious training. He often expressed gratitude to his slave master for treating him so well. Moreover, his intensive study of Christianity and the Bible compelled him to conclude that reading or learning to read afforded the illiterate slave the power to learn the will of God through the literal interpretation of the Bible:

> Get those who can read, to learn you; but remember, that what you learn for, is to read the Bible. If there was no Bible, it would be no matter whether you could read or not. Reading other books would do you no good. But the Bible is the word of God, and tells you what you must do to please God; it tells you how you may escape misery, and be happy for ever. 74

Religion and the Bible was Hammon's order of business. He completely internalized the Pauline be-a-good-slave-go-to-heaven theme so much so that he strongly condemned any thought of slave insurrection. Worrying about being slaves in this life would do the slave no good, he believed, for God would set the slave free "in his own time and way". Furthermore, he reasoned, it did not really matter much, as a mere "forty, fifty, or sixty years" of slavery would seem as nothing compared with the eternity in Heaven that would be the lot of the God-fearing slave, whom nobody in Heaven would "reproach" for being black, or for being "slaves". He considered slaves who elected to resist bondage "the greatest fools." He hoped that the insurrectionists would think about their acts and live as though they believed what he said about "submission and Heaven" to be true, whether or not they

143

actually did believe. 75 He concluded by assuring them that if they were to become Christians, they would "have reason to bless God forever, that you have been brought into a land where you have heard the gospel though you have been slaves." 76

Hammon's discourse was the same as Phyllis Wheatley's and other passive slaves and that was, whatever the evil to the slave, slavery was still a blessing rather than a curse because it had been the means of introducing slaves to the Bible and Christianity.

The reader should read Phyllis Wheatley's "On Being Brought from Africa to America."

> Hammon and Wheatley manifested only one aspect of the duality as it related to the Bible, but there is a duality that prevails and pervades the entire socio-ideological framework of the African American struggle. And that duality bespeaks accommodationism versus separatism, integrationism versus nationalism. It began with the slaves, took ideological formation with Frederick Douglas and Martin R. Delaney, and sustained itself through the Nation of Islam and the Civil Rights Movement. It now reveals itself in the ideology of Minister Louis Farrakhan and the Reverend Jesse Jackson; and what is very interesting is how this ideological duality has embraced Imam Warith Deen Muhammad (accomodationist) and Minister Farrakhan (separatist).

The principle of duality manifested and applied itself to those slaves who sought a biblical interpretative rationale for insurrection or freedom. Some slaves such as James Curry even saw slavery as a contradiction according to God's decrees in the bible:

> My uncle had a Bible, which he lent me, and I studied the Scriptures. When my masters family were all gone away on the Sabbath, I used to go into the house and get down the great Bible, and lie down in the piazza, and read, taking care, however, to put it back before they returned. There I learned that it was contrary to the revealed will of God, that one man should hold another as a slave. I had always heard it talked among the slaves, that our forefathers and mothers were stolen from Africa, where they were free men and free women. But in the bible I learned that God hath made of one blood all nations of men to dwell on all the face of the earth. 77

There can be no doubt, that some slaves interpreted scripture in such a way that God favored retribution for the slaves, Jesus died to save humanity, and Moses led the Hebrews out of slavery. 78

To the slave that was resentful of submissive bondage, the Bible was a source of strength for their struggle at psychological and physical liberation. Some very interesting examples are the biblical characters that became intimate, personal friends or close relatives to some slaves.79 Several slave songs proclaimed, "Jesus is my bosom friend," another stated, "I'm going to talk with King Jesus by myself," and still others told about warm, friendly kinfolk--"Sister Mary," "Brother Moses", and "Brother Daniel."80

This God of the Bible was the slave's personal God and he was committed to justice and he was more than willing to drown the pharaoh's army of slave holders to save the Hebrew children. 81

The majority of slaves, or rather an appreciable number were attached to the heaven's glory idea rather than an earthly plight. In other words, the slaveowners and their handpicked clergy were successful at using selectively distorted scriptures as a means of propaganda for conformity. However, some of the slaves through the use of their scriptural interpretation produced their own form of black liberation theology. The famous leaders of nineteenth-century insurrections, Gabriel Prosser, Denmark Vesey and Nat Turner were devout Christians, convinced that their rage to rebel was divinely inspired and biblically sanctioned. Vesey's plan, recalled one of the conspirators, was "about slavery." Another witness testified how the children of Israel were delivered out of Egypt from bondage."

Nat Turner, Godly proclaimed preacher, said a black, avenging Messiah appeared in a dream to call him to action. God told him to "fight against the Serpent, for the time was fast approaching when the first should be last and the last should be first."

> In masters hands, Christianity and the Bible became a litany of secular commandments that sanctioned, justified and encouraged slavery and white supremacy. The Christianity and Bible forged by some slaves rejected bondage and condemned those supporting it.

I thought it necessary to expound on this subject to demonstrate that Elijah Muhammad was not malicious with regard to his position on the Bible. In fact, careful scrutiny shows that he too exposed a dialectical or dualistic position insofar as the symbolic meaning of the Bible; its half-truths versus its half-falsities regarding the physical and mental slavery of black people.

According to Elijah Muhammad, black people were in the church, drenched in the white man's Christianity and soaked in low-self-esteem; therefore, he had to meet black people on their mental level, and that was in the Bible. He systematically and psychologically utilized biblical scriptures to get the attention of black Christians so that they might be guided toward the Holy Qur'an.

Dr. Alauddin Shabazz, religious scholar, and minister under Elijah Muhammad, indicated that Muhammad used some of the following verses to capture black people's attention:

> Genesis (6:1-7, 25:23, 30:25-42, 15:13-14), Romans (11:16-25, 7:9-24) Exodus (24:9-11), 15:3, 33:11, 20-23) Isaiah (3:12, 5:13, 14, 9:2, 40:12-25, 42:1, 19-22, 43:19-21, 53:1-3, 55:4-5, 58:1, 59:10, 14-15, 63:1-9, 65:1-6, 15). He pointed to the evil deeds of Euro-Americans using: 2--Thessolonians, (2:3, 4,7,8), St. John (8:44), Revelations (13:1-18, 17:1-3, 6:8).

These select verses and others echo Muhammad's words and the passion he displayed whenever he discussed the Bible and its relevance for black people. His astuteness of the Bible equipped him to unearth the above verses and more for the mental and spiritual resurrection of his people:

> By translating the Bible, his (the white man) purpose and aim is to keep you blind to even the truth in it. He wants to keep the truth of the Book away from your knowledge and keep it to himself. He uses it to drive others who have not yet caught up with his lies. "Is the Bible a lie, Elijah?" "No. It is not a lie if you understand it. But if you don't understand it, it makes you see wrong. That wrong way you are seeing was put there purposely by the liars to keep you away from the Truth. We don't hate the Bible because we are the makers of the Bible. Theology of Time (p.234)

The last point pertaining to this aspect of our subject is that the Honorable Elijah Muhammad quoted regularly from the Bible and he carefully employed the use of biblical verses that addressed the psycho-spiritual needs and wants of black people. He met black people where they were; thus ministering as far as he could to a spectrum of needs, wants, and aspirations which transcended the spiritual to find their expression in more immediate psychological, economic, social and moral needs. His official Holy book was the Holy Qur'an; however, his instrument of psycho-social warfare was the Bible

His God was the same one he knew as a Christian and a student of the Bible, a fighting God bent on vengeance and the liberation of his people. He proclaimed this God to be a "Black God" who came in the person of Master Farad Muhammad.

Elijah Muhammad, more than anyone else who was acquainted with the Qur'an and its English translations, popularized the Holy Quran's purity and spiritual exegesis. He single handedly put more Holy Qurans into the hands of black Americans than the Ahmadiyas who were exposing members of Garvey's UNIA to their brand of Islam, and the immigrant Muslims who tended to totally avoid the black community.

His knowledge of the Bible and its inconsistencies, contradictions, and repetitions demonstrated to him that the Holy Qur'an was (is) indeed The Holy Book. With that in mind, he accepted the fact that for most black people the Holy Qur'an was (is) a unique mental and spiritual emancipator. He argued that the Qur'an could extricate black people from their moral and mental imprisonment simply because the Qur'an was (is) the True Word of Allah. It was (is) a book that cannot be disputed and for Muhammad it was (is) a book that Europeans could not dismiss. He said that Europeans (former slavemasters) recognize the Qur'an to be a book full of truth. The Bible is full of prophecy he said, but the Qur'an was (is) not a book of prophecy as such it was (is) a guide. The Qur'an is a message directly to Prophet Muhammad. Elijah Muhammad's profound appreciation for the Holy Qur'an was based on a passionate love and respect for its God ordained directives. Some of his comments regarding his love for the Qur'an were as follows:

> The book that the so-called American Negroes (Tribe of Shabazz) should own and read, the book that the slavemasters have but have not represented it to their slaves, is a book that will heal their sin-sick souls that were made sick and sorrowful by the slavemasters.

Bishop Henry McNeal Turner's position on the Bible was akin to Elijah Muhammad: The white man's digest of Christianity or Bible doctrines are not suited to the wants, manhood growth, and progress of the Negro. Indeed he has colored the Bible in his translation to suit the white man, and made it, in many respects, objectionable to the Negro. And until a company of learned black men shall rise up and retranslate the Bible, it will not be wholly acceptable and in keeping with the higher conceptions of the black man....We need a new translation of the Bible for colored churches.

This book will open their blinded eyes and open their deaf ears. It will purify them.

The name of this book, which makes a distinction between the God of righteousness and the God of evil is Glorious Holy Qur'an Sharrieff. It is indeed the book of Guidance, of Light and Truth, and of Wisdom and Judgment.

This book the Holy Qur'an Sharrieff, is not from a prophet but direct from Allah to Muhammad (May Peace and the Blessings of Allah Be Upon Him) not by an angel but from the mouth of Allah (God).

The Supreme Wisdom Volume Two (p.66)

The next comment from Elijah Muhammad impels us to look deeper into the ideological and political philosophies of the two main translators of the Holy Qur'an: Maulana Muhammad Ali and Abdullah Yusuf Ali who espoused a political ideology that emanated out of British imperialism and the social class to which they belonged. The Honorable Elijah Muhammad paid homage to both of these scholars by using and encouraging his followers to use both translations of the Qur'an. Initially, he used the Abdullah Yusuf Ali translation; afterwards, he relied strongly on the Muhammad Ali translation. One can speculate about, the reason(s) why he did this later. In fact, one of the reasons is contained in the following comments:

The Holy Qur'an translated by Yusuf Ali uses God most times. That is to make the English readers know what he is talking about. There is also a Pakistani Muslim who translated the Holy Qur'an. His name is Maulana Muhammad Ali. You must remember that they both mean good. But being a Muslim myself and wanting Allah to have all the credit that we can give him without mistake, I love to say Allah. I love to read the Holy Qur'an saying Allah or teaching Allah. Allah is a great name for the Divine Supreme Being because it covers everything. It means All. He is All in All. He, being a Supreme One, is distinguished by calling Him the Mahdi, the Independent God. He is Self-Sufficient. I want you to know this God that the Holy Qur'an teaches us is coming in the Last Days. In the 22nd Sura of the Holy Qur'an it gives the name "Mahdi."

According to Elijah Muhammad, using the English name God to refer to the Supreme Being was too definitionally limited and definitionally interchangeable. The name God denoted polytheism;

therefore, he wanted to give credit only to One God whose proper name is Allah.

Now, I think it is imperative to scrutinize some of the various translations and translators of the Holy Qur'an--especially the Yusuf Ali and Muhammad Ali translations and their accompanying political ideology. After the scrutiny and discussion of the above, it should appear even clearer why Elijah Muhammad showed partiality to the Muhammad Ali translation. There are approximately twenty translations of the Holy Qur'an. The earliest was by Hakim Abdul Muhammad Khan in 1905; this translation was limited in editions, and the translator, according to the research conducted by A.R. Kidwai, (The Message International, March 1992, p.17-20) was not that well versed in Islam. The next translation which was also limited in editions was by Hairat Mirza Dehlawi in 1912, and he too faltered in his noble attempt. The three most important English translations, and there are other translations dating up to 1986 and dating back to 1649, are by Marmaduke Muhammad Pickthall, Yusuf Abdullah Ali and Maulana Muhammad Ali. Kidwai categorizes the translators as Muslim and non-Muslim, and because of Muhammad Ali's early Ahmadiya involvement, he falls into the non-Muslim category.

Some of the earliest translators were Orientalists. Therefore, the Muslim need for translating the Qur'an into English arose out of a deep desire to defeat the orientalist effort. Furthermore, the rapidly increasing number of non-Arabic speaking peoples who were (are) embracing Islam require(d) appropriate translations.

Orientalist and Christian missionary versions of the Qur'an were rooted in Eurocentrism and a long historical aversion for Islam. Thus it becomes reasonable why the Muslims could not allow the sacred text of the Qur'an to be confounded and disrespected. Hence, devoted Muslims laboriously translated the Quranic text as well as an authentic summary of its teachings for the interested European and later American literary audience.

Afterwards, the Muslim translations were (are) also meant to serve Muslims whose only access to the Quranic injunctions was through the medium of the European or Orientalist translations.

It stood to reason that English would be deemed the most important language for the purpose of translation because of the vastness of British colonialism (British Empire). With the exception of Elijah Muhammad was the one most responsible for putting Maulana Muhammad Ali and Abdullah Yusef Ali's translations of the Holy Qur'an into the hands of black Americans. The Theology of Time (p.134).

The Honorable Elijah Muhammad & Minister Malcolm X overcame all of the barriers to Christian philosophy to recruit loyal followers for a religion other than that of their former chattel slave owners.

the Ottoman Empire, Britian had the largest number of Muslim subjects.

The Holy Qur'an has been translated into sixty-five languages, but English has been the most widely disseminated for reasons given above. Thus the English translations of the Holy Qur'an are the ones with the most controversial longevity.

It deserves repeating, the early English translations of the Qur'an by Muslims stemmed from the noble and pious effort on their part to refute the allegations leveled by the Christian missionaries and the orientalists against Islam and the Holy Qur'an.

The translation by Muhammad Marmaduke William Pickthall was considered to be of first-rate quality. Pickthall was an Englishman who embraced Islam and rendered into English The Meaning of the Glorious Koran. His translation was the first by a Muslim whose first language was English. He consulted with scholars in Europe and Egypt before undertaking this noble task; however, former professor at Al-Azhar, Shaykh Muhammad Shakir denounced Pickthall's translation and his collaborators. In 1931, a year after his translation was published the Rector of Al-Azhar also expressed his unhappiness with the translation. Pickthall's knowledge of Arabic was limited which, in turn, produced inaccuracies in his translation, scant explanatory notes, and weak background information.82

Pickthall's political ideology was difficult to categorize because he espoused different political positions at different times; moreover, he is best remembered, aside from his Quranic translation, as a novelist who understood the Near East. Between 1902 and 1921, he published nine novels set in Syria, Palestine, Egypt, Yemen and Turkey. Ideologically, he was a monarchist who believed in the widest possible devolution of authority. He was critical of British imperialism in India, supported it in Egypt--this might explain on one level why the Muslim scholars of Egypt rejected his translation. He was a patriotic English Tory and he opposed war between Britain and the Ottoman Empire; this position, understandably, alienated him from his fellow-Englishmen. 83. Lastly, he was a freemason. His conversion to Islam coincided with the defeat of Turkey and the end of World War I, followed by the collapse of the Ottoman Empire. 84 Pickthall's ideology crept into his translation of the Qur'an. Furthermore, his use of biblical English tended to be a stumbling block for the uninitiated reader of the Qur'an.

Abdullah Yusuf Ali's translation of the Holy Qur'an is the most popular. The main reason for this is the argument that his translation is closer to the Sunni Islamic tradition. However, Yusuf was not an

Islamic scholar in the strict sense of the word. He was a civil servant by profession and he later got involved in politics. More about that later. His copious notes and commentaries are reflective of his command of English; he also tends to paraphrase as opposed to engaging in literal translations. His notes on heaven, hell, angels, jinn, and polygamy are, according to some Muslim scholars, Dr. Kidwai being one, comprised with the pseudo-rationalist spirit of his times. Furthermore, Kidwai believes that Yusuf's interpretation of verses dealing with Quranic eschatology as symbolic, allegorical and figurative is outside the pale of Islam (Muslim World League Journal 12(5), February 1985, pp. 14-17). Kidwai cites a number of verses and commentaries in Yusuf's original translation which are not represented as literal translations. Yusuf, instead views them as allegorical, symbolical....Despite its popularity, Yusuf's translation has been criticized by other Muslim scholars worldwide. The Mujlisul Ulama of South Africa warned the Muslims regarding the danger of the Baatil (untrue, deceptive) and Kufr (covering the truth) commentaries of Yusuf Ali. Imam Ahmed Deedat was one of the main critics of Yusuf's Quranic commentaries.

As a result of these attacks, Amana Corporation has revised Yusuf's translation. What is interesting to note is that Yusuf's translation has been revised more than any other translation. The revised edition is now using Allah in place of God--something that Elijah Muhammad contested for years. The new edition is not as voluminous; therefore, it becomes somewhat easy to deduce that Yusuf's translation had a number of errors, and some of those errors had to be omitted as well as corrected. Furthermore, it can safely be deduced that since Yusuf's translation has been revised more than once, then this new version or translation cannot rightfully be called his translation; on the other hand, it can rightfully be called the translation or version of Amana Corporation.

Imam Warith Deen Muhammad once said that he too was displeased with Yusuf Ali's translation of the Holy Qur'an. He pointed out that Yusuf had at least a trace of racism in him that affected his translation of the Qur'an. One example of this accusation might be Yusuf's willful omission of the adjective black in describing the formation of mankind (Surah 15: 26 & 28, "We created man from sounding clay from mud molded into shape." "Behold, Thy Lord , said to the angles: "I am about to create man from sounding clay from mud mounded into shape"). These verses are in the Arabic editions of the Qur'an, but they are obviously left out of Yusuf's edition. It is this conspicuous mis-translation that led Imam Muhammad to say that

Yusuf's English in constructing Arabic terms were not true to what the Arabic was saying n many instances; in addition to his touch of racist tendencies.

Additionally, Shaykh Ben Bazz of Mecca said, despite Muhammad Ali's short-lived Ahmadiya involvement, that Muhammad Ali's translation of the Qur'an is better than Yusuf's version. With the exception of misinterpreting several verses that relate to the "Promised Messiah," his miracles and the Quranic angelology, Muhammad's translation stays close to Arabic. His translation has exhaustive notes that are both readable and corroborative.

For the sake of historical information and clarity, I think it is imperative to view both Yusuf and Muhammad's social, educational and political background and ideology. Yusuf attended Wilson College, Bombay and later St. John's College, Cambridge. He took the Indian Civil Service exam and earned the highest possible score which enabled him to gain favorable positions with the British Imperial Administration in India. His mastery of English, and his passion for intellectual excellence placed him into the circle of the British and Indian elite. He was appointed magistrate in the Sultanpur and Fatehpur collectorates. His reputation within the Indian Civil Service accelerated, so that by the age of 33 he had held positions of acting Under-Secretary and later Deputy Secretary in the Finance Department of the Indian Government. Yusuf was absorbed in his career pursuits until 1914; at that time, he resigned from the Indian

---

To date Amana Corporation has continued to omit black from Surah 15: 26 & 28.

It stands to reason that every translation of the Qur'an reflects the dogma or ideology of the translator. Therefore the strong criticism leveled against Muhammad Ali is baseless when one addresses Yusuf and other translations. If Yusuf's translation can be revised, why not revise Muhammad Ali's?

Muhammad Ali was a member of a heterodox sect called the Ahmadiyyah which was founded by Mirza Ghulam Ahmad. After Ghulam's death, the Ahmadiyyah split into two subsects, the Qadianis and the Lahorites. The Qadianis believe that Ghulam was the "Promised Messiah" or "Shadow Prophet." Muhammad Ali was a Lahorite, and they held that Ghulam was a Mujaddid (renewer) only. Ali did not regard Ghulam as a prophet (Nabi).

Civil Service for reasons that were obscure. Afterwards, he returned to England and got passionately involved in Indian-British politics.

Abdullah Yusuf Ali was by careful scrutiny a loyal British subject (Monarchist). He played an active role on behalf of the British during World War I; he participated in recruitment campaigns, and as a private in the West Kent Fencibles and as president of the Indian Students' Prisoner of War Fund he actively engaged in various kinds of diplomatic assignments. One must bear in mind that he was not only educated in England, but he was also experienced as a civil servant. Thus he was dispatched to Sweden and other Scandinavian countries, and he was assigned to Serbia for diplomatic purposes.

It is now time to view the historical background of Muhammad Ali before we continue our assessment of Yusuf Ali. In doing so, we must objectively weigh the ideological contrast between these two influential Muslims. As a youngster, Muhammad Ali would secretly attend daily Quranic lessons given at Aligarth by Shibli Numani. He became so proficient in Quranic Arabic that Shibli would invite him into the lecture hall. As a result of his studiousness, Ali was at the top of his class and thereby earned his B.A. degree at Allahabad University where he studied history. He later attended Oxford University. Like Yusuf, he also took the Indian Civil Service exam; unfortunately, he failed. It was this misfortune that, to a certain extent, thrust Ali into the realm of Indian-British politics. His main interests were politics and journalism; however, he did occupy positions of education officer and agrarian commissioner.

While Yusuf was involved in accommodationist politics, Muhammad Ali was devoted to speaking at public meetings in support of Aligarth political affairs. Ali's consistent commitment placed him at the center of Muslim political activity. When the All-Indian Muslim League was formed in 1907, its headquarters were at Aligarth. Ali was by definition a revolutionary (Caliphatist). The Caliphate Movement appealed to Pan-Islamic sentiments, and it attracted Muslims who otherwise remained aloof from politics. Ali founded and edited *Comrade* (English edition) and later *Hamdard* (Urdu edition). When Turkey entered World War I on the side of Germany in 1914, Ali wrote a provocative article titled "The Choice of the Turks," for which he was quickly arrested by the British and

Yusuf was not in the minority when it came to loyalty to Britain. Large numbers of Indians fought for Britain. In 1918, Edmund Allenby conquered Palestine with an army of which two-thirds of the infantry and one-third of the cavalry were Indians.

remained imprisoned for the duration of the war. Ali was interned under the Defense of India Act and his publishing rights were forfeited. Ali became a security risk to the British imperialists; on the other hand, Yusuf became a loyal member of the British Empire.

By the time World War I was over in 1918, Yusuf Ali and Muhammad Ali were solidly entrenched on the opposite ends of an ideological spectrum. Yusuf was a tame Muslim who willingly submitted to British imperial rule; contrarily, Muhammad Ali struggled against British imperialism within the context of Islam, and he was willing to endure the consequences for his actions. Despite their extreme ideological differences, their paths would cross at the Versailles Peace Conference of 1919-1920. This led to the Treaty of Sevres in May 1920. These two meetings actually determined how the former Ottoman Empire would be carved up between Britain and France (Sykes-Picot Agreement). 85.

Muhammad Ali attended the conference to remind Britain of its pledge to Indian Muslims, and that involved Turkey retaining possession of Constantinople and Asia Minor--particularly the land of Arabia remaining under a legitimate Caliph. Muhammad Ali's controlled radicalism pertaining to this issue was rooted in his Islamic fervor. Here is his passion:

> "We hold no brief for the Turks but we are the advocates of India claims. We speak not for the Turks but we speak for ourselves. And here I must explain the nature and shape of Islam which makes this not a Turkish but an Islamic question. Islam does not recognize geographical and racial barriers such as the nationalism of modern Europe...We do not worship in the shrines of nationalism that was for its creed 'My Country, right or wrong'...To the Muslims of India, the Turk is not only a man, but a brother....because he shares with us a common outlook on life and common institutions and laws that materialize that outlook and perpetuate the culture of Islam...."

The schism between Indian Muslims that reflected the ideological differences between Yusuf and Muhammad was not clinched at the Peace Conference. To add to this rift Yusuf Ali had befriended T.E. Lawrence (So-called Lawrence of Arabia). Lawrence was the

The Aligarth was a secondary school patterned in many ways after European models. It was founded in India in 1875 by Sir Sayyid Ahmad Khan. Aligarth College was later added to the Aligarth High School. In 1920, the college became a university.

supposed architect of the Arab revolt against the Turks in the *Hejaz*; furthermore, he had a crucial role in the Peace Conference. Understandably, Muhammad Ali, the Caliphatist, resented the presence of Lawrence who definitely represented British snobbery and imperialistic arrogance. Yet Yusuf chose to establish a friendship with this British intelligence agent in the Palace of Versaille. 86.

The Peace Conference was a pivotal event for Yusuf and Muhammad; it showed them how politically dubious, how ill-informed, and how insignificant their views were regarded. Ali and the Caliphatists held immature, preconceived ideas about Turkey simply because it was once an Islamic Empire; they misconstrued the objectives, long and short, of Mustafa Kamal (Attaturk) and they misread the power struggle between Kamal and Enver Pasha. 87 Kamal was against the Caliphatist, and against everything the Ottomans stood for or represented. Kamal was an extreme modernist who severed his connection to the possibility of another Islamic state. Therefore, when the terms of the Treaty of Sevres were published, the Ottoman Empire was shattered in such a way that confirmed the Caliphatists and Ali's biting apprehensions. Their anguish was further exacerbated when Kamal in 1923 declared Turkey a secular republic. 88.

Although Yusef and Ali stood on opposite ideological ground at the Peace Conference, later the same Peace Conference compelled them to stand on mutual ground. Ali's Pan-Islamic politics had been diffused, and ironically Yusuf felt betrayed by the same Englishmen with whom he had forged an alliance. The Peace Conference had designated Palestine mandated territory, and Yusuf was furious when proposals to partition Palestine were debated in the late 1930s.

Yusuf Ali utilized the various platforms that he had access to in London to speak out against the injustice that was being dealt to the Palestinians. He made the following statements regarding this issue:

It is true that Britain finds herself in difficulty, as she introduced the Jews (into Palestine during the Mandate) as a matter of settled policy, and she cannot abandon the Jews. But the Jews have by their own declaration shown that their ambitions are to dominate the Arab country, and there can be no hope of any peace in allowing them a privileged position such as they claim. If Britain has any conscientious scruples about abandoning the Jews' she should settle them in their own territory. She has no right to take away Arab land and to retain her own hold on an area which she temporarily occupied under the Mandate professedly, in the interest of its inhabitants.'

The Palestine question did not completely sever Yusuf's loyalty to Britain; moreover, what I think transformed him from a sentimental to a disaffected Anglophile was the publication of his English translation and commentary of the Holy Qur'an. Between 1934-1937, Yusuf was principle of the Islamic College in Lahore, Pakistan and it was this period that parts of his translation first appeared in print. Once Yusuf returned to Britain, he cold not have avoided being thrust on the front line of the Muslim community and thereby becoming their spokesman for pertinent Islamic causes. 89.

After the Peace Conference betrayal, Yusuf became more Islamically conscious than ever before. But sadly he never ceased submitting to British standards.

There is no doubt that Yusuf Ali's translation of the Holy Qur'an is a testimony to his love for Allah and his way of life (Islam). He died in 1953 in London and was buried there. 90. He was a sincere man who died mentally unhinged and emotionally broken.

Maulana Muhammad Ali was a thorn in the side of the British establishment. He sacrificed his career and life for Islam and Indian independence. As a matter of fact, the Caliphatists were so intent on gaining their independence they launched the Indian independence movement. It was the Caliphatists who actually laid the foundation for Mahatma Gandi's non-cooperation campaign.. Ali's position on the struggle was clear and poignant:

I have not come to ask for Dominion Status. I do not believe in the attainment of Dominion Status. The one thing to which I am committed is complete independence......I have a culture , polity, an outlook on life and a complete synthesis which is Islam. Where God commands I am Muslim first, a Muslim second, and a Muslim last, and nothing but a Muslim. If you ask me to enter into your Empire or into your Nation by leaving that synthesis, that polity that culture, that ethics, I will not do it....My first duty is to my maker, not to the King.... I belong to two circles of equal size, but which are not concentric. One in India, and the other the Muslim world.

He spoke the above words in London in November 1930; he died six weeks later. However he was buried in Jerusalem.

Now, that we have assessed Abdullah Yusuf Ali and Muhammad Ali's educational background and political ideology, let us by way of the given information, conclude why Elijah Muhummad showed partiality to Ali's translation of the Holy Qur'an. I do not think that Elijah Muhammad knew anything about the history of Yusuf or Ali, but I do believe that Master Farad Muhammad acquainted him with certain Surahs that could be used to awaken black people. Additionally, Dr. Alauddin Shabazz, states that Farad probably was Pakistani; therefore, he was fully aware of what Shaykh Ben Bazz declared regarding Ali's translation being the better of the two. Equally important, was the view of Ali's translation contains good footnotes that were useful in reaching black Christians that were incarcerated in the Bible, and 'emotionally chained to white people.'"

One of the Surahs that Mr. Muhammad used to reach black people, for example, was Surah (20:102) regarding the guilty blue eyes. This surah is not adjectivally clear in Yusuf's translation. Another point that could be assumed as biased on Yusuf's part is his willful omission of Lugman's Ethiopian ancestry. The Surah on Lugman is crystal clear in Ali's translation (31: 1-34). The other selected Surahs were: Surah (2: 14) Surah (27:29), Surah (2: 108), Surah (7:27), Surah (2:14), Surah (7:17). He taught using these Surahs: Surah (81: 1, 6, 7, 12), Surah (101: 1-4), Surah (45: 28, 29), Surah (15: 28), Surah (13: 32) and Surah (44: 10)

These and others were specifically chosen for the purpose of attracting black people to Islam, to the endearment of 'Messenger Muhammad,' and to extricate them from the Bible and Christianity.

NOTES

1. Robert Weisbroth, Father Divine, (Beacon Press, Boston, 1983) pp. 34-51.
2. Wardell J. Payne, editor, Directory of African American Religious Bodies, (A compendium by The Howard University School of Divinity) Howard University Press, Washington, D.C., 1991, pp. 112, 114 & 115.
3. Tony Martin, Race First, (The Majority Press, Dover, Mass, 1976) p. 69.
4. Ibid, p. 69
5. Weisbrot, pp. 74, 96 & 185.
6. Ibid, p. 192.
7. Ibid, p. 195.
8. As Sayyid Al Imaam Isa, Who Was Noble Drew Ali?, (The Original Tents of Kedar, 717 Bushwick Avenue, Brooklyn, N.Y.) pp. 4-5.
9. Drew Ali, The Holy Koran of the Moorish Science Temple of America, p.7.
10. Ibid, p. 18.
11. As Sayyid Al Imaam Isa, p.91.
12. Cyril Glasse, The Concise Encyclopedia of Islam, (Harper Collins Publishers, San Francisco, pp. 151 & 356.
13. Mustafa El-Amin, Al-Islam, Christianity and Freemasonry, (New Mind Products, Jersey City, New Jersey, 19986) p.121.
14. Ibid, p. 121.
15. Ibid, p. 122.
16. Nesta H. Webster, Secret Societies and Subversive Movements, (Christian Book Club of America, First Published in 1924) p. 37.
17. Ibid, p. 37.
18. Malise Ruthven, Islam in the World, (Oxford University Press, New York, 1984) p. 208.
19. Ibid, p. 209.
20. Ibid, p. 214.
21. Ibid, p. 215.
22. Webster, p. 44.
23. Ibid, p. 44.
24. Ibid, p. 284-285.
25. Ibid, p. 49.
26. Mustafa El-Amin, Free Masonry, Acient Egypt and The Islamic Destiny, (New Mind Productions, Jersey City New Yersey, 1988) p. 112.
27. Webster, p. 49.
28. El-Amin, pp. 114-115.
29. Teachings for the Lost-Found Nation of Islam in a Mathematical Way, Problem Number 2.
30. Ibid, Problem Number 5.
31. Ibid, Problem Number 6.

32. Dorothy Blake Fardan, <u>Message To The White Man and Woman in America Yakub and The Origins of White Supremacy</u>, (United Brothers & United Sisters Communications Systems, Hampton, Virginia, 1991) p. 132.

33. <u>Ibid</u>, p. 137.

34. E.D. Beynon, "The Voodoo Cult Among Negro Migrants in Detroit," The American Journal of Sociology, XLII (July, 1937-May, 1938)

35. Beynon, p. 895..

36. C. Eric Lincoln, <u>Black Muslims in America</u>, (Beacon Press, N. Y., 1968) p. 12.

37. <u>The New Crusader</u>, (Chicago), August 15, 1959, p. 1.

38. <u>Ibid</u>, p. 1.

39. <u>Insight, The Washington Times</u>, November 11, 1985, p. 9.

40. <u>Ibid</u>, p. 8.

41. <u>Ibid</u>, p. 8.

42. J.A. Bennett, <u>Gurdjieff: Making a New World</u>, (Harper & Row, New York, 1973) p. 26.

43. Hakim Shabazz, <u>Essays on The Life Teachings of Master W. Fard Muhammad</u>, (United Brothers and Sisters Communications System, Hampton Virginia, 1990) p. 24.

44. <u>Ibid</u>, p. 24-25.

45. <u>Ibid</u>, p. 25.

46. Tynetta Muhammad, <u>The Comer By Night</u>, (Chicago, Honorable Elijah Muhammad Educational Foundation, 1986) p. 81.

47. Shabazz, p. 27.

48. Amos N. Wilson, <u>The Developmental Psychology of The Black Child</u>, (U.B. & U.S. Communications System, Hampton, Virginia, 1978)

49. <u>Ibid</u>, p. 213.

50. Kersey Graves, <u>The World's Sixteen Crucified Saviours or Christianity before Christ</u>, (The Cleage Group, Inc., republished in 1991) pp. 209-210.

51. <u>Ibid</u>, p. 211.

52. <u>Ibid</u>, p. 216.

53. <u>Moorish Guide</u> Vol. I No. 6, Friday, October 5, 1928.

54. Elijah Muhammad, <u>The Fall of America</u>, (Published by Muhammad's Temple of Islam No. 2, Chicago, Illinois, 1973) p. 26 (Republished by U.B. & U.S. Communications Systems, Hampton, Virginia)

55. <u>Ibid</u>, p. 27

56. Excerpt taken from <u>An ABC of Color</u>, p. 90.

57. St. Clair Drake, <u>Black Folk Here and There Vol. I</u>, (University of California, Los Angeles, 1987) pp. 62-63.

58. The basic story is told in Genesis 9, 10. The curse is specifically laid on Canaan in Genesis 9:25.

59. St. Clair Drake, <u>Black Folk Here and There Vol. II</u>, (University of California, Los Angeles, 1990) p. 17.

60. Ibid, p. 17.
61. Ibid, p. 17. Notes are discussed in the text at length.
62. Ibid, p. 17.
63. Ibid, p. 4-5. Notes are discussed in the text at length.
64. Ibid, p. 151.
65. Ibid, p. 152.
66. Ibid, p. 152.
67. Honorable Elijah Muhammad, The Theology of Time, (U.B. & U.S. Communications System, Hampton, Virginia, 1992) p. 107.
68. Salam Magazine, July 196, Vol. I No. I, (Salaam Publishing Company, 1939 Ridge Avenue, Philadelphia 21, Pennsylvania) p.33.
69. C.C. Goen, Broken Churches, Broken Nation: Denominational Schisms and the Coming of the Civil War, (Macon, Georgia, 1985) p. 117.
70. David Brion Davis, The Problem of Slavery in Western Culture, (Ithaca, New York, 1966) p. VII.
71. Ephesians 6:5-8. Also see Colossians 3:22-25.
72. George M. Frederickson, White Supremacy: A Comparative Study in American and South African History, (Oxford University, N, Y., 1981) p. 10.
73. Jupiter Hammon, America's First Negro Poet: The Complete Works of Jupiter Hammon, (Port Washington, New York, 1970) pp. 59-65.
74. Jupiter Hammon, An Address to the Negroes in the State of New York, (Carroll and Patterson, New York) p. 11.
75. Marion Wilson starling, The Slave Narrative, (Howard University Press, Washington, D.C., 1988) p. 57.
76. Hammon, p. 14.
77. John W. Blassingame, Editor, Slave Testimony, (Louisiana State University Press, Baton Rouge, 1977) p. 131.
78. William Loren Katz, Breaking The Chains African American Slave Resistance (Atheneum, New York, 1990) p. 69.
79. Ibid, p. 74.
80. Ibid, p. 74.
81. Ibid, p. 74.
82. Inquiry Magazine Vol. 3 No. 5, "The Translator Novelist," by P. Clark, p. 58.
83. Ibid, p. 57.
84. Ibid, p. 57.
85. Inquiry Magazine, Vol. 3 No. 5, May 1986 "The Monarchist and the Khilafatist," by M.A. Sharif, pp. 54-55.
86. Ibid, p. 55.
87. Ibid, p. 55.
88. Ibid, p. 55-56.
89. Ibid, p. 56.
90. Ibid, p. 56.

161

THE BLACK CHRISTIAN
AND BLACK NATIONALIST
TRADITION OF THE NATION OF ISLAM

Some of the most effective appeals of the Nation of Islam that were, for the most part, inherited from the black Christian and nationalist tradition was the emphasis on ethics, economic uplift, self-help, land, education and patriarchal leadership. Furthermore, the Nation of Islam under the leadership of Master Farad Muhammad and the Honorable Elijah Muhammad inherited the political nationalism of Marcus Garvey, the religio-nationalism of Noble Drew Ali, and Booker T. Washingtonian economics.

Elijah Muhammad's southern Christian background prepared him for his patriarchal leadership role. One must bear in mind that support for a patriarchal family can be found in Biblical scripture. Thus after slavery, the black church laid the foundation for this so-called holy sanction by way of supporting black family life with the father in a position of authority. These freedmen with their families worked land, purchased land whenever they could, worked as un-skilled, semi-skilled or skilled artisans. Elijah Muhammad strongly encouraged patriarchal authoritativeness within the black family, and the land question for him was one central aspect to his leadership. The issue of land was a manifestation of his Christian and rural southern experiences and because black people were so harshly mistreated in the major land controlled by white people. His clarion call for separation was regularly outlined in the *Muhammad Speaks* the

162

Nation's news organ. Point number four of "What the Muslims Want" stated this:

We want our people in America whose parents or
grandparents from slaves, to be allowed to establish
a separate state or territory of their own -- either on
this continent or elsewhere. We believe that our
former slave masters are obligated to provide such
land and that the area must be fertile and minerally rich.

Another part of this request explains why separation was necessary:

Since we cannot get along with them in peace and
equality after giving them 400 years of our sweat
and blood and receiving in return some of the worst
treatment human beings have ever experienced, we
believe our contributions to this land and the
suffering forced upon us by white America, justifies
our demand for complete separation in a state
of our own.

It is important to remember that his father and grandfather were both Baptist preachers, and he was an astute biblical student. Another important point to remember is that Farad Muhammad, the founder of the Nation did not advocate land acquisition, economic uplift, or patriarchal assertiveness. These were Elijah's preachments put into effect after he succeeded Farad.

Interestingly, the Weberian Protestant ethic and capitalist spirit manifested itself in the economic ethic and the conservative value system of these newly found converts to Elijahian Islam. This point bespeaks validity when one understands that Max Weber posited a dialectical relationship, that was, for the most part, synthesized between religious ideas and socio-economic conditions. Religious ideas can have unintentional economic consequences by affecting the spirit, the attitude, the behavior, and the mentality of its believers. Careful scrutiny of Weber reveals that he did not argue that Calvinistic Protestantism created the spirit or the motivational attitudes which affected the lifestyles of its adherents.

To add to these points, it is imperative to cite a study by Gerhard Lenski who contended that there is an interaction between religion

163

and economic behavior. His study was based on his observation of black Protestants in Detroit in the late 1950's:

> *One of the more surprising findings in this area concerned the Negro Protestant churches and their relationship to the spirit of capitalism. We had expected that involvement in the Negro Protestant churches would be negatively linked with commitment to the spirit of capitalism, since the group as a whole lacked a strong commitment. However, such was not the case. Those who were active in the Negro Protestant churches were more likely to express views consonant with this spirit than were marginal members......*
> *Active Negro Protestant church goers actually show a higher frequency of responses compatible with a capitalist orientation than active Catholics.*

Weber proved that Protestantism preceded capitalism. he pointed out that the official teachings of religion are not necessarily those that influence people's behavior. It is people's reaction to those religious teachings, or the need religion fulfills for them that are important.

The Weberian idea manifested itself in the New World assimilationists process of the former slaves. Gradually, these assimilated New World blacks began to drift away from their old ideas about the land and communal property. The transformation occurred everywhere slavery existed in the America's. Even on isolated plantations of the Caribbean where Africans continued to arrive in large numbers, slaves began to express their newly adopted concept of individuality through various kinds of business ventures that were sanctioned by their masters. Sidney Mintz, noted anthropologist, writes this, 'Torn from societies that had not yet entered into the capitalistic world, and thrust into settings that were profoundly capitalistic in character on the one hand, yet rooted in the need for

The Journal for the Scientific Study of Religion No. 21 (June 1982) "From Black Muslims to Bilalian: The Evolution of a Movement," by Lawrence Mamiya.

Quote is taken from *The Religious Factor: A Sociological Study of Religion's Impact on Politics, Economics and Family Life* by Gerhard Lenski, p. 122.

unfree labor on the other the slaves saw liquid capital not only as a means to secure freedom, but also as a means to attach their paternity--and hence, their identity as persons--to something even their masters would have to respect".

In essence, the slaves realized that in the harsh and exploitative new environment they found that survival depended not so much on communal harmony as on individual creativity.

Historically, it is important to understand that a large number of black families even after Emancipation were dependent upon the black mother as they had been during slavery. However, the new economic conditions which resulted from Emancipation placed some black men in a position of authority in family relations. Granted the black woman was still, for the most part, the economic mainstay of the family. Nevertheless, those black men who had assimilated the Protestant ethic, sentiments, and ideas of their former slave masters undertook the task to buy and cultivate land. One point that I consider more than relevant is the fact that these men--who, in most instances, were preachers--accepted this new economic position by re-Africanizing and consolidating it through the black church. Immediately after slavery, the black churches through an African and American synthesis created an ethos of upward mobility; a philosophy of morality which instilled sexual discipline, and an established number of beneficial societies that provided assistance in time of sickness or death. *The Free African Societies* for example were also connected to the black church and they too acted as agents for relief and social and economic betterment.

The black church was an important agency of social control. The black churches undertook as organizations to censure unconventional and immoral sex behavior and to punish by expulsion sexual offenders and those who violated the newly accepted western concept of monogamous mores.

Similarly, the Nation of Islam under the leadership of Elijah Muhammad initiated a program which was usually executed by his male ministers that enjoined the body of his followers to care for the sick and to provide for the needy among them. Sexual promiscuity was not tolerated, for that type of behavior was considered a slave practice. Those Muslims who were found guilty of such infractions were banished or excommunicated from the ranks for a period of redemption.

The rank and file members of the Nation of Islam were required to give a portion of their earnings to charity. This money went for sustaining the temple, buying or renting other buildings for temple services, and for establishing and maintaining an educational program. Part of this money also went toward Elijah Muhammad and his ministers livelihood. Committees were set up for the purpose of assisting those believers who had financial difficulties, and the general membership would always try to find employment for those who were unemployed. In many instances, these unemployed individuals as well as newly released prisoners would find employment and support from within the ranks of Muslim businessmen. This practice continued until the infrastructural disruption of the Nation in 1975.

There was a three year economic program which was in actuality a savings bank. This program was designed, I think, for two reasons, 1. to use the money for various business ventures and 2. to demonstrate to the general African American population the significance of a self help philosophy.

The self help philosophy espoused by the Christian freedmen and the Christian nationalists was rooted, obviously, in survival. It, therefore, stands reasonable why W.E.B. DuBois was correct when he concluded that any study of "economic cooperation among Negroes must begin with the church group." Black church members founded and established churches during slavery and after the Civil War. They pooled their resources to buy land to erect church buildings.

Black churches and their allied institutions like the Mutual aid societies, the quasi-religious fraternal lodges, and the benevolent and burial associations, which often met in the churches, helped to create the first major black financial institutions: the black life insurance companies and the black-owned banks. In addition, the growth of black education in the South before and after the Civil War owed much to black churches. Black church members established schools in the basement of the church, and what is most important to note is that some of these schools later became famous black colleges. There is Morehouse College in Atlanta, for example, trace its origin to a school founded after 1866 in the basement of the Springfield Baptist Church in Augusta, Georgia. Spellman College was started in Friendship Baptist church in Atlanta, and Tuskegee Institute began as a school which met in the basement of Butler Chapel A.M.E. Zion Church in Tuskegee, Alabama. However, under Booker T. Washington's influence the school became a Baptist institution. Drs. C. Eric Lincoln and Lawrence H. Mamiya discuss another important feature of the Black Church:

Black families and churches are (were) involved in a dynamic interactive partnership. Families constituted the building blocks for black churches and the churches through their preaching and teaching, symbols, belief system, morality, and rituals provided a unity--a glue that welded families and the community to each other. After the Civil War, for example, black churches legitimated the informal marital relationships of many former slaves and sought to restore the role of black males as husbands and providers.

In addition, as the only communal institutions in most urban and rural black communities, black churches were intimately involved in the complex network of black extended families.

It is historically clear that the Nation of Islam and other radical black religio-cultural groups carried on the black church tradition of self help and maintained the ideology of the African Christian nationalists. For it was the initial program of the black church that assumed the task of helping black people internalize the Protestant ethic of capitalism.

After Emancipation, the black church was responsible for economic co-operation among blacks. The church also provided the incentive for the pooling of the economic resources of blacks for mutual assistance and insurance companies. It was solely through the black church that the initiative on the part of blacks in securing an education and building educational institutions was manifested . The black church therefore became the most effective agency of social control among blacks in their isolated social world. The pattern of control and organization of the black church has been authoritarian, with a strong man (patriarch) in a dominant position.2

Essien-Udom in his classic work, Black Nationalism (1962) argued that the black church gave black people pride in success, grassroots participation in a national movement, independence from white control and a physical center for social life in the black community. Gayraud S. Wilmore went further and argued that the black church was primarily responsible for the politico-theological foundation of Pan-Africanism and black nationalism.

The patriarchal leadership of the Honorable Elijah Muhammad was predicated on discipline, self love, self-respect, and mutual cooperation. His program of discipline was especially appealing to those who had migrated north and found themselves in abysmal poverty. He painstakingly presented his message to potential converts who were rejected outcasts in a racist, classicist, capitalist society. These individuals were victims of racism, classism and internalized black inferiority. Elijah utilized his impeccable knowledge of the Bible as well as his rural christian and southern experiences to minister to his converts a philosophy that expressed their social psychological and economic needs. Elijah's program of salvation was just another manifestation of an Africanized form of religion acting as a medium through which the black community institutionalized its efforts at black liberation.3

The African or black church tradition left a legacy of radical patriarchs. Many of these individuals espoused a black religio-nationalist philosophy, and some of them had cautious or high regard for Islam and its liberational theology. Churchmen such as Edward Wilmot Blyden who openly respected and acknowledged the theological purity of Islam, but who strongly held to Christianity believing that a racist-free Islamic effront to Christianity would abate the racism of white Christianity. He was a staunch Pan-Africanist or black nationalist that saw African redemption lying in the hands of Africans in the United States and later on the African continent. 4 There was Reverend Alexander Crummell, a missionary, who attempted to transplant Anglo-African ideals to Africa. He considered the uplift of black people as being dependent upon character building and the elevation of moral life. He saw this as the duty of an educated elite. This was in actuality the genesis of the American Negro Academy and the consequent emergence of the idea for the Talented Tenth. He proclaimed that, for the incoming missionaries, Islam was a force to be reckoned with among certain tribes in Africa--especially in Liberia. Crummell later in his life expressed the philosophy of self-help, solidarity, and unconditional race pride. He also accepted and advocated an increasing emphasis on economic and social development in preference to politics and social agitation.

Bishop Henry McNeal Turner was a militant bishop of the African Methodist Episcopal Church. He was the most consistent advocate of black liberation and black Christian redemption.5

He assisted in implanting the spirit of revolutionary Christianity into the independent churches of Africa that were struggling against colonialism and racism. He, like Edward Wilmot Blyden and Alexander Crummell, found much that was praiseworthy and provocative about Islam. He was extremely impressed by the lack of race prejudice in Islam. He often commented favorably on the significance of monotheism in Islam, the lack of alcohol consumption of Muslims, and their dignified apparel. Contrarily, he believed, as Blyden and Crummell, that Africans would remain Muslims only until Black Christians were ready to convert them.

Isalm was a force to Crummell only because it posed a continued challenge to the advent of Christianity among the African masses.

It is, after briefly looking at the visions of these Christian nationalists, befitting to cite Dr. C. Eric Lincoln's analysis of Islam and Christianity within the African psychic:

The memory of Islam, however tenuous was never completely lost to the slave experience. On the other hand, the new Black Americans surged out of the white church and became proud members of their own Black churches -- the African Methodist Episcopal Church, the Colored Methodist Episcopal Church, the National Baptist Convention, Inc. Through all this, there was a memory of Islam, but its time was not yet. It was to be another half-century before that memory would find vocal and physical expression among the hapless Blacks struggling for a negotiable identity and searching for their cultural roots.

"The American Muslim Mission in the Context of American Social History." by Eric Lincoln (Excerpted from _The Muslim Community in North America_ Edited by Earle H. Waugh, Baha Abu-Laban and Regula R. Qureshi)The University of Alberta Press, Canada, 1983)

The A.M.E. Church consistently supported Turner in his efforts to establish kinship ties to Africa. Turner, with the exception of Garvey had the most profound impact on Africa and its Christian ministers. 6 Next, there was Reverend Henry Highland Garnet who was considered by some scholars to have been the most uncompromising, radical church leader of his day. He advocated violence against slavery and referred to Christian preachers such as Nat Turner, Denmark Vesey, and Gabriel Prosser as "noble men". He was among the first to realize that the freedmen might not secure a substantial measure of freedom unless they received some land. He labored diligently on behalf of the freedmen through a number of freedmen's aid societies. His Pan--Africanism or nationalism was so encompassing that he repatriated to Africa and remained until his death. 7 There was of course, David Walker who also advocated resistance to slavery through his Appeal and who fused his African nationalism with conservatism. He did not support emigration to Africa.

As a matter of fact he hoped that black and white Americans would eventually discover some common ground upon which to stand. 8

Needless to say, that there were other Christian Prophets of justice to use historian, David Swift's term, but I am primarily concerned with those who had a direct link to the black nationalist legacy that was bequeathed to Elijah Muhammad.

Both the A.M.E. and the A.M.E. Zion churches were strongly opposed to slavery and were conceptually connected to Africa. The A.M.E. Zion church became known as the freedom church because it was the spiritual citadel for some abolitionists. Frederick Douglas, Harriett Tubman, Bishop Richard Allen, Reverend Absalom Jones two founders of the A.M.E.tradition; Sojourner Truth and others were motivated by the liberation tradition of the black church.

The black Christian nationalists believed that the technological aspects of civilization were destined to develop collaterally with Protestantism. No other form of Christianity could contribute to the civilization of Africa, felt Alexander Crummell, and he attributed the shortcomings of the Haitian revolution to the influences of Roman Catholicism. Both David Walker and Martin Delaney were anti-Catholic. Although they represented a people who were victims of Anglo-Protestant culture, they chose to direct their disdain toward Roman Catholicism.9 Protestant Christianity was an essential element of Anglo-African nationalism. Thus Protestantism was an aspect of African redemption.10

The Universal Negro Improvement Association (UNIA) and African Communities League flourished in the United States from 1909 to 1927; it was the largest mass-based protest or nationalist movement in Black American history. No other twentieth-century protest movement achieved the wide appeal enjoyed by the UNIA. It had many times the membership of the NAACP. On the other hand, two organizations whose memberships may have approximated that of the UNIA were Father Divine's Peace Mission and Elijah Muhammad's Nation of Islam both were directly influenced by the Garvey movement and the Christian nationalist movement. One of the major appeals of the UNIA was its religio-political nationalism.

Religion within the Garvey movement included a coherent and compelling way of looking at God, man, and the world, and at the meaning of the black experience in Africa and America.11 Churchmen held a number of posts in the UNIA, and what is equally important is that the one hundred and five men who signed the "Declaration of Rights of the Negro Peoples of the World" (which was adopted in August 1920 as the "Magna Charta" of the Black Race) at least twenty-one-or one in every five were men with church authority. Additionally, at least one of the seventeen women who were signatories to the document, Emily Christmas Kinch, had been a missionary in West Africa. 12 There is no doubt that the clergy played a monumental role in enabling Marcus Garvey to formulate the religious; and theological foundations for the UNIA. As a consequence, Garvey enjoined his theologians to work rewriting theology from a black perspective, or "through the spectacles of Ethiopia."

Garvey was astute enough to realize the importance of the black churches to the eventual success or failure of his movement; therefore, he devoted sufficient attention to issues of religious diplomacy and theological concerns.13

Professor Wilson Moses makes an interesting point about Garvey when he states that Garveyism was orthodox black nationalism modified by an urban environment, an industrial rhetoric, and a militant spirit that was the heritage of the Great War. The evangelic movement that Garvey headed embodied elements of both the new and old black nationalism. Garvey, like his predecessor nationalists focused on the civilization and Christianization of Africa as the first steps toward universal emancipation of the African race. Like the early black Christian nationalists, Garvey insisted upon such ideas as "Divine Apportionment of Earth," "Purity of Race," and "God as a War Lord."

There is no doubt that Garveyism was philosophically and religiously connected to Blyden, Crummell, Turner and Garnet. In Fact, E. Franklin Frazier considered the movement to be more of a religious than a political experience. Religion within the Garvey movement included a coherent and structured way of looking at God, man, and the world and at the meaning of the black experience in Africa and America. Moreover, the essence of Garveyism or Garveyite religion comprised the movement's ability to relate a black nationalist ethos to a general conception of the racist American religious, political, and social setting.14 As I pointed out earlier, Garvey also preached the importance of a Black Messiah and the need for the visualization of a Black God. In essence, Garvey Africanized Christianity and Muhammad Africanized Islam. Thus the ideological basis of the Nation of Islam is very much akin to Black Christian and Garveyite Nationalism.

A number of ministers--Baptists, Methodists and leaders of smaller denominations or sects were active Garveyites. Despite the fact that Garvey was oftentimes critical of most preachers as so-called leaders of the race, he did not present an assault on the black religious establishment. From 1921 to 1923, the *Negro World* reported that more than two hundred and fifty clergyman from across the United States were active Garvey advocates. Approximately one third were Baptists, one fifth each was African Methodist Episcopal and African Orthodox, and one twelfth were African Methodist Episcopal Zion. These Garveyite ministers tried desperately to point the black community toward an introspective analysis, to its own strengths and resources and toward an outward appreciation for "darker" races and, above all, to "Mother Africa."

As Randall K. Burkett points out, there were some noted black Christian patriarchs who contributed to the Africanized theological advancement of Garveyism. Bishop George Alexander McGuire, William Henry Ferris and John Edward Bruce (Bruce Grit) were just three who developed a black theology for political Garveyism.

172

Interestingly, Bruce, while steadfastly remaining an Africanized Christian, argued that Islam might in fact be preferred to Christianity in Africa. *"The Mohammedan missionary has the Christian missionary at a great disadvantage in Africa and the Orient in this, that the former not only preaches but practices the doctrine of the Fatherhood of God, and the brotherhood of man and he does not consider the black man his inferior before God. The Christian missionary, on the other hand is sometimes obsessed with the idea that he is a superman and is disposed to look down upon the benighted heathen with a pitying contempt."*15

Farad Muhammad and Elijah Muhammad were both master eclecticians and tacticians who clearly understood--especially Elijah--the inner dimensions of the Black community. It was Elijah who extended the black Christian and Garveyite philosophy into a realm of tangible pragmatism. The Weberian idea was an adjunct to his program of self help and economic uplift. The program of the Honorable Elijah Muhammad strongly emphasized the development of an independent black economy from farm land to retail outlets. The strict code of moral consciousness encouraged thrift and saving. His followers ascetic lifestyle forbade frivolous behavior like dancing, sporting events, and buying fancy clothes and cars. Mr. Muhammad even enforced rigorous eating habits; Muslims were to eat one meal a day or one meal every other day. No Muslim was expected to be obese. In fact, believers were weighed upon entering the temple. If a believer was considered overweight; he or she had to pay five cents for each extra pound. It was this no nonsense ethic which gave Muslims a reputation for their honesty, hard work and discipline.

Weber postulated that it was the internalization of the "Puritan ethic" in the lifestyle of Protestants that unintentionally created the conditions for the breakthrough to a capitalistic economy from a feudal one. In the case of the Nation of Islam, the internalization of the black Puritan ethic combined with the philosophy of black religio-nationalism made that movement interestingly unique in African American history.

Not since the black Christian patriarchs and the reign of Marcus Garvey had a single black man been able to generate so much unquestioning obedience as the patriarchal leader of the Black Muslim movement. Elijah Muhammad utilized his power with the aplomb of the field marshal commanding an army. He demanded loyalty based on his promise of salvation from white oppression through submission

173

to an all powerful, black God. But Muhammad was perceptive enough to know that before his program could be effectuated he had to restore the black man to his position of husband, father and provider.

Slavery robbed the black man of his masculinity and his sense of responsibility; moreover, the black woman was more assertive and creative, since slave conditions and her vulnerability compelled her to be. After slavery, in many instances, her job opportunities and educational level were greater than that of the black man. Elijah Muhammad emphatically taught that the black man had to be adequately equipped to create an income for his family, so that he could get more respect and hence respect himself. *The Muhammad Speaks*, the movement's publication often carried pictures of a typical Muslim family with the father sitting at the head of the dinner table.

The Muslim father was greatly respected and obeyed by his wife and children. Muhammad insisted that the Muslim father must fulfill his role as family provider and protector. Thus it was the duty of the civilized black man to restore dignity and honor to his woman and to himself. Discipline, self-worth and self-respect were paramount under Elijah's leadership, and discipline was especially magnetically appealing to those who lived in abject poverty and whose lives lacked structure.

Elijah Muhammad fiercely exhorted his followers to engage in self-reliance and mutual responsibility. He argued the following:

Put your brains to thinking for self;
your feet to walking in the direction of self;
your hands to working for self and your
       children. . . .
Stop begging for what others have and
help yourself to some of this good earth
...We must go for ourselves....This calls for
the unity of us all to accomplish it . 16

The obsession that Muhammad had for land was reflective of the black church tradition he inherited as a former rural worker, and as an observer of the "back to Africa" philosophy of Marcus Garvey. Muhammad never relented in his quest-real or contrived-for a national territory or "some of this earth that we can call our own". He stated the following at most of his major addresses:

174

"We are not asking for land that originally
belonged to the European people. We are
asking for the earth that originally belonged
to us. We are going to have a place on this planet
that we can call our own. I don't care where it is:
whether we are going to have an isle in the Pacific
or Atlantic oceans, or if we have to pick up a piece
of this country, we are going to have some land. We
are not going to wait for Moses to come and tell us
that he will lead us to any promised land and we are
going to take some of it."

The slogan that "necessity is the mother of invention" was
certainly crystallized by the slaves and their determination to be cast
into the arena of human viability. The origins of the black self-help
philosophy were grounded in the attempts of slaves to help each other
survive the emotional and psychological horror of the plantation
system. Therefore, Elijah Muhammad's economic ethos of uplift for the
black masses that included thrift, moral values, industry and
discipline was an extension of slave and black church survival
techniques that had an Islamic label. 17

Moreover, Elijah Muhammad's repetitive preachments were very
akin to the early black preachers and Christian nationalists. These
ministers of liberation preached the common sense message of saving
for a rainy day, learning to read and write, getting an education,
supporting the family, finding a job and raising the children to be
respectable and responsible. 18 Muhammad recognized as did his
predecessors the inextricable relationship between economic self-
reliance, self-sufficiency and socio-political power realities.

*"What's the use of being free," if you don't own
land enough to be buried in?"*
Quote from a former slave.

Muhammad also understood the rudiment principles of the capitalist
economic system by the establishment of a network of small businesses
and farm enterprises. 19

The economic program of the Honorable Elijah Muhammad constantly exhorted the black man to do something for himself and to stop
being so dependent on white America to provide him with sustenance.
Muhammad put forth his message first through the Pittsburgh

175

Courier and the Los Angeles Herald Dispatch newspaper. Then, in 1960, he launched his own newspaper called *Mr. Muhammad Speaks*. His program for uplift of impoverished black people laid the foundation for what was to become the most controversial and yet successful black religio-natonalist movement to date.

Elijah Muhammad always stressed the importance and the necessity for individual and race identity. His contention was that as long as Black people lacked knowledge of themselves and their own kind they could not possibly liberate themselves mentally or psychologically from a European value system. Hence their economic dependence on caucasians would remain intact. Muhammad also inherited the black press tradition from the liberation minded slave and black churchmen such as Reverend Samuel E. Cornish along with John Russwurm started the Freedmen's Journal and later it was called *Rights of All* (1827 & 1837). Frederick Douglas started the North Star , Martin R. Delaney started his Mystery and, of course, there was David Walker's Appeal . From a religio- nationalist standpoint, Duse Muhammad Ali produced his *African Times and Orient Review*, Garvey produced the *Negro World* and Noble Drew Ali started the *Moorist Guide*. *Mr. Muhammad Speaks* which later became Muhammad Speaks maintained its inherited black Christian and nationalist tradition.

Let me briefly discuss what psychologists have to say about the issue of self-awareness and its importance for psychic survival in an environment that denigrates and even negates African humanity. From a psychological standpoint, the term self refers to those aspects of experience which the individual considers to be "I" and "me." Gradually, through experience with the world, what is self comes to be distinguished by the person from everything that is experienced as "not me." Dialectically, the self implies that in every person there is the feeling of being a functioning unit organized to achieve certain

The question, "Who is the original man?" was a provocative question whose answer was grounded in a psychological baptism of blackness. The answer: The original man is the Asiatic Blackman, the Maker, the Owner, the Cream of the Planet Earth, and the God of the Universe was no more than an immersion in black self-concept and self-esteem.

goals in life. On the other hand this organization or patterning is made up of a variety of different personal tendencies and characteristics. Self and self-concept, while standing for the cohesiveness of the individual are also multifaceted.20 Thus, a person's self-concept is an interconnected collection of the various ideas, images and feelings that he or she holds about the self.

Equally important to note is that an individuals self-image, or self-concept, is considered one of the most basic and crucial components of his personality. It deeply affects not only his relationship to himself but his relations to other people and the world at large. A realistic and even a marginally realistic self-evaluation and a full measure of self-acceptance and self-esteem are regarded as foundations of healthy (mental) adjustment. A consistent, well-organized conception of one's ideals, goals, abilities and possibilities gives one a sense of personal identity and a point of departure for developing, through self-appreciation and self-love, a lifestyle that is conducive to the betterment of the world.

Elijah Muhammad fully knew and understood these elements of human psychology; in fact, I maintain that he was a master untrained psychologist. He fused myth with historical fact to agitate and arouse the consciousness of black people. His favorite themes were Knowledge of Self, Love of Self, Understanding of Self, and Getting Knowledge to benefit Self. For Elijah Muhammad, the black man and black people were supreme entities created by their black God, Allah. Knowing thyself and thy God eliminated self-hatred.

He made the following statements that were designed to mentally resurrect the black man and woman.

Love yourself and your kind. Let us
refrain from doing evil to each other,
and let us love each other as brothers,
as we are the same flesh and blood. In
this way, you and I will not have any trouble
in uniting. It is a fool who does not love him-
self and his people. Your black skin is the best,
and never try changing its color. Stay away from
intermixture with your slave-masters' children.
Love yourself and your kind.21

It must be pointed out that his message to the black woman was that she was the "Mother of Civilization and Queen of the Planet Earth." She was the first nurse. She was the first teacher; therefore, she deserved protection, respect and love. He argued that the black man would never be recognized until he safeguarded his woman.

The Nation of Islam, despite its denunciations of white people, were very much in conformity with the Black Christian Ethic of acquiring middle-class social and moral ideals. Besides the ban on tobacco, narcotics, and alcohol, members of the Nation were admonished against gambling, fornication, marital infidelity, dancing, idleness, lying, stealing, excessive sleeping, discourtesy- -especially toward the elderly and women- - loud talking and loud laughter. Additionally, personal cleanliness, the meticulous care of their homes, frugality, sobriety, diligent, honest work, and obedience and respect for European American civil authority. These were moral obligations that coincided with Islam and Christianity.

Interestingly, another aspect of middle-class ideals was the Muslim attire. Elijah Muhammad forbade his followers to wear any type of African garment because of its probable tribal identification. Muslims were enjoined to wear a business suit, tie, usually a bow tie, white shirt, and conservative style shoes. Muhammad stressed the importance of keeping the shoes polished, the shirt starched and pressed and the suit clean and pressed at all times.

The Nation of Islam and the Black Church were both conscientious practitioners of the Puritan Ethic, the exception was the fact that the Nation's operative principle was Islam. There is no irony or paradox in the above principles; the goal of middle-class ascension demands rejection of a so-called lower-class subculture. Thus, the emulation of certain positive standards of the dominant society is acceptable.

The point that Elijah Muhammad's major target was not the white man as much, but the slave-mentality of so-called lower-class blacks requires repeated emphasis.

The Puritan or Protestant Ethic was dialectical in that it was the front from which flowed both the preternatural horrors of imperialism in Africa and the beneficent incentives to chastity, honesty, frugality and hard work in rural Southern black communities and churches.

Muhammad, throughout his leadership reign, spoke vociferously to the begging slave-mentality of black people. His language, especially during the last year of his life, was more piercing for black people than for caucasians:

"It actually hurts me to hear our people-and some of them are leaders-- over there begging the white man to give them something. Give you nothing--you can give yourself something now. Whatever he has given to you and me that is freedom to go for self, you don't need anything else

since you claim the earth and he's living on it and it belongs to you and you are not intelligent and smart enough to dig out of it right under your feet... so don't blame him for digging up that which you were not digging up."

Muhammad's unyielding mission and message was to eradicate the slave-mentality that had robbed black people of their self-respect, and kept them dependent on European Americans. The pursuit of economic independence contained in the program and message of Muhammad was not geared toward self-indulgence, but for the good of the entire black community. The Black Muslims like the Black Christians were like the Puritans of old; their objectives and their vision was metaphysical or transcendental, but their methods and operations were creative, resourceful, mundane, and economically beneficial. Max Weber demonstrated quite clearly that ideas may generate consequences that create the very conditions which negate ideas. By working in behalf of the glory of God, rationalizing, and exercising every effort to cultivate God's laws for God's majesty, the Puritan, black or white, invariably resorts to secular forces in industry, commerce, and science that oftentimes undermines the ecclesiastical values he initially sought to propagate.

The Nation of Islam's eschatology, despite its familiarity with other millennium, or what one could very easily call today fundamentalist sects, did not serve as a battle plan directing its members or blacks in general toward a cataclysmic confrontation with European Americans. The essence of their eschatology was deeply rooted in the moral and spiritual reform of the Black race.

The Muslims were not uncontrollably possessed by their ecstatic or militant impulses; on the contrary, they responded to the message of Muhammad by transforming themselves from an "underclass" status into practitioners of law-abiding, middle-class Puritan ethic, from have-nots into haves interested in securing and sustaining a viable material and psychological existence for themselves and for the black community.

They accomplished their material and moral goals by employing particular psychological constructs that directly and tangibly addressed those blacks who were severely deprived of a moral and financial base. They devised a concomitant system of controls, responsibilities, and identifications, through the use of the Holy Quran, the affirmation of history, the rhetorical rejection of white society vis-a-vis the confirmation of Black or African supremacy that allowed for the attainment of those goals.

The consequences of the movements utilization of these various disparate concepts can be measured by the dramatic decline of despair and destructive psychology. Thus the Nation of Islam's durability and strength was based primarily on its social and psychological treatment of the black dispossessed. Religion in the strict sense of the word was not the most important feature or attraction of the Nation. Those blacks who gravitated toward the movement did so because they needed something to belong to, they needed and yearned for dignity and self-respect, and for a means to material, moral, spiritual and emotional regeneration.

I believe it was the failure of the Honorable Elijah Muhammad to totally divorce himself from the American Protestant ethic that put him in ideological hot water with the black nationalists.

The teachings of The Honorable Elijah Muhammad had a great impact on Christian preachers & their flocks. The above photo documents one of the, reportedly, secret meetings Dr. Martin Luther Jr. had with Mr Muhammad.

Michael Parenti, "The Black Muslims from Revolution to Institution," 1964 Social Research 31: pp. 175 - 194.

BLACK MUSLIM AND WHITE CHRISTIAN ESCHATOLOGY

W. D. Farrad and Elijah Muhammad encouraged their followers to purchase radios and to read the books of Joseph Rutherford, the successor of Charles Russell, the original leader of the Jehovah's Witnesses. Rutherford claimed to be the spokesman for the Creator, and he considered himself a prophet. Rutherford radically transformed Russell's teachings. It is the teachings of Rutherford and the Nation of Islam (Farrad and Muhammad) that attracted attention during the 1930's that in turn provoked serious concern and interest.

It is true that Rutherford was one of the few white men that gained a favorable position with Elijah Muhammad. It is equally true that both groups or movements held similar attitudes toward the dominant American society, and both groups berated the Christian church. Muhammad and Russell forbade their followers from joining and fighting in the U. S. military, voting, saluting the U. S. flag, and standing for the national anthem.

Professor William A. Maesen, sociologist, wrote a revealing paper that presents a comparative analysis of the eschatalogical teachings of both movements. According to Maesen, the doctrinal similarities are too close to be accidental. He surmises, with some evidence, that a direct influence upon the Nation of Islam was possible, but gravitated more toward the supposition that the similarities had more to do with their common position as sects and their isolation culture. One argument that Maesen raises against direct influence was the issue of the flag salute. He points out that the Nation of Islam took this position in the early 1930's and that the Jehovah's Witnesses did not formalize its position until 1934 or 1935.

Additionally, Maesen shows that the Nation did not adopt any of the Witnesses teachings after the 1930's. For example, the Black Muslims did not oppose blood transfusions; a position the Witnesses took during the 1940's. Also, the Black Muslims condemned the Witnesses activities in parts of Africa.

1914: DEFERRED END TIME

The Jehovah's Witnesses believed that the end of the "Gentile times" must come in 1914 when the righteous rule was to begin. They believed they were to be taken to heaven in 1914, but discovered "expansion work" must take place first.

181

The Nation of Islam taught that the rule of the white man was over in 1914, but because the so-called Negroes lacked the knowledge of self Allah delayed the final judgment. The year 1914, was always stressed in Muslim meetings.

BATTLE OF ARMAGEDDON

The Witnesses anticipated the Battle of Armageddon which was supposed to end Satan's rule.

The Nation also anticipated the Battle of Armageddon, which for them, meant the termination of "white rule." In fact, a blackboard always stood at the front of their temple asking the question who will survive the war of Armageddon?

144,000

In 1935, the Witnesses preached that only 144,000 elect people would survive the Battle of Armageddon, of whom only about 50,000 would still be on earth, consequently eliminating resurrection.

The Nation of Islam taught that 144,000 black people would survive the Battle of Armageddon since Allah permitted his Messenger, Elijah Muhammad to reconvert only that number to Islam. (Rev. 14:1)

I should point out that Elijah Muhammad exhorted his followers to go after the "dead," all black people, but the prevailing belief was only 144,000 would be saved. Biblical scripture was also used to highlight the 144,000 elect of God.

MILLENNIUM NOW BEGINNING

Witnesses taught that the millennium, the last 1,000 years after the 6,000 from the creation of Adam, began in the 1870's. Maesen shows that the date for the end of the 6,000 year period was changed later to 1975.

The Nation of Islam taught that the world was in its last 1,000 years after the 6,000 following the grafting of the "devil" (white man), but the millennium began in 1914.

NON-IMMORTALITY OF SOULS

The Witnesses taught that there was no such event as immortality of the soul nor external hellfire. Instead, the dead are asleep until the judgment.

The Nation of Islam rejected the belief in the immortality of the soul, but they did believe that heaven and hell were states of conditions on earth. For Muhammad, hell was racist oppression in America; thus since the white man was responsible for hell in black people's lives, that demonstrated that he was the devil. The best way to extricate from hell was to accept the teachings of Elijah Muhammad and his God, Allah in the person of Master Farrad Muhammad.

As a result of accepting this doctrine, and acquiring sufficient racial awareness heaven in the form of peace of mind, money, good homelife, and friendship in all walks of life would be realistically bestowed on the convert.

Furthermore, the Muslims did not believe in a physical life after death (resurrection). For them the only resurrection that existed was mental resurrection. Ponder Elijah's teachings on the subject:

There is no such thing as dying and coming
up out of the earth, meeting your friends
and meeting those who died before you. I
say, get out of such slavery teachings. It
keeps you blind, deaf and dumb to reality.
Get out of it, for if you depend on such,
you will not believe in yourself. When you
are dead, you are DEAD. (Message To The
Blackman in America, p. 168)

Point number five on the back page of *Muhammad Speaks* under the heading "What the Muslims Believe", Muhammad states the following:

We believe in the resurrection of the dead--not in
physical resurrection--but in mental resurrection. We believe
that the so-called Negroes are most in need of mental resurrection;
therefore, they will be resurrected first.

He said in his book *Supreme Wisdom Volume Two*:

Remember the Old Testament (The Torah)
doesn't teach of a resurrection of the
dead, according to Job (Chapter 7:9)
wherein it says, "He that goeth down to the
grave shall come up no more."

Muhammad went on to say:

Surely, there is a resurrection of the dead. It is one of the principles of
Islam, but not the physically dead in the grave yards.

183

Muhammad's main objective thrust was against the teachings of Christianity and its heaven and hell concept. It must be known that Elijah Muhammad did not reject the Quranic injunctions pertaining to heaven and hell: Holy Quran (translated by Yusuf Ali) 8:133, 57:21, 39:74, 56:10, 57:64 refer to heaven: Holy Quran: 104:6-9, 7:38, 50:22, 18:99-101 refer to hell.

The Holy Quran: 6:122, 3:132, 27:80-83 clearly speaks of the mentally dead. Also, Holy Quran: 16:97, 21:95, and 39:42 gives credence to Muhammad's position on the subject.

While the research evidence shows a striking similarity between both groups and no doubt a direct influence upon the Black Muslims, it is more than safe to say that Elijah Muhammad's impeccable knowledge of the Bible also aided him in his scriptural predictions. His knowledge of the Quran was scant and he quoted from it only when certain scriptures were relevant to his teachings.

Essien-Udom (Black Nationalism, 1962) mentioned the Biblical (Old Testament) influence on the Nation of Islam Eschatology. The Old Testament scriptures and images helped to convey the sense of social estrangement of urban lower-class blacks. The Old Testament scriptures also helped to rejuvenate the hope and the spirit of this negated group. God had come to chastise the wicked and to deliver his true chosen people (the Black Nation) for the ushering in the new world.

White Christian eschatology was prevalent throughout the late middle ages. Europe's destitute population repeatedly gravitated toward anticipatory visions of a promised paradise. Groups such as the Adamittes, Flagelants, Joachimites, Anabaptists and the Millennialists were among those who awaited a catacylsmic battle between the soldiers of Christ and the hosts or forces of the Anti-

"Watchtower Influences on Black Muslim Eschatology: An Exploratory Story" by William A. Maesen, Journal for the Scientific Study of Religion Volume 9 Number 4 Winter 1970

hough the assertion persisted in the early years, no documented
vidence has been produced to prove The Honorable Elijah
Iuhammad was ever a member of the UNIA & Marcus Garvey. But
he similarity to Garvey's and Booker T. Washington's Economic
rograms are evident.

Christ. After Armageddon, God's chosen few would live eternally on earth in a state of perfection, totally removed from sin, suffering, oppression, and death. Historian, Norman Cohn, records in his book *The Pursuit of the Millennium* (Harper Brothers, New York, 1961, 2nd ed., pp. 307-319) that these various groups with their eschatological and chiliastic enthusiasm had (have) contemporary counterparts.

Similarly, Father Ronald Knox suggested that the "enthusiastic" apocalyptic sects of the fifteenth to seventeenth centuries bear a striking resemblance to present day religious sects or movements. Knox states that the "enthusiast" is the person who, impatient with the compromises of institutional theology sets out to restore the "primitive purity" and zeal of the early Church. He hopes not to only qualify for heaven but to also excel, and to live in Christ's perfection every day on earth. "Extenuate, accommodate, interpret and the enthusiast will part company with you." He burns with a passion for redemption.

There is a striking resemblance in the manner that the Black Muslims embodied the combined conceptual attributes of Cohn's millenarian and Knox's enthusiast. As we shall see, the Black Muslim eschatology had a familiar structure with the milenarian ideology discussed above.

For the Black Muslims, the ideological similarity is structured like this: First, there was the state of original African purity; the original man and God were Black. Afterwards came the Fall from Grace, the original people were enslaved and negated by the Devil incarnate, the white man, who is a corrupt replica of man called into being by Yakub, the evil black scientist, universally in opposition to Allah's peace and justice. Then came the messenger of Allah who saw through the devil's tricks and snares, and who armed with the truth of Islam from Allah, purged the devil's corruption from the original people. The Messenger was chosen as written by Allah to lead the chosen original black race from its state of mental, moral, and spiritual bondage to an anticipated paradise, a separate Muslim nation. The original black people will be restored to their original state, but the devil will meet his destruction at Armageddon, when the wrath of Allah is delivered upon him.

Eric Hoffer, Longshoreman and Self-taught Philosopher, wrote an interesting work, *The True Believer* (Mentor Books, New York, 1958 p.

Ronald Knox, Enthusiasm, A Chapter in the History of Religion (Galaxy, New York 1961, p. 2).

9) in which he inattentively concurs with Knox and Cohn by maintaining that millenarian or "true believer" movements have indeed existed for centuries and that however variegated in doctrine, myth, and aspiration, they share certain essential ideological features which give them a family resemblance.

The True Believer, according to Hoffer, can be found playing the main role in all mass movements, and who is noted for his or her uncompromising devotion to an all-consuming cause, his need to submerge himself or herself in some authoritarian body which promises collective salvation, and his or her intense--usually his-- personal frustrations and hate-filled opposition to a "devil", be it capitalism, communism, facism, Jews, foreigners or people of African descent.

The Honorable Elijah Muhammad wrote: "We believe we are the people of God's choice, as it has been written that God would choose the rejected and the despised. We can find no other persons fitting this description in these last days more than the so-called Negroes in America."

ELIJAH AND BOOKER

"The Black economy idea is neither myth nor concrete reality. The ingredients exist and merely await skillfull organizational use and application. America is a nation that abounds in many myths and many realities. The greatest myth is that of democratic capitalism, which has never existed for all groups in America. Minorities could not have won their way into different levels of economic status if it were not through some form of group economics--either capitalistic or cooperative." Harold Cruse *The Crisis of the Negro Intellectual*, p. 315.

The above quote from Professor Cruse revolves around his conten- tion that the Nation of Islam's economic program was nothing but a form of Booker T. Washington's economic nationalism. Washington and Muhammad urged their followers to engage in economic self-help, black unity, law abiding practices, vocational training, stay-out-of-the civil rights struggle agitation, and separate from the white man and his form of morality.22 According to Cruse, Booker T. practiced moderate accomodationism and moderate economic nationalism as opposed to Elijah Muhammad who preached and practiced moderate

Muhammad Speaks (September 27, 1965.)

economic nationalism and militant separatism.23   Booker T. and Elijah understood in their own way the dynamics of an emerging capitalist economy and the need to play the capitalist game according to the rules and politics of the market place.

Therefore, realistically speaking, it seems that Elijah and Booker were both advocates and practitioners of moderate separatism and pragmatic economic nationalism.   Booker T. preached a form of economic nationalism that laid the ideological foundation for Marcus Garvey and Elijah Muhammad. Booker T. was often fond of saying, "Up, You Mighty Race, You can accomplish what you will." That motto was utilized by Marcus Garvey who was motivated by Booker T., leadership wise; he was also encouraged programatically by Booker T. Washington.

The Booker T. motto was also an inspiration for Elijah Muhammad; he placed it inside the Muslim Temples and schools--The Universities of Islam. Muhammad not only founded independent schools dedicated to qualifying black people for their future--as did Booker T.-- but he also established a five point economic security plan that coincided with Booker T. Washington's emphasis on racial pride and self-help through economic cooperation:

1.   Recognize the necessity for unity and group operation.
2.   Pool your resources, physical as well as financially.
3.   Stop wanton criticism of everything that is black
      owned and black operated.
4.   Keep in mind--jealousy destroys from within.
5.   Observe the operations of the white man. He is
      successful. He makes no excuses for his failures. He
      works hard in a collective manner. You do the
      same. 24

What was extremely important in Booker T. Washington's outlook was his ideological emphasis on agriculture and rural land ownership. He constantly deprecated migration to the North where, he said, the Negro was at his worst and insisted that Negroes should stay on the farmlands of the South. Since all peoples who had gained wealth and recognition had come up from the soil, agriculture should be the chief occupation of Negroes, who should be encouraged to own and cultivate the soil. While he called Negroes the best labor for Southern farms, he optimistically looked forward to an independent yeomanry respected in their communities.

Booker T.'s other major thrust of interest was education. At the heart of Tuskegee's objectives was Booker T.'s belief that education should be made common, that is related to the needs of the masses. He strove to make the meager funds available for Black education perform the noble task of elevating the race. Each Tuskegee graduate was to become a missionary spreading enlightenment to the black masses trapped in ignorance and poverty.

Similar to Washington, Elijah Muhammad's purpose of education was designed to develop the minds of Black people and to advance the spirit and the welfare of Black people. Central to his education theme was the idea that the kind of education for which blacks should strive was agricultural industry. Muhammad felt Black people should learn how to do best all the things that would enable them to function at the best level as agriculturists. He believed that buying land and becoming a stable property owner in the community was the surest way to becoming a self-determining people and to compel Caucasians to see blacks as respectable hard-working people who were an asset to the community. Muhammad sought through his teachings of agricultural and vocational education to help black people to live a decent life.

Muhammad was concerned about education of a pragmatic and utilitarian nature, and he wholeheartedly accepted the "Protestant Ethic" of self-help and hard work. He often said, "He will be helped who helps himself." It was only in this manner could the Black man and woman achieve security of any kind.

Booker T. constantly criticized black people for seeking higher education rather than practical education, for their loss of places in the skilled trades, for the lack of morality and economic virtues, and for the tendency toward agitation and complaint. This position was dualistic in its nature. Because in its positive aspect, he placed emphasis on the study of history. He urged blacks to be proud of their history and their great men. Race pride, race solidarity, and love of race emanated from a people who honored its heroes. He showed considerable pride in the all-black communities; in fact, he supported the black state in Oklahoma and the black town of Mound Bayou, Mississipppi. He strongly and sometimes covertly--espoused a high degree of racial solidarity, and especially economic nationalism. He occasionally declared: "We are a nation within a nation," therefore, "in every wise and legitimate way our people must be taught to patronize racial enterprises."

Muhammad was also dualistic in his approach to education for blacks. While he urged agricultural and vocational education, he also advocated intellectual development by way of obtaining knowledge in languages, the sciences, history and religion. He frequently made these statements regarding education:

The acquiring of knowledge for our children and ourselves must not be limited to the three R's-- reading, writing and ritematic . It should instead include the history of the Black Nation, the knowledge of civilization of man and the universe and all the sciences. It will make us a greater people tomorrow.

We must instill within our people the desire to learn and then use that learning for self. We must be obsessed with getting the type of education we may use toward the elevation and benefit of our people-- when we have such people among us, we must make it possible for them to acquire this wealth which will be beneficial and useful to us. 25

The above statement attests to the fact that Muhammad's ultimate aim of education for blacks was not only the same as Booker T. Washington's, but his idea of education was to give blacks the broadest and most complete knowledge of arts, sciences, literature and history of all nations in general and the Black or African nation in particular.

For Muhammad and Washington, purposes for education were intrinsically connected to the philosophy of economic self-reliance. Self-education was utilitarian in purpose. Muhammad like Washington taught and preached a philosophy of self-education, self-reliance, and a rigid adherence to the Weberian "Protestant Ethic" of "hard work" and higher education as a path to freedom , justice and equality. The purpose of education to Muhammad and Washington was to enable black people to do something for themselves, to condition the mind and heart to think logically and to feel sympathetically towards the pain and injustices of Black people. And equally important was to strengthen the will to act in the interest of the common good.

Education, then, for both of these leaders, would be an education for Black people which would develop leadership for the race and also develop each person to his or her fullest capacity, that is, academically, vocationally, professionally, and intellectually.

Booker Washington developed a strong following among black Baptists, and Tuskegee Institute was considered an unofficial black Baptist institution. Although Washington was a political conservative, his economic unity or "Negro support of Negro business" was the only path toward economic progress and uplift for a largely rural and destitute people. The gospel of wealth that Washington preached espoused the major values for the Protestant ethic: thrift, industry and self-help. He felt that "economic accumulation" and the "cultivation of morality" were the major means of black acceptance in American society. By demonstrating their worth through frugality, hard work, and achievement, the African American's economic progress would lead to social equality and political rights. 26

Similar to Muhammad, Washington placed emphasis on racial pride and self-help through economic and moral development; contrary to Muhammad, he insisted that interracial harmony and white good will were prerequisite to black people's advancement. Washington never relented in his faith in whites, nor his love for the south.

He was known for his acceptance of financial aid from noted white capitalists such as Andrew Carnegie, and Jewish financiers such as Julius Rosenwald. His philosophy of racial solidarity was radical--considering the era---but his philosophy of interracial harmony was conciliatory.

Muhammad, on the other hand, was fierce in his denunciations of white America. White America was the collective devil, the embodiment of evil, and was destined for destruction by Allah. For Black people to seek harmonious relations with white people was to invite their doom. Why was this the case? Because, according to Mr. Muhammad, the white race was a grafted race. Grafted out of the Black race by a black scientist named Yakub, this grafting process took six hundred years to complete. As a result, this made the White race completely different from the black, brown, the red and the yellow races namely because it was the first that had no black genes (some would call it melanin today) and the first that was not muslim by nature.

Maulana Ron Karenga summed it up best when he said"*It was necessary for the Honorable Elijah Muhammad to call the white man the devil because black people considered him to be god.*"

As I mentioned earlier, Elijah Muhammad was a master psychologist who employed-after the disappearance of Farrad-the use of racial language to dismantle the theory of the white-god concept (white supremacy). He did this through the use of racial reverse psychology by stating:

The original man, Allah has declared, is non other than the Black man. The black man is the first and last, maker and owner of the universe. From him came all brown, yellow, red and black people. By using a special method of birth control law the black man was able to produce the white race. 27

Again, because the Black race and the White race were extreme opposites by nature, an ethnic or racial synthesis (social interaction) was inconceivable and impossible. Muhammad stated the following:
The time has arrived when it must be told the world over. There are millions who do not know who is the original man. Why should this question be put before the world today? Because it is the judgment between the black and white and the knowledge of the rightful owners of the earth. 28

From a psychological standpoint, the Nation of Islam and its racial epithets provided its members and many blacks a means by which they could both release and control their feelings toward a hostile white society. The verbal attacks against whites, and the muslims display of uniform strength gave blacks a sense of power and self-assuredness. Thus within the so-called black ghettos, the black Muslims hurled their imprecations, and threats, that revolved around carefully chosen Biblical scriptures, at white America, as they stood surrounded by friendly black listeners.

Despite their fierce racial rhetoric, members of the Nation of Islam were law abiding and respectful of the American constitution. In fact, newly released files of the F. B. I. clearly show that Hoover and his agents did not regard the leader of the Nation of Islam or his followers as a threat to the internal security of the United States. Considering these facts, it is my belief that the language of the Nation of Islam--especially its racial metaphors--was designed to extricate Black people from the prison of racial, economic and spiritual debasement.

On this same note, the Nation of Islam must be understood as a reaction to the white stereotypes of Black people. For centuries Black people had been told that they belonged to a sub-human race, and white America was relentless in its confirmation of this judgment.

Therefore, the Honorable Elijah Muhammad said to the white American supremacist: "you do not accept us as equals and you segregate us. Well and good, then let us separate." In separating, they psychologically reversed every tenet of the white supremacists. They rejected segregation as a process dictated by and implying white supremacy, and they rejected integration because they regarded it both as impossible and undesirable to contaminate black by association with white. God, Muhammad said was black, original man is black, the greatest contributions to civilization came from blacks, black is pure. White, on the other hand, is soiled and dirty, the whites are a "grafted" rather than an original race, they are war like and irascible. According to Muhammad, it was his mission to inform and prepare Black people (the original people of the earth) for separation and self-government by teaching them to be clean, to support themselves and to love and respect their black brothers and sisters rather than their white enemies.

The major ideological commonality that Washington and Muhammad shared was economic nationalism. Washington founded Tuskeegee and Farrad founded the University of Islam and it was maintained by Elijah and his followers. Washington, founded and headed--with Carnegie's assistance--the National negro Business League and other small business ventures. Muhammad headed--with no visible white support--a multi-million dollar empire.

Interestingly, and paradoxically, is the fact that Muhammad with his racial ideology expanded Washington's economic program to an unprecedented level. Muhammad, for example, masterminded the acquisition of a multi-million dollar nationwide business and farming complex at an astonishing rate that had trained economists and businessmen baffled. At the time, the movement's modern farming operations in Michigan, Georgia and Alabama, comprised close to 5,000 acres of land, boasted a dairy, chicken-breeding and egg-laying plants, more than 8000 head of cattle and more than 700 head of

Bishop Alexander McGuire under the directive of Marcus Garvey Africanized the Bible, Christianity and Jesus. Muhammad, on the other hand, Africanized Islam, God and civilization.

sheep, giant storage silos, a sawmill, apple orchards, a modern cannery and vast tracts of crop-producing and grazing land. He purchased the *Muhammad Speaks* building, which was named for and housed their weekly newspaper. The building provided 60,000 square feet of floor space. 29

Muhammad installed modern offices, and the latest printing facilities, which included a brand-new 70 foot, four-color offset press, and a computerized photo composing room. They purchased a U. S. Government approved meat processing plant and giant walk-in refrigerators for the storage of Muslim-grown produce and meat.

The Nation of Islam under Muhammad's reign completed a number of coast to coast self-help operations that included barbershops, a clothing factory, dry cleaning shops, clothing stores, sheep slaughtering faculties at Chicago's Stock yards, and restaurants that included the Salaam Restaurant, the best eatery on the South Side of Chicago. 30

Mr. Muhammad like Booker T. Washington taught that blacks must extract raw martials from the earth and manufacture them into something useful for themselves. This, he taught, would create jobs in production. He and Booker T. both argue that without land there is no production. Muhammad, Booker T., along with the assistance of George Washington Carver, demonstrated that from the farm comes a people's very existence for it is the farm which feeds, clothes and shelters them. 31

With regard to industrial education, the Philadelphia convention of 1831 adopted a plan "that a college be established at New Haven as soon as $29,999 are obtained, and to be on the Manual Labor System, by which in connection with scientific education they (young men of color) may also obtain a useful mechanical or agricultural progression." Conventions of this sort were common during the three decades preceding the Civil War and they clearly showed that Black people had a deep interest in trade school education. Needless to say, these conventions were never able to follow through on the above resolutions because of their inability to garner required funds for the trade school movement, there were subsequent conventions throughout the 1830's and 1840's that continued to recommend the importance of establishing trade schools. 32

The fascinating thing about history is that it does not record human affairs in an isolated manner. History presents events and personalities in a manner that is wholistic and corroborative.

What I mean by this statement is that my study for this subject amply demonstrated that Frederick Douglas was a strong supporter of the trade school movement, the trade school conventions and in 1848, he served on a committee of five who drew up a position paper that advanced the significance of trades and trade schools. Booker T. Washington not only admired Douglas, but he patterned his philosophy of agricultural and industrial education after Douglas. Washington was aware that Douglas was instrumental in establishing a trade school in Manassas, Virginia. In fact, Douglas went to Tuskegee to deliver a commencement address, saying, "When you are working with your hands they grow larger; the same is true of your heads...Seek to acquire knowledge as well as property, and in time you will have the honor of congress."

Upon careful study, one can see that Washington's advice to "cast down your bucket where you are. . . in agriculture, mechanics, in commerce, in domestic service, and in the professions," was akin to Douglass's advocacy of industrial and agricultural education. Thus the trade school movement and Frederick Douglas inspired Booker T. Washington and Booker inspired Garvey and Muhammad.

Both Booker and Elijah believed that wealth was the ultimate solution to the black man's problems in America. Elijah, of course, extended his belief to the realm of psychological, moral and, theological salvation. Booker and Elijah also encouraged their followers to study the methods of Europeans and Jews to accomplish their aim. For Washington and Douglas, the study of Jews was the best example. For Elijah, the study of the "white man" and his refusal to make excuses for his errors was paramount.

The early Christian nationalists such as Blyden, Crumwell, Garnett and Turner were collectivistic in their programmatic approaches. Washington was a proponent of Black individuality, he said, "Individually, the Negro is strong, organically he is weak." Elijah was a proponent of both individual accomplishment and unity of purpose. In other words, Elijah's collectivistic ideology transcended his advocacy of individual assertiveness. He, therefore, maintained the collectivistic ideology of the pioneer nationalists.

Another difference between Booker and Elijah was their conception of Black economic development. Booker stressed the importance of Black businessmen and tradesmen integrating themselves into the dominant marketplace of society. Therefore, Blacks buying and selling only to Blacks was repulsive to Washington and Douglas.33 Washington consistently advanced the philosophy that Black Americans must compete in the open marketplace. Muhammad's economic philosophy entailed a form of Black economic isolationism, that is, Blacks must buy, sell, and trade with Blacks first; however, he was pragmatic enough to know that whenever Euro-Americans wanted to do business with Black Muslims, work for Black Muslims, or convey some business expertise to Black Muslims it should be accepted with respect and courtesy. Interestingly, a number of Euro-Americans worked for Muhammad in various business entrprises. Furthermore, he advocated trade on an international level--his business contracts with Japan and Peru were unique examples.

Washington worked to make, in time, an easily "assimilated new Negro." He wanted to create a "new negro for a new century", a twentieth century Black Race that would be specifically suited for a new role in American life. Elijah on the other hand worked to make a new "black man ". One that would be perfectly suited to rule the world which was the Black man's destiny. Elijah was wise enough to see that civilization and environment were interacting components that shape and direct man, and man, in turn, manifests those internalized components. Thus for Muhammad, separation was the final solution and the ultimate answer to the Black man's questions and problems.

Elijah Muhammad consistently stated how much respect he had for the economic and educational program of Booker Washington.

There is no doubt that for Muhammad, unity was the essence of "Black Power" and Black success. He. Throughout his forty-four year reign, ceaselessly called for a "United Front of Black Men in America."

Unite my people, and regardless of your faiths and beliefs, form yourselves into one Nation of Brotherhood (the love and help of each other). You will see that unity will solve the greater part of your problems before you know it. 34

In essence, I believe, the commonalities between Washington and muhammad transcended their differences. What must be kept in mind is that both men reflected their social orientation and their environmental circumstances. Both men were mainfestations of their experiences based on their victimization in racist white America . Both men were advocates of the race, one was just more extreme. Again, that was based on experience. Both emphasized the uplifting of the Black masses through economic self-sufficiency and the separation of the races except for non-essential social and business contacts. Both abstained from full political participation as an instrument of black advancement. And, both lacked confidence in direct political action and therefore, advocated social separation as a means of escaping the antagonism of the dominant white society. They felt strongly that no amount of political agitation would succeed unless American Blacks could improve their economical and educational status.

They ascended from the ranks of the unskilled Black workers and they understood their plight better than the Black middle-class intellectuals who often mocked their names and programs.

They tried and succeeded at making the best of conditions as they found them, not as those conditions might exist in the future.

Washington's program of self-help and practical educational training had more of an impact on African nationalists than Muhammad's fierce program of moral and racial redemption. Of course it is safe to conclude that during Washinton's reign, Africa was still under rigid colonial exploitation. Plus his philosophy was more polite and acceptable from a social and religious standpoint. It must be pointed out, however, that Muhammad did attract interest from some curious African nationalists and some immigrant radical Muslims to his movement. In this regard, Malcolm X was the catalytic agent through his militant Black Muslim behavior and his revolutionary rhetoric which indicted white world domination.

Muhammad and Washington believed in and promoted African solidarity. They both criticized and condemned white cruelty and oppression--for Washington it was in the Congo, South Africa, and the United States. Muhammad condemned white rule world wide. They were motivated less by their Africanistic redemptive policies than by their need to demonstrate the impracticality of American Black emigration to a colonized Africa as a solution to racial problems in the United States. Both leaders held a deep personal interest in Africa and the plight of Africans. Their attitude toward African nationalists was favorable; however, their support for African repatriation was pragmatically discouraged.

Industrial education among blacks had a long history before Douglas, Washington, and Muhammad emerged as national leaders. A generation before Washington founded Tuskegee, black people advocated, usually through church leadership, industrial education for very much the same reasons that he did, except that they did not phrase their ideas in terms of accommodation.

Washington, on the other hand, believed that black Americans should undertake the task of going to Africa as teachers and technical assistants. He argued that Black American colleges should train able African students. As a result of this proposal, Tuskegee made a significant contribution to African educational development. In fact, Washington's philosophy influenced African intellectual leaders and colonial officials. Needless to say colonial administrations embraced the Tuskegee model of Black achievement.

Moreover, the example provided by Tuskegee Institute was followed by numerous educational institutions established in Africa, including the Zulu Christian Industrial School of Natal, the South African Native College at Fort Hare, Cape of Good Hope, the Lumbwa Industrial Mission of Kenya, the Mittel and Gebilfen Schule of German East Africa (Formerly Tanganyika) and Achimota College in the Gold Coast (Ghana). Muahmmad's influence in Africa is difficult to measure; one thing is for certain and that is that Malcolm X and Muhammad Ali gave African nationalists a renewed hope during the post-colonial era. Equally important, Muhammad's racial nationalism which declared that Africa was the birthplace of man and thus making the Black man the original man was the extent of his contribution. Muhammad was more of a staunch supporter of "Africans at home." However, during the last ten years of his mission, he directed Africans all over the world toward each other. This was verbally and pictorially presented in the <u>Muhammad Speaks</u>.

Marcus Garvey who considered himself as more closely allied to the philosophy of Washington--the success ethic, racial improvement and practical education--was the only other nationalist that had a wide impact on African affairs. Even though Garvey's economic program did not equal Muhammad's, he nonetheless established a base for African redemption based on Booker T. Washington's examples. Indeed, Washington left a unique legacy for Garvey and Muhammad.

Garvey read *Up From Slavery* and was inspired by Booker's tenacity and business acumen. He believed, like Booker T. and later Elijah, that economics was essential. Successful political action for these men could only be founded on an independent economic base. Garvey and Elijah both excused Washington's accomodationist policies by attributing his actions to skillfull pragmatics for that time.

ELIJAH MUHAMMAD AND THE BLACK PROFESSIONAL

Although the Black Muslim movement was thought to attract mostly the poor and uneducated, it held up as its ideal a pattern that was distinctly a middle-class ethos. As indicated earlier, this pattern followed some of the economic and black consciousness tenets of Booker T. Washington. It was ironic and even paradoxical that the Protestant Ethic of saving and industry was practiced so conscientiously by Blacks that had abandoned Protestant Christianity. Still the Honorable Elijah Muhammad's economic program for the deliverance and salvation of the African American was in essence, nothing but pure American Calvinism: "Pool your resources, education, and qualifications for independence." "Make your neighborhood a decent place to live." Build your own homes, schools, hospitals, and factories." "Stop buying expensive cars, fine clothes, and shoes before being able to live in a fine home". "Build an economic system among yourselves." These were the exhortations of Muhammad for the duration of his leadership.

Many illustrations in the _Muhammad Speaks_ , the Nation of Islam's publication, placed emphasis on the theme of middle-class respectability. There were usually pictures showing a couple with children in a well furnished living or dining room.

There were, on a number of occasions, advertisements in Muhammad Speaks encouraging the purchase of suburban houses, the importance of home ownership and suburban living. The paper almost always portrayed the horror of ghetto-living.

The Muslims avoided public places of entrtainment, but did much of their socializing or entertaining in the wholesome atmosphere of their homes. The appeal of middle-class ideals was often placed within the context of obligation. The masses were obligated to achieve respectability and status. Moreover, certain professional members in the Nation were highlighted as paragons of educational and financial success. The best and most practical way of achieving this success was by adhering to the program of "Messenger Muhammad" which stressed thrift and cooperative responsibility.

The Nation of Islam, like all mass based movements, attracted those from the lower socio-economic classes. However, history shows us that, Nationalist groups such as the Garvey movement and the Nation of Islam have swayed some black intellectuals and college students in their organizational direction. There is no doubt that the Nation comprised an overwhelming number of illiterate black migrants. But Muhammad's strong emphasis on economic self-uplift tended to transform his followers from one economic status to another. In other words the Nation of Islam epitomized "upward mobility."

To my knowledge, research pertaining to the number of black professionals who were in the Nation during the early periods (1930's, 40's and 50's) is non existent; however, we can safely surmise based on some scant documentation that there were a small number that had obtained either a college degree or a vocational diploma. On the other hand, for the majority of the masses, today sociologists would call them members of the underclass, the uphill climb away from social, educational, and economic debasement was based on their tenacity to excel. Therefore, Elijah Muhammad, through his religio-nationalist ideology, advanced his followers from a lower-class status to a upper-lower class status. In other words people who once had a very meager education, whose lives and family ties were stormy, and who lacked concrete life-style formation were motivated to transform the status of their lives.

A number of Black Muslims attended trade or vocational school to study barbering, brick masonry, carpentry, welding, auto mechanics and shoe repair. Some, I might add, that went to prison for draft-evasion, studied various types of trades while incarcerated. Upon completion of these courses, they pooled their resources and opened up small businesses in their respective areas of study. Others worked for various union or non-union factories. The few Muslims that established their own businesses also hired, whenever possible, other unemployed Muslims.

The women, for the most part, worked as domestics and they assisted with various Nation of Islam duties. They were the backbone of the Nation during the period that the men chose prison over fighting in the U. S. military. It must be noted that a small percentage---again there is no substantial documentation--of these women also went to trade schools and studied courses such as sewing, typing and general secretarial skills. These sisters, as they were called, were responsible for the well-being of children and the sick; they were responsible for the financial stability of the temple, and they assisted greatly in administering educational instructions. It was these sisters and some brothers who actually maintained and implemented the program of Elijah Muhammad during the harshest times.

Many of these sisters and Black women in general were the main-stay of the family. Their work as domestics, in some instances,

200

provided them with some type of provisions which allowed them to have some extra money. The employer might provide them with carfare, meals and "toting privileges", that is, they were allowed to take left-over food home. But these women were resourceful and creative, they supplemented their incomes by taking in lodgers, doing hair, making clothes, and selling home-cooked meals. Whatever the occupation, make no mistake about it, these women contributed greatly to the alleviation of impoverishment in the Black community.

World War I and World War II opened up some unskilled and semi-skilled job opportunities for the Black migrant. The best places to measure this employment pattern is in Chicago where a large percentage of Black migrants settled, Philadelphia, Detroit, New York, and New Jersey. Despite the heinous practice of Northern racism, most of these migrants presented themselves as exemplary workers.

Elijah Muhammad constantly urged his followers to give a good hard days work, to be on time, and to be responsible. The Black Muslims vigorously applied themselves to an abject situation, and through a sense of amelioration overcame many obstacles that were endemic to urbanization. As I indicated earlier, because the Muslims were known for their work ethic, they usually obtained jobs faster than other blacks.

Again, the Black Muslims pooled their resources from these jobs; they set-up small businesses, and even purchased buldings for temple meetings. If a building was in need of repair, the brothers united and refurbished the entire structure. It was this kind of activity, along with Muhammad's economic program, that gradually enticed the black middle-class to take another look at the Black Muslim movement.

To reiterate, Black nationalist movements tend to appeal to a certain number of black professionals for whatever the reason(s). I surmise that those black professionals who were unable to contend with racism were apt to seek an emotional and psychological release within a group setting that acted as a mechanism for internal conflict resolution.

Prior to the death of Malcolm X, a number of university and college students emotionally gravitated toward the teachings of Elijah Muahmmad. In fact, I maintain that Malcolm was able to attract three disparate elements into the nation: 1. the ex-convicts, 2. the urbanized street radical, and 3. the radicalized university and college student. Malcolm's brash demeanor, his intellectual bravado, and his rhetorical appeal impelled students who had become frustrated with the non-violence message of Dr. King to assert themselves in a way that intimidated white America.

The Nation of Islam had done a better job of rehabilitating the black urban poor than all the official social, penal and religious agencies assigned to that task. Many black and white sociologists, psychologists and penologists acknowledged that the "Black Muslims", as they were called, had done to exemplify black pride and dignity, and to foster group unity, than most of the more reputable middle-class organizations.

Elijah Muhammad was a very wise tactician. He knew that in order to build the economic empire that he envisioned he would need black professional assistance. Thus, his appointing Malcolm as his national spokesman, and his granting Malcolm permission to go on college campuses fulfilled two purposes; first, he was carrying out his mission to reach as many of the 'mentally dead so-called Negroes" as possible. Second, he was showing the black middle-class that his teachings could produce individuals as intellectually competent as they. Proof of this contention is contained in the fact that more than a dozen educated ministers spoke on college campuses for Muhammad. Some were Minister Pasha esq. from Ohio, Asley X, a U. S. diplomat who spoke three or four languages, and Minister Majied from Boston, who had a masters degree. The media catapulted Malcolm because he was the most visible.

Whenever a black professional accepted the teachings of Muhammad he or she was inevitably placed in a position of influential authority. The reason for this explains itself. For examples, Louis X Walcot popularly known as Louis Farrakhan was an accomplished musician and former English major became the National Representative for Elijah Muhammad after the death of Malcolm X. Lonnie X Cross, who became Lonnie Shabazz, now known as Abdel Alim Shabazz is a noted doctor of mathematics. He quickly became a minister at Temple No. 4 in Washington, D. C. Lucius X who was affectionately called Minister Lucius was an elder in the Seventh Day Adventist Church, a 33 degree mason, and a Bible scholar; he too upon acceptance of the Muslim doctrine, became a minister and was placed at Temple No. 4 before Lonnie Shabazz. There was Minister James Shabazz, he later became Sheikh James Shabazz, who was not only a minister, but an untrained educator in the University of Islam. There was Leo P X McCallum now called Abdul Salaam; who was an important emissary for the Nation and he provided a number of other services. He was and is a professional dentist. Then, of course, there was John Ali, a former FBI employee, who became the National Secretary. A Christian

202

minister from Powhatan, Virginia brought his entire congregation into the Nation. He was later known as Minister David X. Needless to say, there were other black professionals that taught various courses in the Universities of Islam, who were members of the rank and file, and who held administrative positions.

I would be remiss by not mentioning some of the early professional sisters in the Nation. There was Bayyinah Sharrief who attended the University of Khartoum in Sudan. She contributed weekly articles to the _Muhammad Speaks_ and also acted as an educator and emissary for the Nation. Portia Pasha, received a degree from the University Sorbonne in France, she was an educator and captain of the Muslim Girls Training sector of Temple No. 4.

Again, there is no widely disseminated information on the approximate number of black professionals who entered into the Nation during its first forty-plus years. One thing is certain and that is that the most visible black middle-class arrived in the later 1960's and early 1970's.

The early 1970's was the apex of Muhammad's appeal to the black middle-class. Interestingly his racial-nationalism surrendered to a more pragmatic economic platform. His denunciations of white America were toned down to suit this pragmatic purpose.

Other Christian ministers, jazz musicians, professional boxers and intellectuals such as Dr. Boyce E. Jenkins embraced either the theological or the economic program of Muhammad. In some cases, it was both.

Minister Louis Farrakhan was speaking on a number of college and university campuses at that time, and he also gave in-depth lectures at West Point to black cadets. He spoke to black police officers; some converted and formed black policemen's self-help organizations. As a result of Farrakhan's articulatory skills, musical background, and religious astuteness, a number of entertainers accepted the teachings of Elijah Muhammad, or contributed money to his cause. For example, the late Sammy Davis Jr. contributed money, Mahalia Jackson, noted gospel singer, gave donations and openly declared her respect for the program of the Nation. Rock singer, Joe Tex, who became Yusuf Azziz, became a minister for Elijah Muhammad and went on a national speaking tour. Members of the Delfonics singing group accepted the teachings of the Nation, as well as members of Kool and the Gang, another singing group. Other noted musicians that accepted the teachings of Muhammad were jazz artists such as James Moody, Sonny Still, Adam D. Rice, and members of the rock group, the Five Stairsteps. Otis Redding and Jesse Belvin were either members of the

Nation, or their open advocacy gave the impression that they were members.

After a brief hiatus following the death of Malcolm X, the Nation of Islam catapulted on the national and international scene. Several Arab states, including Libya's Muhamar Qaddafi, either loaned or gave Mr. Muhammad millions of dollars for his future projects. He was also given wide respect in Africa, parts of the Carribbean, Arabia, Turkey and Egypt, and in various parts of the United States. Former Mayor, Richard Daly, once an adversary of Muhammad bestowed respect on Muhammad by openly declaring that his office and the City of Chicago recognize Muhammad as a positive force in that city. There was an Elijah Muhammad Day accompanied with the key to the city.

American Indians accepted Muhammad's teachings; furthermore, there were some Hispanics (namely Puerto Ricans) who joined the Nation through the Bronx, New York Temple.

What will be surprising to many is the fact that some European Americans either verbally acknowledged Muhammad or tried to become a member of the Nation of Islam. I am compelled to say that those European Americans who endorsed Muhammad were obviously not ideologically or psychologically Euro-Centered, but they were intellectually, and emotionally 'Righteousness-Centered." Two unique examples are Seifullah-Ali-Shabazz from Clifton, New Jersey who is a dedicated Muslim and an unswerving believer in Elijah Muhammad, and Dr. Dorothy Blake Fardan, noted scholar and Muslima, has not only written a book Message to the White Man and Woman In America which extolls the teachings of Elijah Muhammad, and she has always acknowledged the quality of his leadership.

From 1969 to 1974, the Nation of Islam reigned supreme as a unique alternative organization for disgruntled Black Americans, people of color, and people with a revolutionary spirit.

Beginning around 1969, a year after the grand opening of the Salaam Restaurant and Your Supermarket, Mr. Muhammad enumerated his future objectives. Ads appeared in the Muhammad Speaks on a regular basis requesting the assistance of qualified teachers, technicians, nurses, language specialists, scientists, agriculturalists, machinists. . . . There was also a regular request encouraging his followers to "qualify" themselves by way of studying math, science, languages, world history, and Islamic culture. These delineated overtures in addition to the acquisition of a black bank in Chicago and other properties prompted the black middle class to reassess the program not so much the religio-nationalist aspects of Elijah Muhammad, but his economic consequences for black

Americans. Let me interject here and say that I believe that black people who followed Muhammad did so for two main reasons: 1. the early followers accepted him for the religious-nationalist message considering the popularity of that ideology at the time, and 2. the, what I call late followers, people who accepted his message for its potential, also many of them felt proud to identify with a movement that challenged White America on Black America's terms.

Mr. Muhammad's major overture to black professionals occurred in 1960 at the Savior's Day Convention. At the time, he cajoled, ridiculed, intimidated and even politely pleaded with them to unite under his leadership with their various skills for the good of the total Black Nation. This was his appeal:

Let's unit into a great nation, Get behind me you professional people. Back me up. . . . Why do you tremble when I ask you to join me? Join up with me and you won't have to open your mouth. I'll do all the talking and take all the chances. Just don't throw stones at me. If I had one million Negroes behind me today the other nineteen million in the United States would be free tomorrow. . . .
With your diplomas you are ready to rob your own people just like the white man.

Immediately, after this appeal, some black businessmen and educators either joined the Nation, or worked in behalf of the economic advancement of the movement. The <u>Muhammad Speaks</u> carried black business ads on a regular basis. Plus, the Nation's Afro-Asian Bazaars (today's black expo) always welcomed and promoted black businessmen.

Initially, the black professional looked at the Nation of Islam with jaundiced eyes. The Nation, to them, represented nothing more than a group of lower class cult members. As a consequence, they ignored the Nation and did not see a need to take the movement seriously. After all, the black professional had to maintain his psuedo status of white respectability. Thus by ignoring or willfully denying the existence of the Nation the black professional's social and intellectual credibility retained its so-called maturity. For to know something about an organization that spewed out such anti-white and anti-American venom, meant that the black professional had taken off his badge of status.

With the exception of the small number of black professionals that accepted the teachings of Elijah Muhammad, the black politicians were among the first to openly acknowledge the redeeming message of

Muhammad. This relationship lasted until the death of Muhammad in 1975. Hulan Jack of New York, Adam Clayton Powell of Harlem, Richard Hatcher of Indiana, Carl Stokes of Ohio, Kenneth Gibson of Newark were just some of the black politicians at different times that extended respect to the Honorable Elijah Muhammad. One could very easily surmise that this homage was predicated on political interests, but one must remember that the Muslims at that time were not registered voters, nor did they advocate voting in a traditional manner. The Honorable Elijah Muhammad felt that a Muslim politician was what Black America needed. However, he recognized Adam Clayton Powell as a courageous politician and went on to say "We must give good black politicians the total backing of our population."35 Muhammad believed that traditional politics was the white man's sophisticated game of thievery. Therefore, I think these black politicians recognized Muhammad because of their black constituents, the possibility of Black Muslim voting strength, political verbal support or because the mood of the era impelled them to do so.

Let me conclude by reiterating that among the black professionals, Muhammad's call for black unity and economic uplift was not totally devoid of appeal. The unabated racism that the black professionals experienced increased their race-consciousness, and for some, made them candidates for Elijah's message. It was through Malcolm X, and Louis Farrakhan that some of these professionals such as tradesmen and small businessmen concluded that they should join or support Muhammad's program or perish. Muhammad argued persuasively that the "white man would never treat the black man with justice," so

State Senator James. L. Watson (D) of the 21st District that encompassed Central Harlem, New York introduced a bill on February 4, 1963 in the senate which provided equality of religious freedom and rights to all faiths, including the followers of the Honorable Elijah Muhammad, in New York state's penal and correctional institutions.

MUHAMMAD SPEAKS, Vol. 2 No. 16 , April 29, 1963

therefore, the black man must "join unto his own kind and do something for self." Black businessmen fully comprehended the realistic profundity of these statements because racism and integration had virtually destroyed their black consumer base. Muhammad's plea that only race pride and a determination to forge a united front could offset the white man's subterfuge of integration which was nothing but an alternative plan to keep the black man in his place.

Malcolm and Farrakhan articulated this position so well that the black professional envisioned a new economic and social beginning that challenged the white man and his racist perception of them.

Moreover, the idea or attitude of some of the black middle class, which was, in part, emotionally based, indicated that if white America did not let them be a part of their society and enjoy the fruits thereof then they would join Elijah Muhammad and the Black Muslims. Those who did not fulfill those childish threats adopted certain aspects of the Black Muslim movement and thereby established various types of grass roots organizations. The Black Panther Party is a unique case-in-point. The format of the Panther's newspaper, for example, was patterned after the Muhammad Speaks and members of the party used confrontational rhetoric that was similar to the Black Muslim ministers--especially Malcolm X.

There is no doubt that the Black Muslims or Nation of Islam, to a certain extent, transformed the ideological structure of the black middle class to become more agitational and less tolerant. Furthermore, the Nation of Islam impelled the black middle class to review their historical and cultural connection to Africa and their social, political, and historical link to the American black masses.

NOTES

1. Sidney W. Mintz, <u>Caribbean Transformation</u> (Chicago, Publishing Company, 1974) p. 155.
2. E. Franklin Frazier, <u>The Negro Church in America</u> (Schocken Books, New York, 1963) pp. 33-34.
3. C. Eric Lincoln, <u>Race Religion and the Continuing American</u> Dilemma (Hill and Wang, New York, 1984) p. 164.
4. Gayraud S. Wilmore, <u>Black Religion and Radicalism</u> (Second Edition, Orbis Books, Maryknoll, New York, 1991) pp. 116-117.
5. Wilson Jermiah Moses, <u>The Golden Age of Black Nationalism, 1850-1925</u> (Oxford University Press, New York, 1978) pp. 66-76.
6. Wilmore, pp. 122 & 132.
7. Sterling Stuckey, <u>Slave Culture: Nationalist Theory and The Foundations of Black America</u> (Oxford University Press, New York, 1987)
8. <u>Ibid</u>, pp. 123, 128-129.
9. Moses, p. 47.
10. <u>Ibid</u>, p. 48.
11. Randall K. Burkett, <u>Black Redemption Churchmen Speak for the Garvey Movement</u>, (Temple University Press, Philadelphia, 1978) pp. 6 & 9.
12. <u>Ibid</u>, p. 9.
13. <u>Ibid</u>, p. 10.
14. Tony Martin, <u>Race First</u> (Greenwood Press, Westport, Connecticut, 1976) pp. 69-71.
15. Excerpts are taken from a lecture by John E. Bruce which was delivered to the Boston Division UNIA. September 9, 1923.
16. "Mr. Muhammad Speaks" <u>Pittsburgh Courier</u>, August 9, 1958.
17. C. Eric Lincoln and Lawrence Mamiya, <u>The Black Church in the African American Experience</u> (Duke University Press, Durham, 1990) p. 243.
18. <u>Ibid</u>, p. 243.

19. E. Curtis Alexander, <u>Elijah Muhammad on African American Education</u> (ECA Associates, New York, 1981) p. 51.

20. Adelbert H. Jenkins, <u>The Psychology of the Afro-American</u> (Pergamon Press, New York, 1982) p. 28.

21. Elijah Muhammad, <u>Message To The Black Man In America</u> (Muhammad Mosque of Islam No. 2, Chicago, 1965) p. 33.

22. Harold Cruse, <u>Rebellion or Revolution</u> (William Morrow and Company, Inc. New York, 1968) p. 211.

23. <u>Ibid</u>, p. 211.

24. Muhammad, p. 174.

25. <u>Ibid</u> p. 41.

26. Lincoln and Mamiya, p. 247.

27. Muhammad, p. 53.

28. <u>Ibid</u>, p. 53.

29. Hans J. Massaquoi "Elijah Muhammad: Prophet and Architect of the separate Nation of Islam", <u>Ebony</u> Magazine, August 1970, pp. 80-81.

30. <u>Ibid</u>, p. 81.

31. Muhammad, p. 173.

32. Moses, p. 96.

33. <u>Ibid</u>, p. 97.

34. Muhammad, Elijah, <u>Supreme Wisdom Volume</u> two (Temple of Islam Inc., Brookland, New York) p. 84.

35. Elijah Muhammad, <u>Message To The Blackman In America</u> (Muhammad Mosque of Islam No. 2, Chicago, Illinois, 1965) p. 173

ELIJAH MUHAMMAD'S LAST SERMON

Some casual Nation of Islam observers mistakenly believe Elijah Muhammad had reached an ideological impasse. They reason that Muhammad's lack of formal education, the repetitiveness of his nationalist teachings, and his unswerving loyalty to Master Farad Muhammad were/are the major factors for their conclusion.

Paradoxically, as far back as 1964, Mr. Muhammad exemplified what could be termed today as a conservative or accomodationist posture with regard to his leadership goals. I maintain that Muhammad was more conservative in his programmatic teachings than most people realize. Clearly, his last sermon which was delivered February 26, 1974 reflects, to a great extent, that he was directing the Nation of Islam toward practical involvement in the larger society. Mr. Muhammad never discontinued his plea for a separate territory; however, there was a considerable shift in emphasis over the years, especially in his last speech:

"What must be done?" Get up and let's go and do something! We're trying to do something with whatever the white folks will let us have. We're trying to do something with it to make them feel that they didn't give it over to a bunch of lazy fellows that wanted to sit down and turn our face back to them, begging them to carry us right on."

He continues his speech by placing the burden of proof on the black man, not on the white man:

"I say that the Black man in North America has nobody to blame but himself. If he respects himself and will do for himself, his once slavemaster will come and respect him and help him to do something for self."

In the above, there are philosophical variables that are similar to Booker T. Washington's accomodationist policies and which bear similarity to black contemporary conservatives. As discussed in the chapter titled Elijah and Booker, both of these men were products of

210

the black Puritan work ethic, and both--Muhammad patterning after Booker--espoused basically the same economic philosophy. As we scrutinize Muhammad's words above, let us once again bring some of Booker's words to the forefront. Booker called for black self-improvement geared toward being independent. He believed that the best way for black people to advance was through independent industrial education. In his Atlanta Exposition Address in 1895, he said, "Cast down your bucket where you are--cast it down in making friends in every manly way of the people of all races by whom you are surrounded." Booker believed as did Muhammad that social equality for blacks would be best acquired through "severe and constant struggle" and not by "artificial forcing," and that while social equality should be granted to blacks he believed it was far more important that blacks be prepared for the exercise of equality. Both Booker and Elijah wanted blacks to wage their greatest and foremost struggle from within to conquer economic deprivation by applying themselves to practical educational skills to advance their conditions and regain their dignity and self-respect.

In another section of Muhammad's speech he accentuates his conservative or moderate position:

"Rouse him (black man) up and tell him to get up--if you can't pull the tractor pull the plow. I don't believe in us now, in this modern time lying down on the white man looking for him to give us something. He gave us something. He gave us something when he gave us freedom."

Muhammad, in another section, states:

"We must remember that the fault is not in the slave-master anymore; since he says you can go free and we say today he is not hindering us--it is we who are hindering ourselves. Give justice to whom it is due. We glorify in making fun and charging the slavemaster with keeping us a slave. he can't hold you a slave now; you are holding yourself a slave."

In another section of his sermon, Muhammad maintains his emphasis on blacks assuming responsibility for their actions:

"I say to you, my beloved brothers and sisters, give justice to where it belongs and don't try to rob people out of justice. If the white man, and he has, freed you and me to go to work for self and you go all around the earth, he doesn't object--you go wherever you want to. And he is not to blame today; you are the one to be blamed."

211

Throughout this historic speech, he exhorted black people to bear the burden of responsibility for their lack of economic progress, and their lack of ethnic unity. In this speech or sermon, the white man or slave-master was no longer the impediment to black advancement, or the external enemy. The "Devil" was now a mentality; that is, a conceptual demon that was (is) dwelling within black people and satiating itself on psychological projection. Muhammad knew that in order to properly raise black people above their moral weaknesses, their thinking had to be properly raised.

Thus, maintaining the concept that the white man was the devil prevented black people, who tenaciously held to that belief, from seeing themselves as they really were, and that concept generated attitudes of intolerance, antagonism, ineptitude, injustice, and irresponsibility. Muhammad was very clear and poignant on this issue when he stated:

"If we say there goes the devil, then don't try to fashion after him if you say you're righteous. We are not raised up to sit around and make mockery of people; we were raised to show the world what righteousness looks like and what it feels like to be righteous."

Muhammad was unconsciously, employing the use of basic psychotherapy--namely addressing the child like tendency of black people to utilize a defense mechanism or projection for their faults. Blame the white man, blame racism which was (is) the unconscious defense mechanism of shifting the blame or imputing their faults to EuroAmericans. Black people employ projection as a device for exonerating themselves from responsibility and justifying faulty, misguided behavior. Muhammad was, during his leadership and especially the last two years of his life, trying to usher black people out of a narrow-nationalist frame of reference and into a responsible human philosophy. His following statement from his sermon clearly manifests that he was passionately directing black people toward what the Holy Quran calls a self-accusing spirit, or a controlled developed conscience that demands perfection:

"This is a very sly and spooky way that we have of dumping the burden on someone else. Right is right and we are of the nation of righteous. Take our place among the righteous doing right. I love you. . . .But I love you to do something for self and stop putting your fault on the slave-master."

212

Muhammad's moderation of expressions of hostility toward the European American male was demonstrated with this comment from his sermon:

"What I am trying to say to you, we cannot put all the fault on the white people. No he doesn't deserve us charging him with all the fault because you are free, and to make it clear to you Allah came and gave to you a flag representing freedom, justice, and equality. We hoist the flag right here on this soil. He didn't say take it down. Nope--he did not hinder you from hoisting your own flag right beside his."

Mr. Muhammad, in another section, shows that he was more concerned about black self-actualization than he was about European American racism:

"Now, since you have known self and now you know your once slave-master and he is not trying to hinder you from being yourself I say be yourself. We all love to be equal with other people who are equal. Well then, do something to make them to accept us as their equal. We can't sit up there on the curbstone and tell him to come and sit down with us--no! We are a lazy people who like something for nothing; that is what we are--lazy."

Muhammad echoed aspects of Booker T. Washington's themes on economic independence, self-improvement, and a disdain for slothfulness and petty complaints. Neither man sought assistance from the Federal Government or tried to persuade caucasians to do anything but allow them and their people the opportunity for unhindered self-development. Additionally, neither man believed in social or sexual integration with caucasians; they insisted that both races could maintain harmony and interact on a business level separate and apart, but yet as one.

"In all things that are purely social, we can be as separate as the fingers, yet one as the hand in all things essential to mutual progress."-- Booker T. Washington.

The Nation of Islam was, surprisingly, such an accomodationist movement that the FBI, after a certain period of time, ceased regarding it as an internal threat to security. In fact, it was regarded by J. Edgar Hoover and his inside agents as nothing more than a

213

verbal race-based protest movement whose members were law-abiding citizens.

The Honorable Elijah Muhammad exhibited an accomodationist posture, that even extended beyond Booker T. Washington's, as far back as 1964. On most occasions, Muhammad discouraged his followers from voting. To participate in the political system was in effect to condone European American corruption and European American dominance of that system. As mentioned in previous chapters, Muhammad never completely ruled out future electoral participation. In 1964, he called for 'a full-scale struggle on the political front to elect, particularly in areas where so-called Negroes predominated, black representatives dedicated to the struggle for the advancement and welfare of their people and the weeding out of black political puppets used to maintain white supremacy." Even though his tone was not like the civil rights leaders, his proposal sounded like any interest group attempting to work within the system. No mention was made of separatist goals; only a call for unity at the polls with the NAACP.

Around this same time, scathing attacks against civil rights leaders began to subside. Malcolm X even called for a "common front" with the NAACP and other groups; this appeal was later repeated by Mr. Muhammad himself, in "A Call to All Black Leaders." Muhammad seemed willing to dismiss the fact that the objectives of the civil rights organizations were diametrically opposed to his own, and that caucasians play(ed) exclusive parts in those organizations. Muhammad went so far as to allot full page interviews in the *Muhammad Speaks.*

Scholars such as Dr. Michael Parenti contend that as far back as 1960 Muhammad toned down much of his fiery rhetoric thereby revealing his sensitivity to the charge that he was an uncompromising "hate teacher". As a result, little or no reference was made to white people

Members of the Nation were strongly discouraged from wearing Afro-hairstyles, African garmets of any type, or participating in any type of traditional African ceremonies (Kwanzaa). Muslims were encouraged to dress and look conservatively, that is, business suits, white shirts, dark shoes, ties, clean shave, and neatly trimmed hair.

as "devils," and more emphasis was placed on "Black Pride", rather than "Yacub's teachings." Dr. C. Eric Lincoln speculated that muhammad's early overture to accomodationism could be attributed to his new appreciation of the weight of the external and internal (agents) forces against him, and his desire not to antagonize those forces to the point of destroying the movement.

Muhammad's last sermon was the apex of a fourteen year inclination toward political and economic accomodationism. Professor Harold Cruse uses a fairly accurate description of Muhammad as being a conservative nationalist. Interestingly, Malcolm's contention with Muhammad prior to his suspension and subsequent break with the Nation was that the program had grown conservative, and that Muhammad refused to become embroiled in the "broad civil and human rights struggles."

Another similarity between Booker T. and Elijah which bespeaks conservatism, or some might call elitism, was their pragmatic propensity to assiduously cultivate "national representatives."
In other words, Booker T. brought within his circle numerous black aristocrats who were willing to acquiesce to his leadership in return for his assistance in securing jobs and political preferment. Such a practical arrangement benefited both Tuskegee and the individual.

Muhammad selected, beginning with Malcolm X, men who were articulate, men who possessed a stimulating demeanor of sorts, and men who were considerably learned--religiously, politically, and historically to be his National spokesmen. These men were, for the most part, academically elite. Malcolm, through persistent reading, analyzing, and applying, was undoubtedly in that category. There was Dr. Abdel Alim Shabazz, noted mathematician, there was Bernard Cushmere, now known as Jabril Muhammad, noted religious scholar. As in the case of Booker T., all parties benefited from this practical arrangement. Beneath the surface, it made sense to select men who had the interest of the race at heart, who were more than willing to submit to his leadership, and who had the talent or expertise to

Muhammad Speaks, winter issues of 1961.
Muhammad Speaks, October 11, 1963.
Muhammad Speaks, July 1963.
"Call to All Black Leaders," Muhammad Speaks, October 11, 1963. Michael Parenti "The Black Muslims: From Revolution to Institution," pp. 188-190.

properly and adequately delineate the significance of the Black Muslim program.

Amazingly, Minister Farrakhan repeated this pragmatic policy by appointing--before this involvement with the A.I.D.S. crisis--Dr. Abdul Alim Muhammad, a medical doctor, as his National Spokesman. It is safe to say that strands of Booker T. Washingtonism runs deep in the Nation of Islam, past and present.

Booker was born in slavery, grew up in poverty, and struggled through Hampton Institute. Muhammad was the child of slaves, grew up in poverty, and remained in poverty through most of his adult years, and struggled with self-education.

Elijahian and Bookerite teachings are important because they simplistically and pragmatically showed the Black masses how to get out of their moral and economic degradation and how to become self-respecting citizens. Elijah and Booker set standards of achievement and excellence for their followers and interpreted standards of morality and economic principals that were (are) generally highly regarded by black and white middle-class Americans. Both leaders--especially Muhammad--believed that black initiative was the surest way of emancipating Black people from poverty and want.

According to Ron Karenga, cultural nationalist and essayist during the 1960's and 1970's, there were six major aspects to the doctrine of the Nation of Islam as taught by Mr. Muhammad. The first and perhaps the most psycho-spiritually rewarding was the posing of Islam as the true religion of Black people and Christianity as the religion of the slave-master. The second was his daring contention that Allah (God) came in the person of Master Farad Muhammad and was in reality a Black man and the Black man was (is) God The third was that Black people (the original people on earth, emphasis is mine) were a chosen and righteous people by nature. The fourth was that the white man was the devil. The fifth was that separation on a physical, social and political level from European Americans was a divine imperative. The sixth was the strong promotion for Islamic solidarity throughout the world. The enhancer for these six aspects was Muhammad's passionate religio-nationalist belief that non-white people would inevitably overcome all obstacles placed in their path by Europeans because they belong to the original people.

I contend that there are at least two more aspects to Muhammad's doctrine of Islam. The seventh was his unconscious promotion of American middle-class values through a conservative economic nationalism. The eighth was his strong advocacy of Islamic behavior and fulfillment. the last part of his sermon demonstrated, I believe, that he was on an Islamic evolutionary path. His emphasis on Islamic practices and self-independence often criss-crossed. However, near the end of his life, he presented a firm position in favor of Islamic principles and practices. His following comments are succint and clear on this matter:

"If you put on a white dress, clean, spotless and in that dress is unclean, you cannot be respected like that! We cannot go out and tell the public "I am a Muslim," unless we practice the principles of such. We've got to respect and practice the principles of Islam."

He concludes his sermon with this mild admonition:

"I have visited the Muslim world. I have made pilgrimages to Mecca and Medina--and I have seen and I have heard. These people don't believe in foolishness; so I am trying to clothe you not only with the garments of salvation, but clothe you with the principles of our religion. These men are not here to look at you just trying to be Muslims--they are here wanting to know whether or not that you are a Muslim at heart."

The above comments point to the pristine Islamic direction that Muhammad was traveling toward. He had initially refurbished and ameliorated the physical state of the impoverished Black masses. He took them off pork, drugs, alcohol, promiscuous sexual activities, and unchecked spending habits. This was the first stage of the Islamic evolution that he was undergoing, and that he was introducing to his followers. According to the Quran, the first stage of three is called Nafs-el-ammura. At this stage the consciousness of man is centered in his body; this is the animal man. Man or the human being is governed by biological instinct and the desire for power and wealth warp his soul. The human being is arrogant, evil, corrupt and head strong. Human life and human dignity, moral and spiritual values have no meaning. His immediate gratification and interests are what determines his behavior. If the human being at this stage does anything good, he only does it for his own vainglory. Such a human being is on a low level, and is traveling in moral and spiritual darkness.

It was this stage, Imam Warith Deen Muhammad referred to it as a baby stage, that Muhammad confronted with Master Farad

Muhammad's teachings. Actually, he utilized a physicalized teaching to combat a physical condition.

The Holy Quran calls the second stage Nafs-el-lawwama. this is the stage of the psychic human being. He becomes aware of evil and struggles against it, but it is not that easy to overcome it. This is the dialectical stage of the human being; he moves back and forth between sin and repentance. He is mentally and morally torn asunder. Elijah Muhammad through the use of unorthodox religious catechisms raised the consciousness level of the black masses. He was trying to prepare Black people to wrestle with this dualistic stage of development.. In order to do this, he employed the third aspect of his doctrine which stated that Black people were righteous by nature, and their submission to Allah (God) was (is) their only salvation.

The Quran calls the third and final stage of human consciousness Nafs-Mutmaina. This is the stage that Muhammad expressed in the last part of his sermon. At this stage the light of Islam (truth) triumphs over the darkness of ignorance and moral and spiritual deficiencies. The mind becomes free from self-discord, pain, sorrow, disappointment, arrogance, corruption, fault-finding and avariciousness. The mind finds peace and complete satisfaction in Islam and the Holy Quran. Thus, the human being has completed his sojourn to Allah (God) and is ready to become an agent (vicergent or Khalifah) of Allah (God) on earth.

I truly believe, based on his last sermon, that Muhammad had evolved to the point that he was striving to establish a balance between the physical and material needs of Black people and the spiritual and moral dictates of Allah (God). Muhammad knew that the human being was not created without an aim and purpose, and that life is a constant challenge for him. Islam and the Quran provides the human being with guidance for his felicity in both his present and future life. As Allah (God) teaches in his Quran, life consists of worshiping and acting in accordance with his aims which are based on truth. This is what, I think, Muhammad meant when he said that Islam must be in our hearts, and we must actualize the principles of Islam.

Abdulla Yusuf Ali, Quran, Sura: XXXVI, verse 61.
Quran, Surs: LXXXIX, verse 27.

In conclusion, Muhammad's usual slogan of, "money, good homes, and friendship in all walks of life," was designed to remove poverty and global isolation from the masses of African Americans. This slogan gradually surrendered to the affirmation of spiritual consciousness. Stated another way, his stress on materialism or physicality became subordinate to Islamic-spiritual consciousness. Spiritual consciousness represents a differentiation between being and owning; however, this does not mean that a spiritually conscious person needs to abandon his or her possessions. Muhammad clearly understood that a human being without individuality is no human being at all. Let me be clear before I continue; I do not mean that a human being should engage in unchecked avaricious behavior as spelled out in capitalist societies, and as we will see, Mr. Muhammad resented the actual position of the human being, both separated and attached from his beingness. Ownership or possession of things reflect the me-ness and tends to transform blank things into meaningful objects. These things or possessions are what gives a certain kind of individuality to the human being.

Muhammad became aware of what this desire for things which superseded the desire for spiritual consciousness was in effect doing to his community. Some Nation of Islam members got involved in various types of illicit activities such as armed robbery....Muhammad dealt with this issue in this manner:

"Take somebody's property?--take nothing.
Just take that which God has given to you
and make something out of it. You take
nothing--you go to war with no man!
No--you go to war with yourself.
Trying to rob people out of their
own--that's wrong. The earth is too
large. Well, he has taken it from me
you say. Well, you let him do it. I
don't blame him....If you're going to
let him take it, well, that's okay."
"All we have to do is go to work and
try and make the best out of what He
(God) has given to us, and stop looking
at other people's property, looking for
them to give you theirs. You don't
take anything."

The above comments are undoubtedly from a man with a spiritual and ethical consciousness.

Possessions or ownership of things or objects are part of a dialectical continuum. By that I mean that objects are necessary for the human being, but they are also illusory. The objects owned or possessed provide an essential illusion of permanency. Philosophically speaking, by claiming a part of the object or material world the human being establishes his or her being over against the flux of time, where all things or objects change and pass into each other, including most decisively, our own organism and those beings we love. Spiritual consciousness understands this dilemma and accordingly holds its possessions loosely. Islamic-spiritual consciousness knows that nothing really belongs to the self because the self does not belong to itself but to beingness, which belongs to God.

Hence, spiritual consciousness treats property or objects as a necessary illusion, and regards them no more, or less, seriously than it does its own individuality. In essence, Islamic or even Christian spiritual consciousness is not swayed or mystified by the possession of objects, nor does it make property relations into a sacred idol.

It is this level of reasoning that tells us that there is nothing spiritual about theft, which is almost always violent. Muhammad's comments on this subject made a unique distinction which was simply a question of respect for the other human being and his property, that is, he recognized that self-aggrandzing behavior would be violent, and indicated what should be done to move away from violence. Thus, the individual's personal property may be an illusion, but it remains as what necessarily constitutes one's being and cannot be expropriated without expropriating that being.

There is no doubt in my mind that the Honorable Elijah Muhammad was indeed a masterful teacher and a courageous Muslim leader. May Allah (God) grant him a place in paradise.

About the Author

Adib M. Rashad (James Miller) earned a Bachelors of Arts Degree in history, and a Bachelors of Arts Degree in Philosophy. He later earned a Masters of Arts Degree in Philosophy and a Masters of Arts Degree in Adult Education. He also has diplomas in Mathematics and English.

He has taught in private and public schools as well as on the college and university level. He has and does write articles for various well known publications. He also authored <u>The History of Islam and Black Nationalism in the Americas, Aspects of Eurocentric Thought Racism, Sexism and Imperialism,</u> and a <u>Tribute to John G. Jackson</u>. He has traveled and resided in Nigeria, Ghana and Liberia. Additionally, he has traveled to Hong Kong, Romania, Thailand, Switzerland, India and the Peoples Republic of China.

He is presently an Educational Consultant and history teacher.

Selected Bibliography

Ali, Muhammad, Maulana My Life A Fragment An Autiographical Sketch (Sr. Muhammad Ashraf, Lahore, Pakistan, 1946)

Anderson, D., James The Education of Blacks in the South, 1860 - 1935 (The University of North Carolina Press, Chapel Hill, 1988)

Angell, Ward, Stephen Bishop Henry McNeal Turner and African American Religion in the South (The University of Tennessee Press, Knoxville, 1992)

Armstrong, Karen Holy War (Anchor Books, Doubleday, New York, 1988)

Armstrong, Karen Muhammad A Biography of the Prophet (Harper Collins, San Francisco, 1992)

Aptheker, Herbert American Negro Slave Revolts (International Publishers, New York, 1978)

Clark, Peter Marmaduke Pickthal: British Muslim (Quartet Books, London, 1986)

Davis, Arthur, Redding, Saunders, J., and Joyce, Ann, Joyce The New Calvacade African American Writing from 1760 to The Present Volume I (Howard University, Washington, D.C., 1991)

Davis, T. Charles, and Jr. Gates, Henry, Louis The Slave's Narrative (Oxford University Press, New York, 1985)

Dawley, Alan Struggles For Justice (Harvard University Press, Cambridge, Mass., 1991)

Duignan, Peter & Gan, H. L. The United States and Africa (Cambridge University Press, New York, 1984)

Esposito, L. John Islam and Politics (Syracuse University Press, 1984)

Fardan, Blake, Dorothy Message To The White Man and Woman in America (United Brothers and United Sisters Communications Systems, Hampton, Virginia, May, 1991)

Fromkin, David A Peace To End All Peace (Henry Holt and Company, New York, 1989)

Genovese, D., Eugene In Red and Black (The University of Tennessee Press, Knoxville, 1984)

Goldenson, M. Robert The Encyclopedia of Human Behavior Volume II (Doubleday & Company, Inc., 1970)

Harlan, R., Louis Booker T. Washington Volumes I & II (Oxford University Press, New York, 1972 & 1983)

Huggins, Irvin, Nathan Black Odyssey (Vintage Books, New Ork, 1990)

Jones, Jacqueline Labor of Love, Labor of Sorrow (Basic Books, Inc., New York, 1985)

Kemal, Aziz, Abdul Islam and The Race Question (Islamic Book Publishers, Kuwait, 1982)

Lewis, Bernard Race and Slavery in the Middle East , (Oxford University Press, New York, 1990)

Lincoln, Eric, C. Race Religion and The Continuing American Dilemma (Hill and Wang, New York, 1984)

222

Lynch, Hollis Edward Wilmot Blyden Pan-Negro Patriot (Oxford University Press, 1967)

Jr., Martin, E., Waldo The Mind of Frederick Douglass (The University of North Carolina Press, Chapel Hill, 1984)

McFeely, S., William Frederick Douglas (W. W. Norton and Company, New York, 1991)

McMurry, O., Linda George Washington Carver Scientist and Symbol (Oxford University Press, New York, 1981)

Meir, August Negro Thought in America, 1880 - 1915 (The Unviersity of Michigan Press, 1963)

Mellon, James Bullwhip Days The Slaves Remember (Weidenfeld and Nicolson, New York, 1988)

Miller, Chester, John The Wolf By The Ears Thomas Jefferson and Slavery (University Press of Virginia, 1991)

Mortimer, Edward Faith and Power (Random House, New York, 1982)

Moses, Jerimiah, Wilson Alexander Crummell A Study of Civilization and Discontent (Oxford University Press, 1989)

Quarles, Benjamin Black Abolitionists (Da Capo Press, New York, 1969)

Thomas, D., Lamont Rise To Be A People A Biography of Paul Cuffe (University of Illinois Press, Urbana, 1986)

Vincent, G. Theodore Voices of a Black Nation: Political Journalism in the Harlem Renaissance (Ramparts Press, San Francisco, 1973)

Weber, Max The Protestant Ethic and the Spirit of Capitalism Unwin Hyman, Boston, 1990)

Willis, Ralph, John, Editor, Slaves and Slavery in Muslim Africa (Frank Cass, New Jersey, 1985)

Wood, G. Forrest The Arrogance of Faith (Alfred A. Knopf, New York, 1990)

Yee, J., Shirley Black Women Abolitionists A Study in Activism, 1828-1860 (University of Tennessee Press, Knoxville, 1992)

223

SUPREME WISDOM AND EMPOWERMENT OF THE PEOPLE:
The Legacy of the Honorable Elijah Muhammad
By
Dorothy Blake Fardan, Ph.D.

I think there is only one way I can speak of the historical and human impact of the Honorable Elijah Muhammad and that is how he continues to live in the people. My introduction to Islam through the teachings of Elijah Muhammad was by way of one who came from the grassroots, the Lost-Found in the hellist wilderness of North America; one who like many had encountered Islam, knowledge of self, through the Hon. Elijah Muhammad while struggling to survive in the streets, schools, and prison houses of ruthless overseers and protectors of the American social system.

It was by coming to know and see these living examples of Elijah Muhammad's students and followers that I witnessed the power of this Messenger's teachings. These were people who bore no status nor import in American society, who in essence were expendable and nameless to both authorities and the general citizenry. When I heard their stories, stories like those of brothers who had led the most treacherous of lives in their efforts to survive as men, strong black men, in the face of vicious white supremacist institutions, and how they began to rise up into unfettered manhood through the teachings of Elijah Muhammad, I knew this was the power of Allah (God) alone. When I encountered sisters who had at one time been lost and lonely in the streets of America, unknowing and oblivious to their own self-destruction, and then who came into clarity about themselves through the teachings of Elijah Muhammad, I understood the presence of Allah in this mission; for if the woman was lost and found, then a nation had been recovered and saved for future generations.

This was a powerful thing happening, in the streets, the homes, in the hallways of housing projects, in the bars and clubs even; this was a grassroots teaching one on one. Somebody got the Message and passed it on. Black people in America were stirring, coming alive, more than ever before. While there had always been slave rebellions and some form of strong resistance to white oppression, and the swelling tide of Black Power under Marcus Garvey, this was a fresh new surge of Black people empowerment, for it not only organized a body politic, but

224

it revitalized and restored Black people's spiritual, divine originality. Those who had been seen as the least, the most unlikely to be powerful human beings, those who had been made into "negroes" by white oppressors, these were standing up now and acting powerful, speaking with Supreme Wisdom. The seed was planted and grew from the 1930's onward.

Years later, hearing brothers recall long periods of solitary confinement in the prison holes of North America simply because they were Muslim and followers of the Honorable Elijah Muhammad, let me know this was a powerful seed of wisdom and human empowerment. Equally impressive were the instances of men and women demonstrating increased determination to persevere as members of the Nation of Islam despite overt obstacles and clandestine forces on all sides attempting to destroy this movement. These were the years of true wilderness, when others may have been weak-hearted and clung to the security of white Christianity and service submission to the promise of "better times." Elijah Muhammad often stood alone with his Nation, defiant and uncompromising.

The uniqueness of Elijah Muhammad's mission in delivering Islam was his being able at the same time to break the power of "color" over the personal and collective lives of Black people in North America. James Baldwin once wrote: "the question of color, especially in this country, operates to hide the graver questions of the self." And Elijah Muhammad wisely understood that for his people to understand themselves they would have to understand the "white man" and his time of rulership; understand how color under the white man's rulership dictated the people's every move in the ongoing life of white America. And concomitantly, Black people, he taught, would have to understand who they were and when their time of rulership was and would be once again. He did not attempt to deliver or explain Islam apart from uncovering and exposing the social womb of the white man's rule. He understood that his people would rise up into the consciousness of "muslim", that is, a universal human consciousness, only after they rid themselves of the dead weight of white images, mindset, and black self-hatred. All parts of the self-being (physical, emotional, mental and spiritual) had to be purified of these impurities. Islam via Elijah Muhammad penetrated the very entrails of America cutting away the facade of white superiority and exposing the potent, latent, and immense beauty of black being.

No other imam, emir, scholar, mullah, or king could come from afar into this beastly society and unlock the prison bolts on the inner self of the Black man and woman in America, although one did come, not as a mullah or proclaimed scholar, but as a common laboring man and as a "thief in the night", moving quietly in and out of the Wilderness of North America, long enough to plant a seed. His name was W. Fard Muhammad and he sought a fallow field in which to plant the seed of Islam, the Supreme Wisdom, and found it in Elijah Poole, later to become Elijah Muhammad. It was in the field of himself that Elijah Muhammad cultivated this Gift from Allah, finally growing it into food for his people, food of liberation. No old world Muslims could be the vehicle for this immense task, for they had not been under the boot of a southern cracker, but Elijah Poole had. Nor had they been chained to destitute urban ghettos that had rendered a people landless and with no exits to their past or future. But Elijah Muhammad had known it all: the venom of raw southern racism and plantation capitalistic economy, and the cold northern tyranny of urban masters and a mercantile capitalist economy.

So it was, when I traveled through the streets of North America with my husband, the one who had introduced me to Islam and Elijah Muhammad, I saw the story repeated over and over again. We were "on the road" those years (1971-85), so to speak, and towns and cities came and went as fast as greyhound buses and trains pulled in and out. These places and people remained imprinted on my mind as long as a month or year's stay permitted. Sometimes it would be in a bus station, or some dim little club on the black side of town, and there he or she would be: someone who had been in the Nation, or was in the Nation, or someone who had simply heard about "those Muslims", someone who might apologize for still drinking or smoking, and then look you straight on and bear witness: "I'm on the wayside now, but that's my heart . . . .Islam, I-self-lord-and-master."

Or it might be around a barrel fire in some city, like Chicago, D.C., or Nashville, and the men would be discussing deep things; things about life and times and purpose, and inevitably, Islam would come up, and the Honorable Elijah Muhammad, and they would, for some sacred few moments, bear witness. They traded prison stories and talked about Elijah Muhammad "saved my life". And if a "dead" bystander (a Lazarus) would join in and unwittingly disrespect or misunderstand Elijah Muhammad and Islam, the discussion would grow heated and the defenders of Islam and the Messenger would rise to the occasion.

Greater numbers were in the street who had never "joined the Nation" perhaps, but who bore witness. They were soldiers all the same, who would put their life on the line for those who were in the Nation, who tolerated no disrespect of Elijah Muhammad's name.

They knew things that had changed their lives, even if they didn't go to the temple (mosque) or have their "X". They knew things like not eating pork, and learning to love black self, and who the original man was, and how to respect black women as sisters, and who the white man really was. They knew how they had been "put to death" by a white Jesus; Elijah Muhammad had taught them about the "graveyard" of the Bible, and then showed them how that Bible was to be read in relation to themselves. They most often learned these things by foot soldiers who came through their neighborhoods, maybe selling papers and fish. These fishers of men carried supreme wisdom along with the papers and fish, dispensing it throughout the streets, among the people.

Everywhere we went, there were witnesses. Elijah Muhammad lived in the streets, in the people. It was something of a sacred trust, it was the presence of Allah. In Canada we would meet brothers who had crossed the border, escaping further oppression in the prisons of the United States; or we would encounter those fleeing the oppression of Vietnam, some having "deserted" the war because they had seen a greater truth and mission. And true to pattern, there would be some who "tuned in," who had somewhere at sometime encountered the Nation, Elijah Muhammad, and Islam. And if they hadn't, they were hungry for his message, longing for self clarity, searching for some handhold whereby they could make sense out of the past and make purpose out of the future. It was also in Canada that I saw the bridge that the Nation provided for communication with the native indigenous people. The teachings of Elijah Muhammad provided a conduit for the native indigenous person's sense of All-Being and sense of ravishment by the white man, to flow into the sensitivity of the Muslim, the black man and woman who also understood the tyranny of the white man's rule.

In Jamaica we lived in a poorer section of Kingston, and my husband lost no time in moving about the streets, sharing the teachings. A brother called McKenzie was a strong ally, and was quickly drawn to Islam and the Nation. The three of us would ride the over-crowded buses to Crossroads and on to other destinations, and en route, the two of them would play tapes by Minister Farrakhan, imparting the teachings of Elijah Muhammad. The crowds would either stretch to hear or toss their heads and roll their eyes in denial. But there in Jamaica I saw the great love and respect the people, the grassroots people, had for Marcus Garvey and for Elijah Muhammad and Islam. They knew of the Nation mostly through the tapes or appearances of Minister Farrakhan. Even in Trenchtown, where raggae was conceived and reborn each day, the Rastas and musicians felt kinship with members of the Nation. They knew: One God, One Love, One Destiny.

This "living" presence of Elijah Muhammad within and among the people was brought home to me probably in no better example than the one that follows. It was 1975, Washington, D.C., following the physical departure of Elijah Muhammad, and the subsequent leadership of his son, Warith D. Muhammad, over the Nation. Since I was Caucasian, I could not enter the Nation until the doors were opened under W. D. Muhammad.* One day I was at a bus stop at 14th and U Streets, NW. I was in fact on my way to the Mosque on New Jersey Avenue. I noticed a tall, slender young black man restlessly pacing back and forth on the corner, also apparently waiting for the bus. He spoke freely with the people there, and occasionally glanced my way, probably because I was Caucasian and dressed as a Muslim. All of a sudden a button popped off his coat (one of those long maxie coats they wore those days), and it rolled towards my foot and the curb. I stopped it, picked it up and handed it to him. That was his entree to inquire: "Are you a Muslim?" I said yes and he wanted to know which mosque I attended. When I told him, he replied with some doubt, "I was just there Wednesday, and I didn't see you then." I was in the midst of explaining about my belonging to the Mosque at 4th and New Jersey, when the bus came, and the people gathered at the corner to board began to move towards the door. When I got on, all seats were taken but one, which the young man with whom I had been talking, was about to sit in. He looked up as I stood, appearing somewhat annoyed, and said: "Here, you take the seat. But I tell you the truth, I don't like white people, never have, don't trust'em, but I respect Elijah Muhammad." Despite the teachings about devils, he knew the Honorable Elijah Muhammad would respect a Muslim, no matter the color.

What I felt all throughout America, was that Elijah Muhammad laid a foundation for Black men and women to walk the streets as new men and women, with pride and love for themselves, and with 360 degrees worth of knowledge that equipped them to confront situations at any given time and with any given person. He laid the foundation for those to come much later on down the line: young revolutionaries who would possibly not even know his name or know much about him and the teachings. Elijah Muhammad lives today in the "X" caps, because Malcolm X lives, and Malcolm X lives because Elijah Muhammad was his foundation.

228

From what I could see, every other black organization or movement that evolved after the formation of the Nation of Islam owed its consciousness and viability among the people, to the work of Elijah Muhammad. The Nation's mission to teach love of Black self and its defiance, rejection of and separation from white America, formed the backdrop to the '60's revolutionary movements. This is not to say there were no internal problems within the Nation, no need for self-criticism, nor that a new fresh spirit was not spawned in these new generational movements. But the Nation's legacy of uncompromised vision about the Black man and woman in America inspired the revolutionary articulations of not only Malcolm X, but the Black Panthers, and subsequent nationalist formations.

And today, in the 1990's, in the aftermath of the L. A. rebellion, the substance of the teachings of Elijah Muhammad has never been so clear and "on time." Where many other stood awed in the wake of so-called "violence," and still others showed disbelief and continued to extend appeals to the white power structure for some signs of justice, the members and supporters of the Nation of Islam calmly, firmly , and with continued clear vision, reminded all: you were told many years ago of this day to come. Only those from the street level, the most grassroots point, sometimes the most desperate spot, understood what happened in L.A. and spoke the truth. They are usually called "gang members" or former members, and they most often had credentials from the prison houses nearby. And as to be expected, during their incarceration, somewhere and at sometime, they got a touch of Supreme Wisdom, whether straight from the Nation, or from the Five Per Centers, or some other organization.

Supreme Wisdom covers all areas of knowledge, all geographical regions, all planetary life. It is simple, mathematical pure truth, based on natural facts. It is universal, and covers all the problems of color. In the end, it will destroy white supremacist power and the rule of the white man; will destroy its diabolical social and economic system. It will also guide those called Caucasians out of whiteness and into knowledge of self and peace with the universe. It will also as a form of justice destroy those holding on to white power. It will, as Elijah Muhammad said it would, carry the world into the Hereafter, a new order of things. It will resolve issues of color, racism, power, and injustice. Supreme Wisdom is the knowledge and power of Allah.

Thus it is, when I walk the streets of America, and hear and see the evidence of Wisdom as it grows out of the words and actions of Black men and women preparing to take on the rulership of a righteous social order, I know and understand the full scope and power of the impact of the Honorable Elijah Muhammad on not only America, but the world. There are some who become disturbed at the diversity of Black liberation groups, some who see conflict between the various organizations, and some who ask who is the real this or the real that, but I am never much disturbed at the variations on a theme, for I can always hear the theme song in the cacophony of voices, understanding that the theme arose out of the initial, essential 360 degree Message embedded in Supreme Wisdom. It is this Wisdom that Elijah Muhammad bequeathed to his people, and ultimately to anyone willing to face truth. This was and is the empowerment of the people, the Wisdom living in the people. And I am reminded of the old people's saying: "Don't forget the bridge that carried you over."

* Issues concerning the various expressions of the Nation after the departure of Honorable Elijah Muhammad have been addressed in past publications or forthcoming ones.

AN OBJECTIVE ASSESSMENT OF
ELIJAH MUHAMMAD

by Dr. Alauddin Shabazz

The Honorable Elijah Muhammad, (May he rest in peace and the mercy of Allah engulf him and ensure his status in the next reality one of bliss and nearness to Allah) a man among men. A champion of the poor, disenfranchised and oppressed people of America and the world. A man who constructed men from the mire of American society, a society rooted in 'white supremacy" and "Black inferiority". A man who took the minds of millions out of the sky, looking and waiting on a mystery pallid God to do for them what they could do for themselves, as other intelligent people were doing for themselves, in the name of Allah--a man who understood, evidently, the Quran where it states... That man can have nothing but what he strives for; that his striving will soon come in sight" (53:39,40).

The Honorable Elijah Muhammad (R.A.) was one of the greatest Muslims that ever lived. He was indeed more of a 'Sunni" Muslim than the self-proclaimed "Sunni" Muslims who issue diatribes against him, if "Sunni" means following the example of Nabi Muhammad (SAW). The first 10-13 years of the history of the mission of Nabi Muhammad should be studied more critically before one even attempts to discern the Islamic property of the manner in which the Honorable Elijah Muhammad advanced his Muslim followers.

As all human beings, Elijah Muhammad had faults and made mistakes--this includes Nabi Muhammad, the seal of the prophets (PBUT)--no human being is/was or will ever be infallible. It is indited in the Holy Quran (325:45 & 16:61) that no human being has earned life or the next life to come--and Nabi Muhammad was the first addressee of this fact. For anyone to say that any human being is/was perfect or sinless is obnoxiously absurd and is akin to shirk/anthopomorphism which is, according to Quran (4:48) is the only unforgivable sin.

The teachings of the Honorable Elijah Muhammad were rather controversial; and to many so-called white people, even contumacious. If history is authentically recorded in the hadith of the bible, the same was true of the teachings of Moses and Jesus (PBUT) to religious leaders esteemed by so-called white people and so-called Black people alike. For the most part, Elijah Muhammad's teachings were based on/in bible and world history. The bulk of what he taught was/is corroborated by not only history and the scriptures, but also mathematics, biology, genealogy, DNA, anthropology, archaeology and melanin content.

This is not to say that each and every conclusion reached by the Honorable Elijah Muhammad were correct. Some were inaccurate. A good example was his position of the "show-down" between Allah (SWT) and the nations of the earth--He said that 1965 and 1966 was "going to be fateful for America, bringing in the fall of America.' He said regarding"the doom of America," that what was "going to happen in 1973 and 1974' would certainly change the minds of many" about following a doomed people", etc. (See "Message to the Black Man," pages 268, 270 & 272). Prophet Jesus (AS) is considered by billions of people to have been the actual "son of God", nay "God incarcerated/incarnated." Yet some of his conclusions were inaccurate, according to the bible hadith--peruse St. Matthew (24:1-35) especially verses (34 & 35) for example. Some Jewish scholars and historians point out "mistakes" made by Christ Jesus in another of their hadith (St. Mark 11:11-14) where it is reported he denounced a fig tree for not yielding fruit to appease his hunger, though it was not the season for a fig-tree to bear fruit. Surely "God incarnated would have known that fact. But this is deception on the part of some Jewish authors of the scripture translation. Christ Jesus (AS) was employing a simile. He was using symbolic speech.

The "fig-tree" in scripture represents the Jewish people. Jesus' words in St. Mark (Chapter II) is expressed again in a slightly different way in St. Matthew (21:10-46). The key connection is cited in verses (43-46). We have heard the term 'family tree". We all have one. the 'tree' cited in Genesis having a 'knowledge" of "good and evil" is symbolic of a wise people--the snake was in the tree. The human body is symbolized also as a tree and rightly so. We should all study the analogous aspects of said.

The Honorable Elijah Muhammad was a student of the bible prior to being mentored by one, called in the early 30's, W.D. Fard. Most of his teachings were right out of the bible. This includes the making of the devil, the mother ship, the coming of God in the person, the mental resurrection, the birth of W.D. Fard, the Fall of America, the white race being a race of devils, etc. We will, Insha Allah, point all of this out in the scripture itself before we conclude.

The concept of a chosen people is misunderstood by millions. Such a people exist but it's not any one race or so-called religion per se. The chosen people of the creator are those who chose to actualize the will of the creator. The Quran (62:6-8) directs a serious question to a group of people historically known to have arrogantly claimed the exclusive status of a "chosen people." The creator is no bigot in the area of religion, gender, or ethnicity. In the last revelation of divine origin, (i.e. Holy Quran) it is candidly proclaimed that the most honorable people are those most conscious of the presence of the creator attested to by their deeds (49:13). All people in general were created honorable--Quran (17:70/40:64) and beautiful. The acts/deeds of man are the "manifestation" of satanic or Godly influences in man's mind--peruse Quran (37:95, 96; 8:53; 13:11; 9:14; 8:17 and 7:19, 20, 201). Surely Allah (SWT) speaks the truth.

Imam W. Deen Mohammad has stated that the devil 'came to birth on something that started within lies, weak ideas or wrong thinking.' Negative things that "be-gin to grow a particular disposition in you and pretty soon your disposition is one of evil and wickedness. If they continue to grow, you will take on the mental form of a devil." It is revealed in Quran (7:11-13) that 'Iblis" came into being via an attitude of supremacy and arrogance (i.e. "I'm better" than others be-cause of birth). The matrix of satan is divinely pointed out by creator! We suggest the following verses of Quran be concatenated for a broader panorama (15:26-44; 38:71-88; 18:50).

The last verse cited states that Iblis was 'one of the Jinns." This point of fact must be properly understood. One should read very carefully all of the Quranic citations where Jinns and Iblis are discussed in context. For example, verse 13 of chapter 7 mentions the negative mental germs of 'arrogance" and "meaness." In chapter (15:28, 33) the Quran deals with the first man being created from Black or dark mud, fashioned into shape. (i.e. "...hama-im-masnuun"). Iblis had a problem with this dark man in which the very spirit of Allah (i.e. creator) was placed (verse 29). In chapter (18:50) it is recorded that Iblis was 'one of the Jinns' (This indicates that all of the Jinns did not refuse to submit to Allah's will). It is also indicated that Iblis and his "progeny" (i.e. children or descendants, off-springs) would be so powerful or strong (e.g., military) that people would seek the protection of the Jinn's satanic descendants, rather than Allah.

In chapter (72:6) of Quran Allah reveals how some people took shelter with people of the Jinns and was bereaved of good judgment. Said association was a costly undertaking having an absurd or ruinous outcome. In this very same chapter (72) entitled "Jinn", verses 1-4, states that some of the Jinns (not Iblis progeny, mind you) accepted Quranic guidance and berated other Jinns (Iblis off-springs) for advocating the trinity and anthropomorphism. Notice verses (11-15).

Most Muslims are conversant with Quran (35:27,28) where color is mentioned. Most are aware of (49:13) where Allah states 'We created

233

you from a single entity of male and female, and made you into nations and tribes, that you may know each other..." but few have actually studied said verses with the helping light of history. In the latter verse, at one juncture "created" is employed and at another "made" is employed. Nations and tribes (both plural) were not "created" first like the original prototype, but "made" into such subsequently. How? I am not absolutely sure. Allah says "...that you may know each other". To "know" means "to have a particular understanding of,""to be able to distinguish,""to be acquainted or familiar with." How many Muslims are aware of the fact that according to the Quran (7:27; 18:50) one of the "tribes" cited was developmental satanic in mentality? How many Muslims realize that Allah raised up "prophets" from among the Jinn--peruse Quran (6:130)? Every people received a prophet, a messenger, or a warner and the Jinn/people was included.

Speaking on the Jinns, Imam W. D. Mohammad has stated that "the Jinn is born out of the womb of fiery passions of the physical body.' Where the term "we" is used in Quran, Imam W.D. Mohammad has taught that Allah (i.e. creator) use the term "we" meaning that he is at the source or origin of the creation. He first had to produce some material for other things to use.' He was also taught that "after these materials had been produced, the angels (forces of nature) came into play. It is the forces of nature in the physical body that manifest urges or desires. if your mind cannot handle these urges, the urges grow in power to overcome you."

The Jinn people are those formed by lies, false concepts, etc. Factious and fallacious knowledge goes into the mind and forms one in his or her body. This false knowledge grows and grows in the person until he or she becomes unnatural, or alien to the original upright propensity of human nature. The symbolic teachings of Yacub's history are designed to convey these abstract facts, in a concrete narration, to an un-educated people in the 30's, 40's and 50's.

The Honorable Elijah Muhammad (R. A.) taught that Mr. Yacub had an unusual size head. He was called the "big head scientist." The idiom "big headed" means egotistical, egocentric, arrogant, megalomania, or as the Quran states..."I am better." The Arabic word "Yacub" in English means "Jacob", and the etymology of Jacob means "supplanter" which means "to take the place of, to supersede by deception or tricks, to trip up ones heal. In the bible (Genesis 25:23) "two manner of people" are mentioned. Verse 26 speaks of the birth of Jacob/Yacub and his first deportment. Verses 29-33 ditto. Genesis (27;1__-36 an d 29: 1-3) is also a concise history of Jacob/Yacub's chicanery and exploitation throughout the world. It is stated in

234

Genesis (32:24-30) that the name of Jacob was changed--but his insidious and nefarious nature continued in his progeny,.

The history of Mr. Yacub and the "making of the devil" as taught by the Honorable Al-Hajj Elijah Muhamad (R.A.) was satirical, mythological and concocted but with merits. The graftage of a people into be-ing is liking to the monster Frankenstein made from inhuman exploits. Here was a wise but demented scientist who made an abnormal person, who turned against its designer. The Honorable Elijah Muhammad use to say to 'Black people' who may have entertained thoughts about decrying the evil deeds of the "white devil" to extremes, that the latter could say "...you made me." In this Mr. Muhammad was placing the basic blame of oppression on "Black people." In essence, "Black people" engendered problems for themselves and must remove from themselves "negative germs" that conclude in black suffering and death.

The bible gave Dr. Fard (Imam W. Mohammad said in NYC during a lecture years after the passing of his father that he (W.D.M) "gave W.D. Fard a doctorate" and that the world would not be able to see him (W.D. Fard) in such light until he (W.D.M) "treated their vision"! The bible provided material to use in his (W.D. Fard) concoctions. For example, the book of Genesis (30:25-; 32:24-32) and Roman (11:13-25) and Isaiah (48:7-9, 12) all deal with the grafting of a particular mind-set of people. In the book of Revelation (1:9) John, which is a variation of Jacob/Yacub, states that he, John/Yacub, was on the Isle of Patoms (called 'peniel' in Genesis 32:30/29:25) for two reasons--one is found in Genesis (1:26) 'The word of God" and the other in St. John (8:44). Supporting verses of scriptures used by Mr. Muhammad were: Genesis (6:5,6), Roman (7:22-24), II-Thessalonian (2:3-9), etc.

Coupled with the supra scriptures were citations from books like "The Genetic Code" by professor Isaac Asminov (of Biochemistry) at Boston University School of Medicine (9n 1962) and "Findings in Genetics" by Gregor Mendel. These medical publications dealt with DNA, enzyme, organisms, chromosomes and the chemical language of the genetic body in general. The latter publication by the Austrian scientist, Mr. Mendel, proved that 'Black" characteristics were "dominant" and "white" characteristics were "recessive" where genes were concerned. Books such as these plus history in general educated Al-Hajj Malik Shabazz (a/k/a Malcolm X) and enabled him to substantiate the teachings of the Honorable Elijah Muhammad to a great extent. The collective misdeeds of Europeans and European-Americans was the most potent weapon in the arsenal of the Honorable Elijah Muhammad.

235

Once, while being interviewed by a pallid talk show host, Malcolm told the host that if Mr. Muhammad's teaching on the "white man" being the devil was a lie , white people" could destroy Mr. Muhammad and the Nation of Islam over night. The host asked "how?" and Malcolm replied "by giving black people freedom, justice, and equality and stop being satanic in their behavior, over night." On another occasion, Mr. Muhammad himself was being interviewed and he was asked by the wan host "why do you call white people devils?"...Mr. Muhammad answered with the question "What is a devil, sir?" and the interviewer rendered a definition from Webster...a destructively mischievous person, a wicket person, a slander, and evil spirit, etc..." Mr. Muhammad said 'well, there you have it." It has nothing to do with "skin color", it was based on the "color of the mind."

In the alleged "Autobiography of Malcolm X", pages 174-181, one can find a wealth of knowledge that is indisputable. There is a biblical parallel to said empirical, historical data (Revelation 6:8; 17:1-6, 15-18; 18:2-24; 2:2-13; 3:9). The Honorable Elijah Muhammad pointed the rigid finger of history at the so-called white man it was his own deeds that identified him as demonic. This was hard for most so-called white people to digest, but impossible for them or their carbon copies to disprove. So they mearly repeated the charge over and over again that Mr. Muhammad was a 'hate teacher' and 'a racist' when in truth he was mainly a 'history teacher' and a 'realist' who loved his own people. Allahu'Akbar.

Is it unIslamic for a "black person" to be "pro-black" or seek to better the conditions, elevate the status, and renovate ones own "ethnic group"? What is the position taken by Allah (SWT) in Quran on this question? Read It For Yourself (8:;75; 16:90; 26:214; 33:6; 90:1-18; 2:1777)--to give a few locations. Deen Al-Islam is the 'natural way of life". In the words of Dr. Akbar Muhammad, the youngest son of the Honorable Elijah Muhammad, "Islam has never destroyed the ethnic pride of a people, rather it enhances it." This is extra true for "Black people " when the authentic history of Al-Islam is learned by them. Conventional Islamic teachings omits a copious amount of truth regarding Africans and African-Arabs in the annals of history, during the prior, and after the birth of prophet Muhammad (SAW). There is nothing wrong with ethnic pride, concern, promotion, etc., as long as no injustice is committed against others of another ethnic group.

The Honorable Elijah Muhammad was a just man. He detested the satanic deportment of "white people" and candidly admitted so. He spoke out against such demonic demeanor; the Holy Quran (4:148) allows that. He did not allow his justifiable hatred of the maleviolence

236

of European-Americans to induce him to "swerve from justice" in his relationship with said ethnic group (5:9). Never did Mr. Muhammad advocate violence against anyone save in self-defense Quran (2:190; 4:75, 76; 222:38-41). Those who attempt to parallel the 'Nation of Islam' with the "Ku Klux Klan" are obviously insane, ignorant or agents of obstreperous misinformation.

The Nation of Islam was and is an integral part of the universal ummah of Nabi Muhammad (SAW). There are those who verbally try to deny this, but truth is truth. There are those who claim that Mr. Muhammad and the Nation of Islam were unIslamic because they advocated 'separation of the races', that said were 'separatists"--but listen to Mr. Muhammad's words on 'what the Muslims want.'

> "1) We want freedom. We want a full and complete freedom; 2) We want justice. Equal justice under the law. We want justice applied equally to all regardless of creed, class or color; 3) <u>We want equality of opportunity. We want equality membership in society with the best in civilized society.</u>'

That's what he said.

What intelligent, humane, civilized, creator--loving person or people can take issue with the supra? What authentic 'Muslim', or 'Christian', or Believer in the Creator in general can ponder those 'wants' and call Mr. Muhammad a racist (in the common usage of the term) or a "separatist" in any negative sense? Can any real, sane Muslim espy anything in the cited projections by Mr. Muhammad that's unIslamic? On the contrary, there are purely Islamic/Quranic and in line with the sunnah of Nabi Muhammad. Study the supra three once again. In number two, racism, caste-ism, and religious chauvinism is condemned. In number three, Mr. Muhammad expressed the desire of "equal membership in society," but "with the best in civilized society"--how is that construed as separatism? One might ask, what about the "want" or "a separate state or territory" uttered by Mr. Muhammad? the last part of number four, of "what the Muslims want" answers that question. Mr. Muhammad states..."<u>since we can not get along with them (European-American) in peace and equality</u> after giving them 400 years of our sweat and blood and receiving in return some of the worst treatment human beings have ever experienced, we believe our contributions to this land and the suffering forced upon us by white America justifies our demand for complete separation in a state or territory of our own.' <u>Note the reason cited by Mr. Muhammad that produced this particular want.</u> . So-called orthodox Muslim detractors of Mr. Muhammad evidently do not realize that Nabi Muhammad and his followers "separated" from

Meccan rulers and went to "yathrib", and established his own state due to some of the very same reasons. Study history. Oppression warrant separation according to the Quran (16:41; 29:56) and the sunnah. The hijarah to Abyssinia (i.e. Africa) took place as early as the fifth year of the prophets call to Al-Islam and the second hijarah to Yathrib took place less than a decade later. Both were due to injustice, oppression, lynching, rape, murder...Was either hijarah an integrationist endeavor with open enemies, or a clear endeavor to separate from such oppressors? What was the inducement of the Declaration of Independence in 1776? How did Pakistan come about and why? Why are "mental cruelty" and"ill-reconcilable differences" grounds for divorce in a court of law between two people ? Mr. Muhammad and his followers never separated themselves into an area of the USA, but if they had, it would have been in direct accord with the "sunnah" of Prophet Muhammad.

In all candor, far too many so-called "Sunni" or "orthodox" Muslims are sheer hypocrites when it comes to Quranic directives and the alleged "sunnah" of Nabi Muhammad. The Quran (4:3, 129) clearly states that a man can have up to four wives under certain circumstances but they berate the domestic affairs of Mr. Muhammad. Without proven knowledge, many so-called orthodox Eastern Muslims and their clones repeat the lies printed by the open enemies of Al-Islam and that Mr. Muhammad had sexual relationships with "teenaged" girls. All of Mr. Muhammad's wives were adults. But what if the lies were actually true? Was the alleged "sunnah" followed, or violated by Mr. Muhammad? Let's reason.

According to most Muslim scholars, Aalims , Mullahs, etc., Prophet Muhammad (SAW) had a sexual relationship with a nine year old female (A few scholars say 12 years old. Aalim Ziauddin Kiramani in his book entitled 'The Last Messenger with a Lasting Message", on page 310, states that she was no less than 17 years old). We are referring to Sister Ayesha (R.A.). Nabi Muhammad was at least 54 years of age at this time. The point being, if the record is anywhere near the truth, Mr. Muhammad cannot be charged with an act that was not in accord with the 'sunnah."

And what about the charge of having sexual relationships outside of marriage? Most Muslim historians claim that Maria, the Egyptian copt who gave birth to Ibrahim, Prophet Muhammad's last son, was a slave-girl of the prophet. In Bukhari and Muslim hadith there are reports about more female mates of the prophet's that he wasn't married to. <u>I crave Allah's forgiveness for having to mention such rubbish about Nabi Muhammad (SAW) in order to rouse the conscience of the captive Muslim intelligentsia. I do not subscribe to the filth alleged in the ahadith that I know our Nabi was above.</u> But, say the history was true and Muslims in America were to follow said 'sunnah', prisons would be filled with Muslims for child molestation', 'statutory rape', 'white slavery" and civil-rights violations copiously. Again, let us be clear, we do not subscribe to all that is written even by Arab/Muslim scholars, under the caption of the "seerah" of Prophet Muhammad (SAW). We cite these histories alleged by Aalims, Imams, Mullahs, etc., only to show the 'unbalanced" convictions of "some Muslims."Authentic Mu'minum use one and the same ruler to measure the conduct of all people." Malcolm X--here was proof of the positive effects of 'Islam as taught by the Honorable Elijah Muhammad" to his people.

The Malcolm X that the masses esteem is the product of the teachings of Mr. Muhammad. No question about it. NO matter how J.E. Hoover, his negro agents, and the Jewish controlled press was successful in deceiving and manipulating Malcolm and members of the NOI into camps hostile to each other, Al-Islam continues to grow in African-American circles.

At this juncture we will point to some misconceptions held by some people, regarding Malcolm, due to misinformation. First, it is wrong to think that Malcolm didn't know that there were people considered/labeled "white" by certain classifications that were Muslims and who made Hajj every year. Was Malcolm physically blind? No. What did he see in Mecca, Arabia in 1964 that he did not see in 1959? Nothing in particular. Malcolm always knew that Muslims of all complexions made Hajj to the holy city of Mecca Arabia. He had debated Muslims in America who in this country were considered "white". We suggest that the book entitled "When the word is Given", by Louis E. Lomax, be pursued by all who wish corroborations on this point--especially pages (58, 60-63, 89, 116, 120-122, 140) Alex Haley knew all this prior to his alleged 'Autobiography of Malcolm X' in 1964.

The Honorable Elijah Muhammad gave Malcolm the Arabic/Muslim name Malik Shabazz before 1961. On page 69 of the Supra book by Lomax, he points this out. Dr. E.U. Essin-Udom, in his book entitled "Black Nationalism", points this out on page 177. For Alex Haley to even suggest that Malcolm acquired a new name in Mecca in 1964 was fallacious because he (Haley) knew better. Here is my proof: Alex Haley, in May of 1963, did an interview with Malcolm for Playboy Magazine (for whom he worked) in which he (Haley) was candidly and clearly told by Malcolm that his 'real Muslim name' was "Malik Shabazz". This was prior to the departure of Bro. Malcolm from the Nation of Islam and his mentor, the Honorable Elijah Muhammad, and his 1964 Hajj in Mecca. Think about it.

When "The Autobiography of Malcolm X is perused with a focused mind, the misconceptions that have been slipped into the minds of many are detected. For example, on page 340, Malcolm said it was his "experiences in America" that had led him "to believe never could "there "exist between the white and the non-white" a spirit of "unity and brotherhood". He went on to state: "America needs to understand Islam, because this is the only religion that erases from its society the race problem. Throughout my travels in the Muslim world, I have met, talked to, and even eaten with people who in America would have been "considered white" - but the white attitude was removed from their minds by the religion of Islam.' Ponder that.

Malcolm went on to state "We were truly all the same (brothers)--because their belief in one God had removed the white from their minds, the white from their behavior, and the white from their attitude. I could see from this, that "perhaps" if white Americans could accept the oneness of God, then "perhaps", too, they could accept in reality the oneness of man--and cease to measure, and hinder, and harm others in terms of their differences in color." Prior, he felt that the "white attitude" and "white mind-set" (e.g. white supremacy, better than thou conviction) prevalent in European--Americans was incorrigible.

The Honorable Elijah Muhammad was correct, the "white man" can't go to mecca on Hajj. He was talking about exactly what Malcolm finally understood. In the "lessons" the question was asked "Who is the colored man"? Answer, the "so-called white" Why? Color dominates his mind. He coined the terms "red Indians", "yellow peril," etc. etc. Malcolm said on page 333 of his alleged "Autobiography" ... That morning was "when I first began to reappraise the white man." It was when I first began to perceive that "white man" as commonly used means complexion only secondarily. Primarily it described attitudes and action. In America, "white man" meant specific attitudes and actions toward the black man, and toward all other non-white men.

Here again, while in Arabia, brother Malcolm began to understand, without knowing it, what Elijah Muhammad meant by the "white man is the devil." Man means "mind", teaches Imam W. Deen Mohammad and the study of etymology. Some may contend, "Mr. Muhammad did not mean it that way, he was talking about physical flesh." But the syntax "so-called white man," used by Mr. Muhammad in the "student enrollment," clearly depicts the clear intended point that something is amiss at best. He was pointing out a lie, a prodigious one--not a little "white" one. Check out the synonyms for "white" and think about so-called white people in America.

Few people, including some members of the Nation of Islam, realize that Mr. Muhammad taught that in the ummah of Al-Islam color has no place. This is plainly acknowledged by the most Honorable Elijah Muhammad. He knew that Muslims would be found in every ethnic group of people on the planet earth. He used to praise the Muslims in Turkey for having genuine faith in Deen Al-Islam.

In an article printed in the late 50's, under the caption of the "Significance of prayer", Elijah Muhammad wrote in part..."The prayer service is divided into two parts, one to be said in private and the other to be performed in congregation, preferably in a mosque. While the private part is meant simply for the development of the inner self of man, the public part has other ends well in view: Ends, that, indeed, make the Islamic prayer a mighty force in the unification of the human."

Mr. Muhammad, in that same article, went on to boldly state "There could be no more leveling influence in the world. Difference of rank, wealth and color vanish within the mosque and quite a new atmosphere, an atmosphere of brotherhood, equality and love, totally different from the outside world, prevails within the holy precincts." Malcolm knew all this prior to his departure from Mr. Muhammad's mentorship and the Nation of Islam per se. In the common atmosphere of so-called "Christian" America, such was not the case. But to the contrary it was a dire reality. See "Message To The Blackman", pages 138-139.

In continuation, Mr. Muhammad pointed out..."In fact, the five daily congregational prayers are meant, among other things to carry into practice the theoretical lessons of equality and fraternity for which Islam stands; and, however, much Islam may have preached in words the equality of man and fraternity of the community of Islam, all this would have remained a dead letter, had it not been translated into the everyday life of man through the institution of five daily congregational prayers..."

According to Alex Haley's book on Brother Malcolm, page 352, Malcolm said "....The muslims of "white" complexions who had changed my opinions were men who had shown me that they practiced genuine brotherhood. And I knew that any American white man with a genuine brotherhood for a black was hard to find no matter how

241

<u>much he grinned</u>." Note what actually changed Malcolm's opinion, it was the actual "practice" or "genuine brotherhood" that he never ever witnessed in America from so-called "white" people, even those "Muslims considered white."

Malcolm said, according to the supra, page 335, that Dr. Abd'ir-Rahman Azzam, an Eastern Muslim scholar, related the fact of Nabi Muhammad's (SAW) black Lineage and explained "how color, the complexities of color, and the problem of color which exist in the Muslim world, exist only where, and to the extent, the area of the Muslim world has been influenced by the west.' It was "western influence" that engendered "differences based on attitude toward color" in the so-called Muslim world. The Honorable Elijah Muhammad pointed to this "influence" in his catechism on "who is the colored man?" part of the answer was "skunk of the planet earth." Why was this allegory used?, because a skunk ejects a malodorous secretion that influences the environment in which it resides. The remarks Dr. Azzam made to Malcolm were correct and a witness to the teachings of Mr. Muhammad of the "so-called white man" of America.

It's very important to realize that Malcolm was no fool. He was fully aware of the fact that what he saw in Mecca, was not the reality of America. When he returned to America, from Mecca, he said..."My attitude here concerning white people has to be governed by what my black brothers and I experience here, and what we witness here--in terms of brotherhood" (The Autobiography of Malcolm X page 362-363). He was a realist. The Hajj did not blind him to the bare realities of the world at large, especially the USA.

Racism, bigotry, male-chauvinism, and corruption do exist in so-called Muslim world. Slavery, which was condemned by Nabi Muhammad (SAW) was reinstituted by certain Arabs. It is a historical fact that some Arab, some Africans, and some Afro-Arabs who call themselves Muslims were evil participants in the slave trade. The Honorable Elijah Muhammad and Malcolm knew this history well. Many of the Arab-Muslims who were slave traders had made Hajj. Slavery was legal in some Arab countries including Arabia, even until the 1960's. Such was/is unislamic.

According to the "Freedom of Information Act" records on Malcolm and the Nation of Islam, agents of Hoover's FBI and other evil experts of chicanery, manipulated the split and eventual rancor between Malcolm and his benefactor, Mr. Muhammad. A lot of misinformation, malfeasance, and malignant plots were put into full play for years before the scheme, designed to negate the love, unity and respect that existed between MR. Muhammad, Malcolm, Ali, Farrakhan and other

242

members of the Nation of Islam, met with any success. We all are victims of an evil plot .

Malcolm was not easy prey. He did not succumb to the plot until he became bitter, and he didn't become bitter until he was made to believe that Mr. Muhammad had put a hit on him, and his family. The Honorable Elijah Muhammad did no such evil. Prior to that juncture in his orchestrated departure from the Nation of Islam, Malcolm still supported his mentor and the Nation of Islam. He was aware of the fact that agents and hypocrites in the Nation of Islam were creating problems for him.

In Alex Haley's book on brother Malcolm, page 428, it is reported that Malcolm said "My home was bombed by the Muslims!" Then on page 433, it is reported that Malcolm said..."he was going to state that he had been hasty to accuse the Black Muslims of bombing his home. " According to Mr. Haley, Malcolm said "Things have happened since that are bigger than what they can do. I know what they can do. Things have gone beyond that." He was waking up. Malcolm went on to say "a part of the whiteman's big maneuver" was keeping the black man fighting himself (page 433). He saw the scenario of the satanic scheme. When we peruse Malcolm's remark concerning Elijah Muhammad's first public statement about him (page 197), last half of the page, and examine the works of J.E. Hoover and his agent in the Nation of Islam, we must admit Mr. Muhammad was right and exact.

What Malcolm said on page 198 of his alleged "Autobiography" paragraph one and two, was absolutely true. Just a few days prior to his murder, Malcolm expressed a desire to reunite with the Honorable Elijah Muhammad. Charles Kenyatta was correct when he stated, according to David Gallen's book entitled "Malcolm As They Knew Him", page 77,..."ten or fifteen minutes before he was assassinated, if Elijah Muhammad had asked him to come back, he would have come back" rather than working through the recently formed MMI or founding the OAAU, "Malcolm," Kenyatta says, "Would have preferred to stay (with the NOI). No question about it, that I do know." I concur with that conclusion because of Malcolm's own words to me, after his departure from the NOI.

Wallace D. Muhammad (a/k/a Imam Warithuddin Mohammad) had uttered basically the same deprecative charges against his father that Malcolm made. Wallace returned to the NOI and publicly recanted and asked forgiveness--he was welcomed back with a loud ovation. The same would have been true for Malcolm.

The misinformation projected to the public that Mr. Muhammad was jealous and envious of Malcolm's fame is just that, misinformation. He, by the grace of Allah (SWT) made Malcolm. He wanted Malcolm "to become well known," so he would become "better known" -- but warned Malcolm that he would become "hated" when it happened, "because usually people get jealous of public figures" -- see Haley's book on Malcolm, page 265. Again Mr, Muhammad's wisdom espied the end results of Malcolm's ascension into distinction, respect, etc. On page 387 of said Autobiography we find a statement from Malcolm that was to be a dedication of said publication. But when we read the dedication in the beginning of the book itself, we find something else. How did this conflict happen? Malcolm never saw the completion of his alleged "Autobiography." The question comes to mind, was the agreement Malcolm made with Mr. Haley (see page 387) honored? It's dubious. We now know the whole chapter was omitted by Mr. Haley. Was Mr. Haley an agent of the government too?

There is much more to be said regarding Brother Malcolm, a true Mujahideen whom we love. But due to the time I will conclude by saying, remember the conversation Malcolm had with Alex Haley on February 20, 1965, in which he said, "The more I keep thinking about this thing, the things that have been happening lately, I'm not at all sure it's the Muslims. I know what they can do, and what they can't and they can't do some of this stuff recently gong on...The more I keep thinking about what happened to me in France, I think I'm going to quit saying it's the Muslims." The murder of Brother Malcolm was designed by wicked members of the FBI and CIA and carried out by poisoned-minded members of Mosque 25, Newark, New Jersey.

"Black people," Christians and Muslims and others, must not allow the press, which is mainly controlled by "some" Jews who see themselves as some "special people" merely because they claim a chosen status in the symbolic eye of the Creator, to deceive and divide us regarding Malcolm's murder. Surely if Elijah Muhammad, Minister Farrakhan, or Imam W. D. Mohammad had anything 'whatsoever' to do with the Sinister assassination of Brother Malcolm, the government would have charged them with some complicity. However, even the FBI, who worked night and day for years to destroy the Honorable Elijah Muhammad and the Nation of Islam, never issued an iota of an indictment on either.

The FBI knew, that, Mr. Muhammad did not want any harm whatsoever to come to Malcolm. The powers that be knew that Malcolm was loved by Mr. Muhammad. They loved each other.

"Certain" Jews, powerful Jews, are endeavoring to assassinate Brother Farrakhan by suggesting in books that their companies print, movies on Malcolm that they promote, finance and provide the "spin" that dominates, overtly and covertly, the movie that Spike Lee 's name is associated with on Malcolm X that he and Mr. Muhammad were in some way involved with the murder of Brother Malcolm.

It is a well known fact, that certain Jews in power hate Minister Farrakhan and want him dead. They have made the repudiation of Brother Farrakhan the litany of all wanna-be leaders, polka dot politicians, journalist, etc. that beseech their blessing, support, and eulogies. Certain Jews induced Jesse Jackson to punk out over and over and over again; they have him jumping through hoops ..backward.

The detestation of some Jews for Farrakhan, the Palestinians, Al-Islam, etc., is rivaled by only the hatred their progenitors had for Jesus the Christ (A.S.) , 2000 years ago-they hated Jesus and obtruded their vituperation on the government of that day--peruse the bible (St. Matt. 21: 23-46; 23:1-15; 26:57-60; 27:11-25; St. Luke 11:53-54; St. John 5:1-16; 8:31-40; 1145-53; 18:34-40__, and today they are doing likewise to Farrakhan, Dr. Leonard Jeffries, etc.

Why do they hate Farrakhan and berate him, and why do some wish for his death? It is because he has exposed them. He has made the masses aware of the role some Jews played in the slave trade that is documented by Jewish scholars, historians, etc. The bold stand he takes on the Palestinian issue is seen by certain Jews as a warrant for his death. Unlike Jesse Jackson and some other leaders, Brother Farrakhan is no chameleon--he is his own man.

The Honorable Elijah Muhammad taught love and concern for self and kind first, and then others. He feared only Allah. His Islamic intentions and devotion is without question. It's witnessed in his works. He never sold out to the negative powers that be. He was bent on the renovation and elevation of "black" people, first and foremost, and people of color all over the world. NO one, not even Mecca, could coopt him in the worship of the gods of this world who resided in the White House and the Kremlin.

The Monarchy of Mecca and other Arab states no longer turn to Kaaba, they turn to the "white house". They clearly beseech the protection and guidance of the President of the United States, instead of Allah (SWT). They have actualized the Holy Quran's emission of them (25:30). They submitted to U.S. Presidents the will of George Bush and his nefarious coterie of skull and bones, and rejected the will and guidance of Allah (3:28, 100, 102--105, 118; 4:139, 144; 49: 9-13; 64:13). All Muslims must study Quran (2:120 and 5:54, 58, 60)-- surely Allah speaks the truth. Arabia and many other Arabic states have become satellites of America. They are Pawns in the game of the great satan.

The Honorable Elijah Muhammad was well aware of the fact, that for the most part, Mecca and other so-called muslim countries had gone astray. He saw the unIslamic deportment in the so-called Muslim world and refused to partake of said. When told that Mecca and some other so-called orthodox Muslims rejected him, he boldly replied "I am not sent by Meccca". He was also aware of what was written in Quran (9:97-107; 49:14) about certain Arabs. He knew about their involvement with slavery, etc. More than likely he was aware of the fact that the Quran (49:13) was revealed to check the bigoted mentality of some Arabs toward Bilal Ibn Rabah (R.A.) and others of his hue - humanity.

Imam W. Deeen Mohammad said, after the passing of his father, that, "What the world has known as Al-Islam, is a corruption of Al-Islam". He went on to say that "the scholars of Al-Islam were lead astray from the Sunni of Prophet Muhammad...This is a fact!" The pathetic state of the "Muslim world" is proof that it is astray (24:55; 8:66). A billion or more Muslims, with some of the wealthiest countries in the world, and yet without one jot of the influence exerted and exercised by a 'welfare state" of less than their numbers. This is disgraceful and an infradig to the name "Muslim" and the name "Islam".

There were no "Kings" and "princes" in Mecca during the time of Prophet Muhammad. Shura was established by him and followed by those who adhered to his sunnah. "Kings" and "princes" and other monarchies witnessed in the "Muslim world" is diametrically contrary to Quranic guidance and the Sunnah of Prophet Muhammad (SAW). It is evident that said monarchies are dictators who conceive that Allah is 'in the person" of whomever is the presidency of the United States--what is more anthropomorphic than the "submission of the Will" of the monarchs of Kuwait, Jordan, Morocco, Iraq, etc, "to the will of Bush" or "the will of Clinton" and the Jewish controlled, lilly-white Senate and Congress?

Shirk is the order of the day in todays so-called Muslim world. Still some "Sunni" Muslims in the east and the west have the audacity to charge Mr. Muhammad with shirk. The Muslim world today and the Muslim world of 1400 years ago, what is the difference? That is the real question. The Honorable Elijah Muhammad said..."If you want to talk to Allah, read the Quran' he said that Allah was a power "higher than man." These are the type of teachings that must be emphasized more than his allegorical or arcane ones that were a medicine concocted to rid a people of their self-dejection, self-disdain, inferiority complexes, extreme European adulation, and self-destructive behavior.

All medicines have some side effects other than the positive effects it was concocted to induce--especially if used beyond a given time. Ponder Quran (6:67; 13:38-42); the Honorable Elijah Muhammad recognized the principle in this and endeavored to implement the same by changing the tone and emphasis of his teachings as time went on.

Mr. Muhammad made mistakes. He was a human being. Prophet Muhammad made mistakes (peruse Quran 17:73-76; 33:3;7; 66:1-3; 80:1-12; 22:52; 93:7) and was reprimanded by Allah. The Satanic Verses pre-dates Salman Rushdie and his book--it goes back to an early Meccan surah. Allah, according to the Quran (2:1116; 13:19; 16:102) abrogates certain verses and causes others to be forgotten. Al-Islam is a progressive movement, a natural progression. Conditions pre-empt divine revelations that ameliorate them and advance humanity. Mr. Muhammad's work must be seen in such light. He was a giant of a man.

When one studies and compares the first 11 1/2 years of Prophet Muhammad's mission, with the last 11 1/2 years of Mr. Muhammad's mission, it is clear that the former contains some aspects with unIslamic ramifications that were rectified during the latter. Again, abrogations were in order due to mental and moral development in the people addressed. For the Arabs, when was Deen Al-Islam perfected in the time of Prophet Muhammad? When was Quran (5:4) revealed? Why not before, for example in the fifth or tenth year? Why not when he first showed in Medina? Why did it take 23 years (17:106) when the Quran was sent down with Prophet Muhammad (7:157)? Why did Allah (SWT) warn Prophet Muhammad not to be so quick to relate the divine dictates to the people (75:1619)?

Allah does not change, nor does his sunnah (i.e. way of doing things)--Quran (33:62). Institutions that are evil cannot be destroyed over night. Fard Muhammad and Elijah Muhammad knew that and measured their concocted medicament according to the mentality of their patients.

As stated earlier, here are some biblical bases for some of the teachings of the Honorable Elijah Muhammad and his mystic mentor, W. D. Farad (a/k/a W.F. Muhammad, Al-Mahdi, etc, who passed in 1992): "The Mother Ship" (Ezekiel 1:4-21, 23-28). The coming of God "in the person of W.D. Fard (Ezekiel 1:1; Isaiah 40:10-14; 42: 18-22; 44:3-11, 21; 63:1-9; 65: 1-6; Jeremiah 5:26-31; 11:9; St. Matt. 24:27,28. 2-Thessalonia 2:3-9). The symbolic birth of W.D. Fard (Revelation

247

12:1-5; Habakkuk 3:3,4, 13; Genesis 36:11, 15, 42; I-Cron. 1:36; St. John 10:33-35; Psalm 82:1-6). Slavery (Genesis 15:13, 14; Psalm 137:1-4; Isaiah 5:13,14; 42:22; Jeremiah 22:13; Ezekiel 1:1; 17:1-6, 22-24; Daniel 1:1-7; Nahum 3:8-13). The Honorable Elijah Muhammad. (Isaiah 11:1-4; 40:13-14; 42:18-21; Jeremiah 23:22; Malachi 3:1:3; 4:5-6). Mental death and resurrection (Job 7:9; Psalms 31:12; 113; Ecclesiastes 9:4-5; 1; Jonah 2:1-10; Micah 4:4-5; St. Luke 15:11-32).

There are many scriptures that lend support to the theological projections of Mr. Muhammad. We should deal with the sources of the concept, convictions, etc., before taking aim at the person who accepts them.

In citing the supra, we only intend to set the record straight. We do not sit in judgment of any servant of Allah, even if we disagree. We are aware of Allah's words in Quran (4:85; 5:8; 4:94, 135; 33:36). May Allah bless us all with more concern for each other, a better understanding of each other and our deen in general (16:53; 42:30; 57:4; 16:11; 10:41; 35:8). We should remember the words of Allah's Messenger and seal of the prophets. . . "a Muslim is not a Muslim until he desires for his brothers and sisters that which he desires for himself." Belief is seen in behavior. Muslim is a state of being, not what a being states.

IMAM ALAUDDIN SHABAZZ, Ph.D.
AKA - ANGELO SHABAZZ
AKA - BROTHER ANGELO

Dr. Shabazz earned a doctorate in Religious Studies/Comparative Religion from the University of Florida. He was ordained and received credentials of clergy from Church of The Holy Monarch Theological School, Daytona Beach, Florida - Doctor of Divinity Degree.

He first took Shahada in 1957, becoming an active member of a small "Sunni Muslim" Ummat. Became an active member of "The Nation of Islam" in 1959, in Detroit, Michigan.

He was appointed National Director of Prisons for the American Muslim Mission, in 1976, by Imam W. Deen Mohammad. He was also appointed "Islamic Contents Editor" of Muslim Journal (by the same) in 1985.

Dr. Shabazz is the author of six books and a number of papers on religion and social issues, Lecturer, Imam, Educational Consultant and a former Minister in the Nation of Islam, cohort of Minister Malcolm X and Minister Louis Farrakhan.

THE HONORABLE ELIJAH MUHAMMAD AND THE BLACK QUEST FOR IDENTITY IN THE U. S.
By SULAYMAN S. NYANG, Ph.D.

Since the death of the late Honorable Elijah Muhammad in 1975, many scholars and students of the Muslim experience in the U.S. have wondered about the Nation of Islam and its future directions. The movement which was led for much of its life by Honorable Elijah Muhammad, went through a transformation after his death. The assumption of the leadership of the organization by his son Imam W. Deen Mohammed, has triggered a reaction from some of the old members. Two tendencies have developed within the old Nation of Islam after the death of The Honorable Elijah Muhammad. The first tendency is towards traditional Sunni orthodoxy and the incorporation of the African-American Muslims in the larger global Muslim ummah. This movement has been largely the result of Imam W. Deen Muhammad's efforts at reform. The second tendency is towards the reassertion of the old philosophies of the Nation of Islam. This is primarily speaheaded by Minister Louis Farrakhan and others who share part of his teachings but oppose his leadership on certain doctrinal grounds. Those who shared much of what Minister Louis Farrakhan claims as true teachings of the late Honorable Elijah Muhammad but are also opposed to his interpretations of the old NOI philosophies, are Minister Silas Muhammad of Atlanta, John Muhammad of Detroit and the five percenters, an originally New York-based gang group that embraced aspects of the NOI philosophy.

The purpose of this study is three-fold. The first is to discuss the teachings of the NOI under the late Elijah Muhammad and to demonstrate how his teachings were inspired by both the American socio-economic and political realities and by the deceased NOI leader's understanding of the message of Islam. The second objective of this paper is to assess the impact of the NOI on Afro-America and on the history and development of Islam in the United States of America. The third and final section of this paper offers a number of conclusions about the late Honorable Elijah Muhammad and his movement in the U.S.

A. The Honorable Elijah Muhammad and the Philosophies of the Lost and Found of Islam: When we look at the NOI and its philosophies we are struck by a certain number of ideas claimed by its founder, The Honorable Elijah Muhammad. The first idea, which is central to the belief of the NOI, was that God is black and that he came in the person of Master Farad Muhammad to save the blackman and woman from the clutches of racism in the American wilderness. This idea had a tremendous psychological impact on African-Americans who found themselves in a social universe where the codes, cues, signs, symbols and signals make the life of the black person nasty, brutish and worthless. Knowing fully well that the black person in America has been devalued by the triple quandary of race, caste and class, The Honorable Elijah Muhammad found in the teachings of Master Farad Muhammad a metaphysical solution to the dilemma of the Blackman in America. There are five ways in which this teaching of God as a blackman affected the black American. First of all, such a teaching became a counter-argument to an implicit doctrine taught by many white Christians of his days. The subtle and not so subtle racialization of Christ through pictures and paintings hung in churches across America has always affected directly or indirectly the consciousness of black Christians. In fact, one of the leading black thinkers of the nineteenth century, Edward Wilmot Blyden, addressed this issue in his famous book, *Christianity, Islam and the Negro Race,* when he lamented the racialization of the Christ image in churches of the Western world. There is no evidence that The Honorable Elijah Muhammad was familiar with the writings of Blyden. However, in discussing his intellectual origins and the manner in which his religious thought developed, it should be pointed out that his teaching that God was black liberated those less sophisticated blacks in Christian Afro-America from the naive acceptance of the racialization of The Christ doctrine of the mainstream Christian churches.

The second way in which this central teaching of the NOI affected Afro-America and the larger U.S. society, was in the self-definition of the members of the Nation of Islam. By defining themselves as *blacks and not negroes,* the members of the NOI radically altered the rules of the naming game firmly established for generations by the dominant white society. Here too we see the teachings of the NOI serving as a system-challenging function. Although in its real life operation the NOI was dismissed as conservative and reactionary by many Black political activists working in the field of civil rights in the U.S., the psychological battle against negative stereotyping of blacks in the U.S. benefited immeasurably from this assault on America's popular definition of the two races. The net result of this NOI assault on the citadel of names would become evident only after the civil rights movement had scored some victories and the message of the NOI was more widely disseminated by the late Malcolm X (El-Hajj Malik Shabazz).

251

Retrospectively, one could successfully argue that the term Black was dignified and elevated from scorn and rejection among African-Americans by the followers of the NOI. Indeed, a future American historian might well argue in the next century that one of the ironies of twentieth century American social history is the fact that the NOI, which was a counterracist racist religious body, created the necessary psychological conditions for many underclass blacks from America's ghettos to rise economically and socially to the point that they could compete with whites and others in the U.S. without any complexes about their blackness. There are certainly many evidences to corroborate such a claim.

The third way in which the central teaching of the NOI affected Afro-America and the larger U.S. society lies in the racialization of the Christ figure itself. By turning the dominant societal image upside down, the NOI projected itself not only as a psychological bull in the white China shop, but it also triggered a subconscious reaction among African-Americans recruited into it. Here two processes are at work. The first tells the NOI follower that God himself is on his side and cosmic powers would be unleashed on America whenever there is a confrontation between the whites and the NOI. This psychological message is clearly stated in the *Message to the Black Man* and *The Fall of America*. In both works the Honorable Elijah Muhammad taught his followers to see themselves as a part of a divine plan. Here we have parallels to how early Christians saw themselves in the coming kingdom of Jesus Christ. Such millenarial expectations serve the purpose of soothing the psychological wounds inflicted by the daily struggles of the Black man and woman in the U.S. The second process at work in this way of understanding and relating to the central teaching of the NOI, transfigures the NOI believer into a pro-active as opposed to a reactive and defeatist social animal on the American landscape. By seeing himself as a divinely favored being whose color is divine and beautiful, inspite of what one reads, sees or hears in American society, this NOI believer becomes intoxicated with this wine of self-adulation. Those believers who tried to alter reality to fit their new image of themselves and of the universe, succeed when their social action is directly compatible with the rules of the dominant white society. Otherwise, their efforts remained fruitless and other's looking at their movement attributed their failures to the unrealism of their philosophy of life. Some American social scientists have dismissed the NOI as a social movement whose cultist teachings are nothing more than ego-boosting myths created to make certain Blacks feel good about themselves. These observations about the NOI are not

252

altogether incorrect; however, it is dangerous and unwise to deny the psychological importance of the NOI doctrine about the color of God in the daily lives of Blacks who have successfully internalized that message.

The fourth manner in which the central teaching of the NOI affected Afro-America and the larger society was in the new mode of discourse it introduced to the Black community. By teaching his followers that God was black and by remaking the world in the image of the Black man, the NOI founding father changed their mode of discourse. Like Adam in the Quran, the new blackman of the NOI is taught the "names"; this is to say, he is now capable of conceptualizing reality for himself. This ability to think differently from the mainstream, to imagine a realm of possibilities different from the world of fantasy created by the dominant media, transforms the NOI follower into a new person who no longer identifies everything good and positive in American society with the white man. This new man of the NOI is now convinced that a black scientist called Yacub created the white man. However fantastic this claim may appear to those outside the NOI, the fact remains that such myths served a number of purposes for The Honorable Elijah Muhammad. Time and space do not allow me to theorize in detail about this manner. I will mention here only briefly and in passing one important consequence of this new image of the world according to the Nation of Islam. By developing such a myth about Yacub and the creation of the white man, the NOI founding father kills two birds of ill omen in the Black community with one stone. First of all, the strong reluctance among blacks in the ghetto to study science was changed by making it appear that science as we now know it was something possessed and perfected by Blacks long before the white man appeared on the face of the earth. This psychological benefit of the myth certainly inspired thousands of African-Americans to take the mighty road to scientific knowledge. Such a road became more attractive when the news went out in the early 1960's that one of America's leading mathematicians had joined the fold. His conversion to the teachings of Mr. Muhammad made it categorically clear to the people of the ghetto that the sciences are not closed to Blacks and indeed Blacks are more historically connected to them than whites and their study of such branches of knowledge simply means a return to the source of one's origins. Related to this psychological point is another one often missed by many of our colleagues analyzing the Nation of Islam under the late Elijah Muhammad. This second point relates to the power of the myth of Yacub. Here one sees the myth telling the black followers of the NOI that white power is built upon the scientific knowledge taken from their ancestor, Yacub. This point not only demystify the white man and his power, but it also sends out the message to the NOI follower that the cosmic forces will join him in the transformation of the world when his mastery of the sciences complements his strong faith in this destiny as a black man.

The fifth way in which the central doctrine of the Nation of Islam affected Afro-America and the larger society became evident when immigrant Muslims from the Old World began to propagate their religion in the United States of America in the second half of the twentieth century. After having been exposed for over sixty years to the NOI philosophy, most white Americans still cannot differentiate between the NOI believers and the other African-American followers of Islam. To these Americans (and here African-American Christians should be included), Islam is either the religion of desert Arabs and Iranian hostage-takers in the Middle East or black followers of Elijah Muhammad and Louis Farrakhan. This picture of Islam is to some extent the result of the bitter encounter between the Nation of Islam and the American establishment. It should be remembered that up until recently, the term Muslim was associated almost exclusively with Black members of the NOI. It is true that there were Muslims from other regions outside the black world, but in the American imagination, local claims to Islam were made only by the members of a small cultist group called Black Muslims. This image of black Muslims became more developed in the late 1950's and early 1960's when Malcolm X (El-Hajj Malik Shabazz) served as the National Minister and Spokesman of The Honorable Elijah Muhammad.

b. *The Nation of Islam and the Development of Sunni Doctrines in the United States of America*: When we look at the history of Islam in the United States of America we see that the rise of the NOI has a great deal to do with the American perception of Islam and Muslims. This view of Islam, as we have just demonstrated above, was the result of the bitter encounter between the members of the NOI and the American establishment. What we plan in this section is to examine the historical relationship between the NOI and the Sunni groups which developed in the U.S. over the last sixty years. First of all, it should be pointed out that the mysterious founder of the NOI, Master Farad Muhammad, was said to be a man from Hijaz in Arabia. But regardless of how the NOI members viewed him, his teachings of Islam were definitely unacceptable to Muslims from the Old World. This doctrinal gulf would remain unbridged until the post 1975 transformation of the NOI by Iman W.D. Muhammad. What made the

NOI unacceptable to the Old World Muslims were the body of beliefs which conflicted with the traditional Islamic view of God *(tawhid)*, man, and history. Contrary to the NOI doctrine, traditional Islam rejected categorically any anthropomorphic association of the Godhead with man. Here the traditional Christianity which teaches that Jesus was the Son of God. Indeed many a traditional Muslim of both the Sunni and Shia variety dismissed the NOI believers as heretics whose knowledge of Islam was shallow and distorted because of admixture with Christian elements.

What was most disturbing to the traditional Muslims in America and abroad was the NOI philosophy of race. Claiming an idealized nonracial view of society, and deeply rooted in the monogenesis of the Quran, traditional Muslims in the U.S. and abroad saw the NOI as an aberration which threatened their identity and their chances of preaching a nonracial universal doctrine. Convinced that their religion was a prescription for racist American society, and determined to make their message known to the American people, these traditional Muslims found the NOI followers a doctrinal thorn in their flesh. Most of these traditional Muslims avoided contacts with the NOI. Only a few opened themselves up to these American followers of Mr. Muhammad. This pattern of relationship continued long after the death of Mr. Muhammad.

Another point of disagreement between the NOI and the traditional Muslims in the U.S. and abroad was their conflicting views of man. As explained in the previous section, the NOI taught its members that God was Black and the Black man has a rendezvous with destiny. This view of the NOI's goes against the traditional Muslim view that all men are children of Adam and color has nothing to do with one's piety *(taqwa)*. Because of this divergence between the NOI and the traditional Muslim community, most of the light skinned Muslims from the Old World and almost all of the native-born white Muslims in the U.S. became estranged from the NOI. This communication gap started to be closed only after Imam Muhammad began his reforms in the late 1970's. The gap is still there and it is not uncommon today to read articles in the Muslim press of America lamenting the chasm between the immigrant Muslims and the native-born Muslims. Much of the conflict and disagreement between the two communities center around issues of pride and prejudice. Pride becomes an issue because the immigrants are as a group economically better off than their native-born co-religionists. This economic disparity has introduced a class element in the relationship. Related to this but not necessarily occasioned by it is the arrogance of many immigrants in projecting

255

themselves as better informed Muslims simply by virtue of earlier exposure to Islam. Such un-Islamic behavior towards fellow co-religionists has certainly created the feeling in the Muslim Afro-American community that many of the immigrants are unwilling to accept whole heartedly Black Muslims.

If, however, the immigrant Muslims are to be blamed for some of the difficulties faced by native-born Muslims in the development of the religion, then the conflict between the NOI and the native-born Sunni Muslims should also be identified as a possible explanation of the crisis. The origins of this dispute go back to the pioneering days of men like Shaykh Daoud Faisal, founder of the Islamic Mission of the United States of America. Shaykh Daoud Faisal became a Sunni Muslim in the late 1920's and would later develop into a strong Sunni Muslim foe of the NOI through his Islamic Mission in the United States of America. The pattern of hostility that developed between the NOI and Shaykh Daoud Faisal would later determine the course of events in the young emerging Muslim community in America.

The pattern of hostility between the small group of Sunni Muslims among the African-Americans and the NOI members became most evident in the late 1960's and early 1970's. During this time two different Sunni Muslim groups emerged out of the Afro-American community. They were as follows: -(i) The Darul Islam Movement; (ii) The Hanafi Movement led by Abdul Haalis. These groups shared a number of things which distinguished them from the NOI. One can list a few of them to show the reason for solidarity among them against the NOI and its teachings. The first and most important point of divergence from the NOI was their affirmation of universal tawhid, a doctrine central to traditional Islam and opposed to the central teaching of the NOI. The second point of agreement they shared against the NOI was their willingness to embrace international Islamic groups and to disseminate their literature. This attitude towards international Islam was not only dangerous from an NOI point of view, but it also entailed the danger of subversion through association. The leader of the NOI was not ready to go this far. A third point of difference between the NOI and its Sunni critics within Afro-America was the Sunni rejection of racism and their denial of the claim that Farad Muhammad was God himself and that Elijah Muhammad was indeed a prophet. To the Sunnis, this was an anathema and blasphemous.

It was indeed against this background that the conflict between the NOI and the four groups developed in the late sixties and early seventies. This conflict was so serious that several persons lost their lives in the struggle for primacy within the African-American community. A close examination of the publications of the NOI and the four Sunni groups, would show a definite pattern of ideological hostility. *The Western Sunrise* of the Islamic Brotherhood, Inc., the *al-jihadul Akbar* and the *taqwa* of the Darul Islam Movement, the al-Islam of the Islamic Party of North America and press reports of statements from Abdul Haalis of the Hanafi Movement reflected the ideological struggle against the NOI. There are several articles criticizing the teachings of the NOI. Black nationalism was subjected to serious scrutiny and the NOI was identified as one of its most virulent propagators. It should be pointed out that during this period in the history of the Islamic Movement in the United States of America, four Sunni groups found the NOI as fellow traveler with the black nationalists of the Black Power period. Evidence for this Sunni attitude can be derived from the contents of articles written against prominent advocates of black nationalism such as Ben Jochanan. Dr. Ben Jochanan is a controversial figure in black intellectual circles for a number of reasons. The most important point of disagreement with the Sunni Muslims is his view that ancient Egyptian civilization was black and Islam, Christianity and Judaism are all derived from ancient Egyptian religion. To him, Africa is the mother of all Western religions although African peoples have suffered at the hands of those who had stolen their legacies from Africa. During what one can now describe as the identity debates of the late 1960's and early 1970's, Sunni Muslims saw themselves as the genuine successors to El-Hajj Malik Shabazz, although they were his bitterest critics when he served as the national spokesman of Honorable Elijah Muhammad.

In our assessment of the legacies of Honorable Elijah Muhammad we cannot help but look at the nature of the relationship between Malcolm X (El-Hajj Malik Shabazz) and his spiritual master in the Nation of Islam. When we examine the available evidence on the nature of the relationship, we find that both men directly or indirectly helped plant the seeds of Islam in the United States of America. Though traditional Muslims now identify more strongly with El-Hajj Malik Shabazz there is ample evidence to show that the Honorable Elijah Muhammad's psychological therapy on the so-called ' inner city Negroes' led to the radical transformation of self we described in the preceding section. It was because of the success of the founding father in producing a new type of black American that Imam W. Deen Muhammad managed to carry out his reforms. This point is often missed by many of those who study the Nation of Islam. Indeed one could argue that the split within the Nation after the death of the founding father was ironically a good testimony to the success of the founding father. He was able to transform his primarily low class religious movement for inner city blacks into a 75 million dollar enterprise with businesses around the country. This institutional edifice testified to the founding father's success in creating a vehicle for social and economic mobility to a people who heretofore thought that the American Dream was not only Satanic but undesirable. The success of the founding father of the original NOI becomes evident if we argue convincingly that his legacies are being appropriated, however, selectively done, by a variety of people. Witness the different interpretations of the NOI legacies by Mr. Muhammad's son, Imam W. Deen Muhammad, and by Minister Louis Farrakhan and Minister Silas Muhammad.

El-Hajj Malik Shabazz's contribution to the direct or indirect development of Islam can be seen in two areas. The first was his single-handed effort at propagating the message of his spiritual master in the late fifties and early and mid sixties. His successful projection of the NOI image across the U.S. media drew the attention of many young blacks who later joined the ranks of the Nation of Islam. Many of these young men and women would attend colleges and universities and through their efforts, Islam would later become more visible in both the black community and the larger society. The second area in which Malcolm X (El-Hajj Malik Shabazz) contributed to the development of Islam in the U.S. lies in his matyrdom. His assassination in 1964 transformed him into a hero for different ideological groups in the U.S. because he was portrayed as the system challenger par excellence, El-Hajj Malik Shabazz has become an icon to the nationalists and a source of inspiration to the Sunnis. On account of this image of him El-Hajj Malik Shabazz is often-times pitted against Honorable Elijah Muhammad and the NOI. This was done at the height of the cold war between the NOI and the Sunni organizations described above. The Sunni groups had a common cause with El-Hajj Malik Shabazz and for this and other related reasons they appropriated the Malcolm X legacy. Evidence of this can be gleaned from the annual revisitation of his legacy by the Muslim press in America.

In concluding this paper we must recapitulate the main points developed in this study. There are twelve of them and I enumerate them as follows:

1.   The late Elijah Muhammad was a social psychological genius who managed to establish a multimillion dollar empire through his effective manipulation of certain ideas with great emotive value.

2.   The founding father of the Nation of Islam was able to create a new image of self for those who followed him. Through such efforts he managed to control his followers and the realities with which they identified under his leadership.

3.   The NOI became a force to be reckoned with largely through the efforts of Malcolm X (El-Hajj Malik Shabazz) and the charisma of the founding father.

4.   The conflict between the NOI and the Sunni groups in the U.S. in the late sixties and early seventies owed its origins to the theological differences between them. These differences were later responsible for the bitter and deadly encounters between the two factions within the Muslim community along the eastern seaboard.

5.   The transformation of the NOI under the leadership of Imam Muhammad showed the irony of the success of Honorable Elijah Muhammad. Here one notes the fact that soon after his death, his organization split between the reformers and the custodians of the old belief.

6.   The split in the old NOI leads us to the conclusion that the evolution of the organization under Mr. Muhammad brought about the co-existence of the future potentials as well as the original seedlings of the NOI.

7.   The late Honorable Elijah Muhammad contributed indirectly to the development of Islam in the U.S. through his effective psycho-therapy and through his exhortations to blacks not to accept the hegemony of the whiteman and to understand and take seriously their role in life and their destiny in the coming mellenium.

8.   Though the international Muslims shield away from the Nation of Islam in the heydays of both Elijah Muhammad and Malcolm X, there is still room to conclude that they respected the NOI leadership and found political utility in what they were doing.

9.   The Honorable Elijah Muhammad's life demonstrated that a man with a message for an oppressed people succeeds only when he is able to recruit and retain members to his organization.

10.   The Honorable Elijah Muhammad, our study concludes, was a man of thought and action who managed to create the Nation of Islam largely because of his ability to make good judgments about those who work for or with him.

11.   The study concludes that, regardless of how one may feel about this man from Georgia, the fact remains that he created one of the largest bodies of African-Americans and Muslims in U.S. history.

12.   The last and final conclusion is that, though Mr. Muhammad did not have a college degree in sociology or social work, his work with

inner city blacks revealed his mastery of the intricacies and subtleties of urban life in America.

Sulayman S. Nyang, Ph.D. is Associate Professor of Government and Public Administration at Howard. He is also the former Chairman of the African Studies Department at Howard. Professor Nyang writes for numerous publications - national and international. He is also the author of two books: _Islam, Christianity, and African Identity_ and _Islam and Its Relevance for Today._ Professor Nyang is a national and an international lecturer; he is an educational and political consultant. He was/is the editor or associate editor of African, Arab and Islamic journals. He is presently working on his third book which addresses African Americans and Islam.

Professor Nyang was born in Gambia, West Africa.

ALLEGORICAL TEACHINGS
OF THE HONORABLE ELIJAH MUHAMMAD

By
Dr. Na'im Akbar

Every ethnic group shares a unique psychohistorical experience which has been shaped by their special experiences as a cultural group. Out of this unique experience emerges a cultural myth which serves as the foundation which unites that group and lays the foundation for their cosmology or particular world view. To the degree that all human beings ultimately share the human psychohistorical experience, there are certain of these myths, images or ideas which are shared by all of humanity. The power and the salience of culture is a reflection of the importance of this unique image. The young are taught the story of the world within the language of their cultural myth and the old are revered because of their mastery of the story. This lies as the groundbed for the values and the social organization which ties a people together. This social unity is fundamental for the protection and growth of a people.

Out of the cultural myth, people develop a metaphor about the human plight and its mastery, based upon the unique language of their collective experience. It is this myth and the derived metaphors which equip people for their collective advancement. Probably the best known cultural myth in western society is that of the Jewish people, because of the general acceptance of the Bible as being the unique historical chronicle of the so-called Hebrew people. Even though there is a general acceptance of the idea that the stories of the old testament represent a chronicle of Jewish history, people rather readily accept this as a story of humanity in general and a reelection of the cosmology of the human race. Whether either of these assumptions if accurate or not is irrelevant to the notion that cultural myths and the allegory which grows out of a people's unique historical experience recapitulates the story of humanity as a whole and plays out the drama of the ultimate forces of the human experience. This drama encompassing the confrontation of good and evil, the image of the Divine and man's relationship to Him/Her, Deliverance, immortality, etc. These profound abstractions must be relayed to people meaningfully in the context of their particular history and experience. Otherwise, the experience of the concepts becomes an

262

alien experience and the understanding of the Transcendent becomes an instrument of human oppression and perpetual social impotence. On the other hand, for those people who identify with the historical allegory as their own, they are empowered by appreciating their unique relationship with the Divine and their unique and special niche in the cosmos. They are empowered by the noble self-image that they share and with an understanding of their prophetic certainty of victory in the ultimate playing out of the human drama.

Though the mastery of such a profound philosophical postulate may sound outside the range of a third grade itinerate preacher of Islam, named Elijah Muhammad, an observation of his work suggests that either he or his teacher(s) did have a firm grasp on this concept. The most meaningful way to comprehend the peculiar language and concepts of the Honorable Elijah Muhammad is to see them as the effort to restore the cultural allegories and myths of a people who were robbed of their peoplehood through the systematic destruction of their cultural myth and ideas. Slavery was not just a social, economic and political condition, it was a fundamental attack on the forces which maintain human solidarity and inspire human beings to take a winning posture in the race of human existence. The loss of these critical elements severed our connection with a long history of being among the frontrunners in the human race. In the teachings of the Honorable Elijah Muhammad, he brilliantly created a new cultural myth to match our current situation and built allegories out of our particular historical experience.

The people held captive for 400 years, in wait for Allah's (God's) deliverance were no longer the Hebrew children crying under the whip of the oppressor in Egypt 4,000 years ago, instead, it became the tearful agony of the Mississippi mother watching her Black son lynched and her daughter raped by cruel white men in 1930, 1940, 1960, etc. The voice coming to bring leadership to a misguided people was no longer an ancient Elijah speaking to a people in a strange land, but the "Little Lamb Elijah" who was promised to come in the last days in the person of this Elijah speaking to the Black man in North America. The devil (evil personified) was no longer a metaphysical creature out of a European medieval image but a "kind of man" whose demonic qualities could be easily demonstrated within the recent historical experiences of any Black man or woman in America.

The limitations of the Judeo-Christian metaphor was easily demonstrable by the treatment of African-Americans at the hands of the Christian teachers. The attractive preference for Islam was clearly superior as a set of images that were more easily adaptable to the

263

situation of the African-American person. Islam became a religious system that could be tied to the historical connection of these people in America with millions of people in Africa and around the world. Despite the historical reality of Arab Muslims participation in the slave trade, the American Black man of the 1930's - 1960's had little knowledge of what an Arab was and even less about his history as a co-conspirator in his oppressed condition. Besides, in the service of creating a workable new Cultural myth, such facts could be dismissed in much the same way that all of the characters in the Bible (many of whom were clearly African nationals) all became mysteriously white and pure in the teachings of Christianity as European cultural myth. Once Islam was established as a system which offered greater validity for the Black man, it became easier to build a sense of identification with the Divine and to believe in the real possibility of Divine intervention.

The idea that God (Allah) had consistently intervened either personally or by a Messenger in the experiences of human beings from the very beginning of time is a prominent reality in all people's religious stories and/or cultural myths. In Ancient Kemit (called Egypt) Divine personages frequently interacted in human circumstance. The same is true in Greek mythology, West African mythology, East Indian, Native American and the cultural myths of all people. This idea is repeatedly followed throughout the Holy Qur'an, the Torah and the Bible. It would seem bizarre that God (Allah's) commitment and demonstration of His intervention in the affairs of other people throughout history would suddenly become an unimaginable occurrence in the affairs of a truly deserving people based upon their persistent faith if nothing more.

In the creation of the restoration of cultural myths produced by Elijah Muhammad, if God could talk directly to Moses and engage in dialogue with Job and walk in the garden with Adam, then why couldn't he come in the person of Master Fard Muhammad to intervene in the oppressive situation of African-Americans? Such an idea should be considered no more absurd than the entrance of God in the person of man in the Cultural allegories of most people. Certainly with a more complete understanding of the theology of Islam, such a concept is the most profound blasphemy. However, one must, at least be willing to question the reason for the considerable success in human reformation, social development and human organization which emerged from such an approach. Myths are never completely correct, be it the myth of a Virginal impregnation or an angel talking to a man in a cave in Arabia. But, neither are myths completely incorrect when understood as an allegory or a picture of a non-physical reality.

The Honorable Elijah Muhammad chose pictures and metaphors that African-Americans could relate to in their 1930 - 1960 state of mind. His definition of "heaven" was not something in the sky. For a people whose orientation was paralytically other-worldly, such an image of transcendent reality rendered them hopelessly passive in the worldly struggle for material advancement. The "pie in the sky" made them ever more retarded in the development of resources for earthly human development. He condemned the sky image of heaven as "spookism." The esoteric image of the serenity of heaven as a place where white angels flew around dressed in white robes, on white clouds paying homage to a white God did not do much to free the human powers of Black people or engender an identification with celestial reality. We were catching so much "hell" down here on earth that he gave us an "earth" definition of heaven as freedom from white oppression and the reestablishment of a Black land. The image that he chose was: "money, good homes, and friendships in all walks of life." For the deprived and isolated Black man, this more accurately portrayed heaven than "gardens with underground rivers."

At the close of this 20th century, we still do not fully understand the depths of the brilliance of the Honorable Elijah Muhammad. History will have to be his ultimate judge. Certainly, he did not present Islam in any form recognizable to the orthodox understanding of the religion. In fact, as we suggested above, he was downright blasphemous as regards many of these accepted images of the faith. Despite this deviation which has made him subject to the condemnation of most Islamic scholars, his success in proselytizing for the faith remains unsurpassed. He succeeded in making "Black " Muslims act more Islamic than many of those who have more recently mastered the Arabic language, are regular readers of Qur'an, have made Hajj to Mecca and reference the Grand Islamic scholars of the last 1400 years. If one understands Islam in its fundamental sense, (free of the complications of eschatology, hermeneutics, jurisprudence, etc.) then one must look at the followers of Elijah Muhammad in a different light.

Dr. Na'im Akbar is a graduate of the University of Michigan. He has served as a professor of Psychology at Morehouse College and at Norfolk State University. He is presently a clinical Psychologist at Florida State University. He is also the author of several books, including *Chains & Images of Psychological Slavery, The Community of Self, From Education to Mis-Education* and Visions for Black Men.

THE REWARDS OF SUCCESS IN LIFE AND IN THE HEREAFTER IS WITH THOSE WHO BELIEVE AND ACCEPT THE TEACHINGS OF THE HONORABLE ELIJAH MUHAMMAD: THE MESSENGER OF ALLAH

By H. Khalif Khalifah

For those of us who believe in the teachings of The Most Honorable Elijah Muhammad, the basic thing that we realize is that in order to receive the full blessings, or benefits that we strive for as believers, we must accept that which he declared himself to be. And less we be misunderstood in anything that follows, Mr. Muhammad told us in his own words that he was "The Messenger of Allah" to us all. He said in the *Theology of Time* (page 6; paragraph 2): "I am the Last Scientist or prophet. But I am not a prophet in the sense of prophets of old. I am a Messenger. The Last One does not prophesy. He has nothing to prophesy. He fulfills that which others prophesied. "

I don't think anything could be plainer than this declaration, especially for those who believe in the fulfillment of scripture; or the ultimate freedom and liberation of African people. The essence of all prophesy is that one day the oppressed will overcome and be liberated from the bondage of the oppressor. Put another way, one day those who are treated unjustly will obtain justice. However, in order to overcome the barriers to the state of freedom from bondage, the oppressed must be taught; and they must accept and carry out certain instructions, individually and as a people. As The One who fulfills the predictions, or prophesy that one day justice will prevail, the Honorable Elijah Muhammad's message contained all of the instructions needed by Black people in North America to reach our ultimate goals of "Freedom, Justice and Equality." Those who reject his message, or accept some and discard parts of it will not realize the promise that was made to those who do accept it. The ones who reject it or do not strive to accept it in total, may well find it in the teachings of some who prophesied in the past; why wait? Why not test that which has proven itself in our own time? Moreover, the formula for our deliverance was given to us through one who was raised from our midst: The Honorable Elijah Muhammad.

So we believe that which The Honorable Elijah Muhammad taught. We see no contradiction in anything that he said did or instructed us to do to be of the rightly guided to success in this life; and in the hereafter. We see ourselves (we who accept his teachings and guidance) as the fulfillment of the great promise that he said would be ours if we believed, accepted, and successfully carried out his instructions. In the *Theology of Time*, Mr. Muhammad made it perfectly clear when he said: "If you believe that I am he, you are a very lucky man." We bear witness, he is right.

The Most Honorable Elijah Muhammad told us that as believers and followers of him, we would have "money, good homes and friendships in all walks of life." And we bear witness that this is so. We have lived long enough in the "Wilderness of North America" to experience and observe material and spiritual poverty (lack of knowledge about self and kind) in many individuals. We have also had the good fortune to experience and observe material wealth and spirituality in others. Without a doubt, those who have material wealth and are also followers of The Honorable Elijah Muhammad are the most successful; and the happiest. Many who may have the material things but no declared spiritual expression, or an expression other than Islam, as taught by The Messenger, do not reflect the peace and character of the ones who are successful, believe and *practice* the teachings.

Those who uphold Mr. Muhammad's name, giving credit where credit is due; the ones who sincerely put into practice his teachings as best they know how, are not only successful according to the spiritual standards of Islam. We also enjoy the respect that is reserved for the just person who reflects a genuine, sincere spirituality.

As the spiritual person realizes, one can "gain the world and lose his own soul." This simply means that one may have all of the material comforts imaginable, but if he or she does not have peace, he or she may also be as miserable as one can imagine. And without knowledge of self and kind (from whence comes spirituality) there will be no peace of mind. Before the preparation of, and teachings of Messenger Elijah Muhammad, we are hard put to find teachings that properly guides Black people in America to knowledge of Self & Kind, Allah & the Devil, the basics that Mr. Muhammad taught. His is a wholistic message: broad and deep enough to reach the total members of society.

As a matter of fact, we know many brothers and sisters who have attained much success because of their acceptance of only parts of the teachings of The Honorable Elijah Muhammad. They accept *this* or *that* aspect of the Universal Formula that he gave to address every concern that a human being is likely to face in life. They use parts of Mr. Muhammad's programs to develop and grow to be successful. But because they may be ones who do not really accept his spirituality, they will not have the peace, or spiritual bearing that is necessary to enjoy the material success.

On the other hand, we know many great, beautiful brothers and sisters who try to live the spiritual teachings of Mr. Muhammad to the letter of that which he taught, but unfortunately, they neglect the aspects that he taught about the acquisition and use of the material blessings, or benefits, the "money, good homes & friendship in all walks of life"). So they too are imbalanced, and may not have the Peace of Allah because their material needs to live in this world are not yet satisfied. However, no matter what their shortcomings may be, if they continue to strive to do the work according to the teachings, they will eventually find the balance with which to be successful as a spiritual and material being. Of course, if they don't evolve to correct use of the material formula (left by Mr. Muhammad), eventually they may find their spirituality becoming less and less harmonious.

Every Muslim has met, or knows of others who represent the two characters described above. We know of, or about rich Muslims, and we know or have heard about good Muslims who have nothing much, except the knowledge of Qur'an, or the teachings of The Honorable Elijah Muhammad. And of course (we pray to Allah that you are of these), we also know of good Muslims who have a good healthy balance of (spirituality) and money (material success). There are also Muslims who appear to have one, or all three, but for one reason or another (that may or may not be known to us), they eventually lose one or the other, or all three. There are always solid reasons for the good as well as the misfortune that happens in our life experiences. In all cases, the basic reason for all good or affliction is the result of our balance or lack thereof. The essence of what Messenger Elijah Muhammad offered to African people is the most vital part needed for the wholistic well being of the Blackman & woman in America. That is "knowledge of self." Since "self" does not live in isolation, but must relate to other entities in the world, it was also necessary to teach the Blackman knowledge of his own people; knowledge of the Devil and of course, knowledge of Allah, The Creator, Sustainer & Cherisher of the Heavens & the Earth.

So whether one agrees, or disagrees that the Honorable Elijah Muhammad was a Savior, A Prophet, a Christ, or simply what he declared himself to be, "The Messenger of Allah," none other than the enemy of Truth, Righteousness and Justice will deny the fact that Mr. Muhammad achieved more with these "broken bits of flesh," as Mr. Marcus Garvey called us, than any man living or dead. If it is money one desires, the Honorable Elijah Muhammad gave us a simple formula to acquire it as well as instructions as how to spend it to obtain and maintain individual peace (happiness). For Believers foolish enough to deny themselves the Saving Grace embodied in his teachings, because of a quarrel or disagreement over the title that he assumed after meeting face to face with Allah, Who came in the person of Master Farad Muhammad, you will receive your just due for such foolishness. *What difference does the name of the vessel make, if one is dying of thirst for the water in the vessel?*

You may be one who accepts Islam. You want to be a Muslim, but you want to find a way to practice other than the teachings of Elijah. Your reasons for feeling this way is because you don't agree with certain practices instituted by Mr. Muhammad to raise Black people suffering from abject subjection in "the wilderness of North America." Futhermore, you may once have been a good follower of Mr. Muhammad, but have forsaken the way that saved your life, for what you may now be calling "pure Islam?" Good! If it is working for you,

270

keep and practice it. Do you enjoy "money, good homes & friendships in all walks of life?" Does your *new way of life* impact on the cause of African people? If you can truthfully answer affirmatively to these, Right on. For even the worse critics of Mr. Muhammad's teachings admit to its profound economic impact on the Black community in America.

On the other hand, for those who deny themselves the Saving Grace (How To Eat To Live, etc.) because they do not want to be a Muslim, you are equally foolish. The Honorable Elijah Muhammad is not requiring that you believe and accept all that he taught. The good that he taught and demonstrated are available in whatever measures you may need: so accept and apply that which you can. Leave the rest alone, if you can. But whether you do or not will not affect those who "have money, good homes and friendships in all walks of life," because of their acceptance of the teachings. The Honorable Elijah Muhammad will be who he is and was to Black people forever. What he was will never change, no matter what we may think or believe. He was with us. He received his mission. He delivered the message. And hundreds of millions heard it; hundreds of thousands heard, accepted and believed what was taught and will spend the rest of their lives striving to practice that teaching. As a duty, we do what we can to teach and disseminate the body of knowledge left by Mr. Muhammad. He told us that "the one who knows the truth, must teach that truth."

BELIEVERS WHO ARE LEAST SUCCESSFUL SPEND TOO MUCH TIME CRITICIZING RATHER THAN PRACTICING

Many great believers in the Messenger spend too much time examining and criticizing those who don't believe; or those whom they feel are teaching contrary to what Mr. Muhammad said would being us the ultimate (in this life and in the hereafter). Now, you may think that one cannot go wrong in using all of his or her spirituality "defending" or making sure that what the Honorable Elijah Muhammad taught is followed to the letter. You may or may not be right. But what is absolutely certain is that your place in paradise will depend wholly on your own conduct; your own practice of that which you say you accept and believe, rather than your adeptness in pointing

271

out the faults in the work of others. In other words, if the time that you should be *practicing* what you say you believe is, instead, spent examining and criticizing what others are doing, you may well win the spiritual battle on earth, but you may also lose your own soul because of your lack of practicing what you preach. We must guard against this possibility. For only through practice will you develop to the attainment of mastery -- over Self; and over the enemy who practices oppression (evil).

The last of what we stated above will be hard for some good brothers and sisters to accept. They appear to have convinced themselves that all they need to do to obtain paradise is to watch over the legacy left African people by the Honorable Elijah Muhammad (and make sure that no one practice it contrary to his instructions). This is not so. If you want success in this life, or paradise in the hereafter, YOU must PRACTICE what you are studying. And you will not be able to determine whether you are even practicing successfully until you can see, appreciate and enjoy the results of your practice.

Not by any means am I saying that the treasures left us by The Messenger should not be protected. But less we forget, his protection will be by Allah. And since there is no spook god, Allah will utilize the Believers in His Messenger to protect him. In other words, if you truly want to be a defender of the Honorable Elijah Muhammad, strive hard to practice what he taught. In more words, demonstrate your faith. If you already have "money," keep practicing the teachings and soon you will have "good homes." If you have money and good homes, you still must keep practicing, you will then develop "good friends in all walks of life." Once you have that great promise ("money, good homes & friendships in all walks of life"), your greatness and qualifications to defend Mr. Muhammad will be self-evident because you will have a balanced life: and balance is what the promise is all about. As a balanced Blackman or woman, you will then be the ideal citizen needed to insure that The independent Black nation that Mr. Muhammad's mission revolved around, will be a free, independent, productive, secure and righteous Black Nation: A Black Super Power.

Now if you are one of the great Black men and women who does not feel that Mr. Muhammd's teachings is the "solution to the so-called

Negroes' Problem" you are free to demonstrate the efficacy of your solution. But be sane, don't deny yourself your birth right. The legacy of The Messenger is for us all: so use and utilize whatever of the Muslims program that suits you. If you are sincere, your efforts will surely be rewarded. If you find it hard to accept what is stated above, this is all the more reason why you should examine yourself, critically. And if it is your job to "defend the Messenger," by all means, do your job. For if you are successful, you have already found your spiritual and material balance and are now enjoying the peace and security that comes with "money, good homes and friendship in all walks of life." In other words, you are successfully practicing the teachings of the Honorable Elijah Muhammad. But if you do not now have the promise, you may well need to spend more time practicing than preaching what you say you know, believe and accept as the surest way to success.

As one who is privileged to hear different sides of many of the most profound events in life, I thank Allah, Who came in the person of Master Farad Muhammad, for the patience to listen for the understanding of any point of view, without necessarily making it my own. Less we forget, understanding does not necessarily mean acceptance. Nor does acceptance necessarily mean understanding. This dramatizes the importance of faith and believing in all aspects of life. And compounds the reasons why we accept the formula for success that was taught by The Honorable Elijah Muhammad, there is proof positive that it works.

Unfortunately, we have too many, otherwise good, brothers and sisters who will not allow themselves the pleasure to hear and understand other views about that which they have already accepted a particular point of view about; yes, listening for understanding is a great pleasure because doing so helps to attain at least one part of the promise of The Honorable Elijah Muhammad, "friendships in all walks of life." For, two persons listening to each other for understanding creates a dynamic creative force; a source from which good friendships grow. Studying the teachings of The Honorable Elijah Muhammad from this perspective, you will grow by degrees for a deeper understanding of Allah's Kingdom. This is Peace indeed!

273

For those who do not understand the science in seeing things from multiple, analytical points of view, perhaps this book, authored by Mr. Adib Rashad will give you some new understanding. For it is obvious that Mr. Rashad is examining, critically, albeit, gently, much of what many of us have accepted to be divine: The work of the Most Honorable Elijah Muhammad.

He (Mr. Rashad) is a close friend and associate. His own deep love, respect and appreciation for Mr. Muhammad has enhanced my own. This book is one that I am of no doubt contributes greatly to the understanding that one must have to become a sincere Believer in Allah, a Righteous Muslim. It will also add to the profound respect and appreciation for the way to "Freedom, Justice & Equality" that was taught by The Honorable Elijah Muhammad. Hopefully, this thorough examination of *The Honorable Elijah Muhammad & The Ideological Foundation of the Nation of Islam*, will aid the seeking souls to see and accept the light. If you do, you will soon attain "good homes, money & friendships in all walks of life."

H. Khalif Khalifah is the Founder and C. E. O. of U. B. & U. S. Communications Systems, Inc. The publishers of *The National Newport News & Commentator and Your Black Books Guide newspapers*. He is the author of The Legacy of The Honorable Elijah Muhammad and six other books, the latest of which is a collection of his writings from 1982 to 1992: *The Words, Acts & Deeds of Khalifah.*

ASPECTS OF EURO-CENTRIC THOUGHT

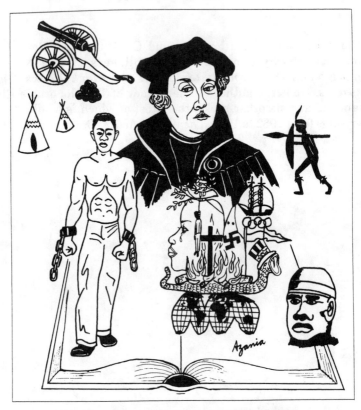

•RACISM •SEXISM •IMPERIALISM

FOREWORD

Na'im Akbar, Ph.D.

By

ABID RASHAD (James Miller)

PUBLISHED BY UNITED BROTHERS & SISTERS COMMUNICATIONS SYSTEMS
1040 SETTLERS LANDING ROAD SUITE D
HAMPTON, VIRGINIA 23669
(804) 723-2696

FROM THE CATALOGUE OF

U. B. & U. S. Communications Systems, Inc.

THE HISTORY OF ISLAM AND BLACK NATIONALISM IN THE AMERICAS

ADIB RASHAD

©MARY E. GREEK MUDIKU 1991

ORDER FORM

PLEASE SEND ONLY A "COPY" OF THIS FORM
Save original for future orders:

. . . .

Name . . . .

address . . . .

City. . . . . State. . . . . .Zip. . . . .

PLEASE ITEMIZE PRODUCTS: & Add Shipping Costs:
Please add $2.00 for first book & .50 for each additional

. . . .
. . . .
. . . .
. . . .
. . . .
. . . .
. . . .
. . . .
. . . .
. . . .
. . . .
. . . .
. . . .
. . . .
. . . .
. . . .
. . . .
. . . .
. . . .
. . . .
. . . .
. . . .
. . . .

RETAIL AND WHOLESALE ORDERS USUALLY SHIPPED WITHIN **48 HOURS**
AFTER RECEIPT (please send money order or credit cards). All prices
subject to change without notice. We do not Back order anything.

THE HONORABLE ELIJAH MUHAMMAD

ENTERTAINMENT AND MUSIC

FOR A COPY OF OUR CATALOGUE:
Call (804) 723-2696
or Write to:
912 West Pembroke Ave. ● Hampton, Va. 23669
FAX OR PHONE YOUR ORDER
(804) 728-1554 (fax number)   (804) 723-2696
(phone number)

PSYCHOLOGY

1. The Isis Papers, Dr. Frances Cress Welsing 14.95
2. Chains and Images of Psychological Slavery, Na'im Akbar 5.95
3. The Community of Self, " " " 6.95
4. Visions for Black Men, " " " 7.95
5. From Miseducation to Education, " " " 4.00
6. The Psych War, La Rue Nedd 5.00
7. The Invisible Chains, Edward C. Graves 9.95
8. African American Identity Crisis, H. and M. Alkebulan, E. Ibrahim 7.00
9. Image In Crisis, Sidney R. Sharif 6.95
10. Phoenix Arising, M.A.Z. Kamau Collier 10.95
12. The Neurological Misadventures of Pri. Man, Edgar Ridley 3.95
13. The Heart of Soul, John L. Bolling 19.95
. . . .

MALE FEMALE RELATIONSHIPS

14. Profusion, H. Khalif Khalifah 5.95
15. The Blackman's Gde to Understanding the Blackwoman, S. Ali 10.00
16. The Blackwoman's Gde to Understanding the Blackman, " " 10.00
17. Black Relationships Mating and Marriage, Ernestine Walker .. 10.00
18. Black Males and the Psychology of Love, Nathaniel Bracey 3.95
19. Are Problems in Relationships the Man's Fault, Kieth T. Wright 7.95

HISTORY

1. The Destruction of Black Civilization, Chancellor Williams $16.95
2. The Rebirth of African Civilization, Chancellor Williams 14.95
3. Africa At The Crossroads, By Prof. John H. Clarke 18.95
4. Real Afro-American History, H. Khalif Khalifah 4.95
5. Hatshepsut, John F. Hatchett 5.95
6. Capoeira, Yusef A. Salaam 5.95
7. Afrikan People and European Holidays..., Bk II 9.95
8. African Civilization Revisited, Basil Davidson 14.95
9. The Making of the Whiteman, Paul Guthrie 10.00
10. A Brief History of Struggle in America, Afoh , Lumumba, et al . 10.00
11. The Secret Relationship Between Blacks & Jews, Nation of Islam 24.95
12. Stolen Legacy, George G. M. James 9.95
13. Stolen Legacy HB, George G. M. James 22.95
14. The Six Black Presidents, Auset BaKhufu 12.95
15. The Five Negro Presidents, J. A. Rogers 2.95
18. 100 Amazing Facts About the Negro, " " " 3.95

HEALTH/NUTRITION

1. How To Eat to Live, Book 1, The Hon. Elijah Muhammad $8.95
2. How to Eat to Live, Book 2, The Hon. Elijah Muhammad 9.95
4. Heal Thyself, Queen Afua 9.95
5. " " Cookbook, Diane Ciccone 9.95
6. The Hog: Should It Be Used For Food?, C. Leonard Vories 2.00
7. What is Safe Sex in the Age of AIDS?, Curtis Cost 4.95
9. Updates on Immuno Defiency Virus.....AIDS, M. and J. Akpan .. 8.95
10. Afrikan Holistic Health, Llalia O. Africa 14.95
11. Animals In Digestive System, Michael Joseph 9.95

BIOGRAPHY

1. John Henrik Clarke: The Early Years, B. E. Adams 10.00/HB 19.95
2. The Autobiography of Malcolm X, Alex Haley 5.99*
3. Marcus Garvey Hero, Tony Martin 8.95
4. The Legacy of The Honorable Elijah Muhammad, H. K. Khalifah . 3.95
5. Bumpy Johnson & Odingo Lumumba, L. Odingo & H. K. Khalifah . 7.95
6. Oh Africa, My Africa, Nancy Sweet 10.95
7. Hey Dummy, Lonnie Clinkscalce 5.95
8. Hath the Lion Prevailed? History of Rasta Fari, John Moodie 6.95
9. A Tribute John G. Jackson, A. Rashad & H. K. Khalifah 2.95
10. Silent Trumpets of Justice, Vonita & Gerald Foster 16.95

ESSAYS, LEADERS, POLITICS

1. Words, Acts and Deeds of H. Khalif Khalifah 14.95
2. Drug Kingpin, David L. Johnson 10.00
3. Pandemonium at the Pentagon, D. Wallace, C. Watson, E. Banks . 6.95
4. Hauling Up The Morning, Tim Bllunk & Raymond Lavasseur 15.95
5. From Kingston to Kenya, Dudley Thompson 10.95
6. Rodney King and the L.A. Rebellion 10.00
7. Reparations Yes!, Lumumba, Obadele, Taifa 8.00
8. Aspects of Eurocentric Thought, Adib Rashad 13.95
9. Aspects of Eurocentric Thought, Adib Rashad 13.95
10. African Fundamentalism, Tony Martin 14.95
11. Guinea's Other Suns, Maureen Warner-Lewis 9.95
12. Carlos Cooks and Black Nationalism, R.N. and G. Harris 9.95
13. Brazil: Mixture or Massacre, Abdias Do Nascimento 12.95
14. African World Revolution, John H. Clarke 18.95

THE HONORABLE MARCUS GARVEY

15. Race First, Tony Martin 10.95
16. The Philosophy and Opinions of Marucs Garvey, " " " 12.95
17. Message to the People, Tony Martin 9.95
18. Literary Garveyism, Tony Martin 9.95
19. Marcus Garvey and the Vision of Africa, ed by John H. Clarke .. 10.00

20. They Stole It But You Must Return It, Richard Williams 9.95
21. Who is the New Afrikan?, Zolo Agana Azania 2.95
22. Aparthied: The Untold Story, Corbin Seavers 5.95
24. The Trials of Flight Lt Jerry Rawlings, Kojo Yankah 9.95
25. Message in America, Mack Chisolmn 9.00
26. The Political Legacy of Malcolm X, John Henrik Clarke 14.95
27. The L.A. Conspiracy, Nasir Hakim 8.95
28. What Should. . . Arrested or Framed by the Cops, A. Muhammad 4.95

CULTURE & EDUCATION

1. The Mis-education of the Negro, Carter G. Woodson 9.95
2. The Education of the Negro, " " " 9.95
3. Black Parents Handbook to Educating Children..., Baruti Kafele . 5.00
4. Goal Setting, Students, " " " 2.00
5. Goal Setting, For Black Folks of all Ages, " " " 2.00
6. Why Our Children are Killing Themselves, Mauri Saalakhan 10.00
7. Africa is not a Country, It's a Continent, Arthur Lewin 9.95